ECONOMIC DEVELOPMENT IN THE CONTEXT OF CHINA

Also by Clement Tisdell

THE 'GREEN REVOLUTION' AND ECONOMIC
DEVELOPMENT (*with Mohammad Alauddin*)

Economic Development in the Context of China

Policy Issues and Analysis

Clement Tisdell
Professor of Economics
The University of Queensland
Brisbane

St. Martin's Press

First published in Great Britain 1993 by
THE MACMILLAN PRESS LTD
Houndmills, Basingstoke, Hampshire RG21 2XS
and London
Companies and representatives
throughout the world

A catalogue record for this book is available
from the British Library.

ISBN 0–333–54225–8

Printed in Great Britain by
Ipswich Book Co Ltd
Ipswich, Suffolk

First published in the United States of America 1993 by
Scholarly and Reference Division,
ST. MARTIN'S PRESS, INC.,
175 Fifth Avenue,
New York, N.Y. 10010

0–9

ss Cataloging-in-Publication Data
ment Allan)
ment in the context of China: policy issues and
ent Tisdell.

Includes index.
ISBN 0–312–08670–9
1. China—Economic policy—1976– 2. China—Economic
conditions—1976– I. Title.
HC427.92.T57 1993
338.951—dc20   92–24485
                                                       CIP

Contents

List of Tables

List of Figures

xi

Preface

This book grew out of a series of lectures and seminars which I gave in China in 1989, mostly to university students and academics. I hope it will improve our understanding of economic development issues generally, particularly those confronting China, and provide a useful assessment of economic policies adopted by China in the post-Mao reform period.

I examine developmental and economic issues from several different points of view. Given our limited capacity for understanding inter-relationships, this seems an appropriate approach. Socioeconomic relationships are so complex that no single paradigm, e.g. the neo-classical, is likely to be adequate for analysing and understanding them. It is through diversity of analysis that we obtain fresh insights and improve our understanding of socioeconomic relationships.

Without my visit to China in 1989 and the help and friendship of those Chinese whom I met there, this book would in all probability not have been written. It was as a result of meeting at Harvard University in 1987 with Professor Mao Yu-shi of the Institute of American Studies of the Chinese Academy of Social Sciences that I became interested in the possibility of visiting China. I was, therefore, delighted when the President of Nankai University (Tianjin), Professor Mu Guoguang, invited me to give a series of lectures to postgraduate students in Nankai's College of Economics. I am also grateful to Huazhong Normal University (Wuhan) for inviting me to give lectures to students and staff, to the International Economic Co-operation Department of the Beijing Second Foreign Languages Institute for an opportunity to lecture to students, and to the Chinese Academy of Social Sciences (Beijing), to Tongji Medical University (Wuhan), to Shaanxi Academy of Social Sciences (Xian), to Shaanxi Institute of Ecology (Xian) and to Tianjin Tourism Institute for opportunities to present seminars. This book has benefited from these contacts as well as from lectures which I have given on social choice and economic planning at the University of Queensland.

For part of my stay in China I was a Visiting Professor at Nankai University and at Huazhong Normal University, and for the remainder of my stay I was an Exchange Fellow of the Chinese Academy of Social Sciences (CASS) and the Australian Academies of Social

Sciences and Humanities. I am grateful for the support provided for me by these bodies.

Parts of this work have benefited from my contacts with Chinese scholars such as Cao Yang, Cheng Fuhu, Hong Zhiyong, Lin Nanzi, Mao Yu-shi, Wen Jie and Yang Ruilong. I appreciate the comments of Dr Joseph Chai, Dr Sukhan Jackson Professor Rodney Jensen and Professor John Longworth on part or the whole of the material used in this book and also those of my students both in China and in Australia. But they are in no way to blame for any shortcomings of this book. I also wish to thank Professor Don Lamberton, editor of *Prometheus*, for allowing me to use in Chapter 4 some of my work previously published in his journal.

The whole of the manuscript for this book was prepared at the University of Queensland and typed efficiently and cheerfully by Deborah Ford. I am grateful to the University of Queensland for its support and to Deborah Ford for her assistance.

Last, but by no means least, I thank my wife, Mariel, and children, Ann-Marie and Christopher, for essential help and for forgoing shared time because of my research and writing efforts.

CLEMENT TISDELL

1 China and its Economic Development in International Perspective

1.1 INTRODUCTION

The main purpose of this book is to consider general development issues and to illustrate and examine those in relation to Chinese policies and experience and conversely, to examine approaches to economic development in China drawing out their general implications, strengths and weaknesses. The coverage is necessarily selective. This book is not intended as a compendium of Chinese economic development.

Ever since the visit of Marco Polo, China and its economic potential have fascinated Westerners. Adam Smith, for example, gave some coverage to China in the *Wealth of Nations*, published in 1776. However, views about the economic potential of China and its prospects for 'modern' economic development have varied considerably. Prior to World War II, Western powers and Japan saw China as a large potential market for their economic production and possibly to a lesser extent as an important source of raw materials for their own industry and economic expansion.

Although the Portuguese were allowed by the Ming Dynasty to set up a trading base in Macao in 1557, the subsequent Qing Dynasty strongly opposed further extension of trade with foreign merchants. Nevertheless, it allowed Canton (Guangzhou) to be used as a trading port commencing in 1685. But trade was restricted by the Qing government and the balance of trade was heavily in China's favour. In 1778 Britain began selling Indian opium to China in an attempt to balance up trade. Chinese attempts to stop the trade in opium eventually lead to four 'Opium Wars' which occurred during the period 1839–60. Each war ended with a treaty opening more Chinese ports to foreign ships and extending trade (Mackerras, 1982; Garraty and Gay, 1972, p. 940).

1

Japan, which had begun modernising rapidly with the Meiji restoration in 1868, soon commenced the task of building an empire and came into territorial conflict with China about control over Korea. The Sino-Japanese War of 1894–5 resulted in the defeat of China. As a result Japan had Taiwan ceded to it and Chinese control over Korea ended and was replaced by Japanese. Korea was subsequently annexed by Japan in in 1910. The Chinese government was required to pay a large indemnity to Japan and to allow Japan to build industries in treaty ports in China (Garraty and Gay, 1972, p. 941). Already Japan was displaying similar imperialistic ambitions to Western countries.

Japan's imperialistic ambitions in relation to China surfaced in World War I. It seized the German port of Qingdao and German installations in the Shandong Peninsula and in 1915 presented China with 'Twenty-One Demands', which resulted in China granting Japan a number of economic concessions. In 1931 Japan occupied Manchuria and in 1937 launched an all-out invasion of China. By 1939 Japan had overrun eastern China and the Chinese Kuomintang government had been forced to retreat to the west. Japan's intentions in relation to China were to make it part of its Greater Co-Prosperity Sphere, embracing itself and its northeast Asian neighbours. Thus its interest appears to have been largely an imperialistic economic one.

After defeating the Kuomintang, the Communist Party of China (CPC) came to power in 1949 and formed a close alliance with the Soviet Union, which ended in the late 1950s when all aid to China was suddenly withdrawn by the Soviet Union. In the period 1950–60 China had little contact with the West and in the period 1960–9 was to a large extent economically and politically isolated from the rest of the world. Zhou Enlai commenced the process in 1969 of opening up to the Western world and President Nixon of the United States proved sympathetic to the establishment of new international relationships. Deng Xiaoping in the 1980s gave further support to the general policy of China's modernising and opening up to the outside world, a policy which continues to be followed by Premier Li Peng.

These policies provide new opportunities for enterprises from foreign countries to trade with and invest in China. Japan, the United States and many other countries have taken advantage of these opportunities. These new policies provide scope for mutual economic gain by China and foreign countries. In the Asian-Pacific region these policies provide new prospects for China's economic development and increase the likelihood that China will emulate the economic development achieved by its near neighbours (Hong Kong, Japan, South

Korea, Singapore and Taiwan). It is also hoped that its economic development will provide spillover economic benefits to those near neighbours and more developed countries in the Asian-Pacific region. Thus it is possible that the type of Greater East Asian Co-Prosperity Sphere which Japan hoped for before World War II may be established without resort to territorial imperialism. With growing fears that the world may become locked into major trading blocs, e.g. the European Market Bloc and the North American Bloc, countries outside these blocs such as Japan and Australia are likely to look increasingly to trade and investment within their own region as providing some alternative economic outlets. In that context the development of China becomes of increasing significance to the economic future of the Asian-Pacific region.

1.2 WHY IS IT USEFUL TO DISCUSS ECONOMIC DEVELOPMENT ISSUES IN THE CONTEXT OF CHINA?

It is useful to consider economic development problems in relation to China because a wide variety of such problems can be illustrated by China's experience, and because China has experimented with a variety of policies and economic structures in recent decades. In addition, leaders of the Communist Party of China, and liberal thinkers in that country, have consistently developed *principles* to support the type of economic development policies adopted by the government, as well as the changes in direction that these have taken. So a well-developed body of economic thought exists, even though one may not agree with all the socioeconomic principles espoused by it. Furthermore, the development problems of China are not unique. Many occur in other less-developed countries which have low levels of income per head, irrespective of whether they espouse a socialist or a private-enterprise approach to organising their economies. It is also instructive to compare China's economic direction and reforms with those of other socialist countries. China appears to have been much more successful, for example, than the Soviet Union in introducing market reforms.

As indicated above, the economic development of China is likely to have several important consequences for the rest of the world. These could include (1) an expansion in international trade which may be especially beneficial to China's neighbours and to other Pacific countries, (2) expanded opportunities for foreign investment in China, (3) adverse global environmental spillovers as a result of

China's economic growth, e.g. as a consequence of the greater emission of greenhouse gases, and (4) a change in the relative economic power of nations which may alter the international balance of military and bargaining power. For example, the relative international importance of China in the Pacific may rise in relation to Japan and the USA; the Chinese sphere of international *influence* might be expected to expand (Klintworth, 1989, Chapter 1).

Of course, another reason to be concerned about the economic development of China is that it affects directly the welfare of approximately one-fifth of the world's population. This provides an anthropocentric reason for concern. In addition, China contains many unique species of wildlife, the giant panda among them, and several natural environments of global significance. For those individuals who are concerned not only about people but also about the conservation of nature, the possible implications of economic development in China have a further interest.

1.3   ECONOMIC AND RELATED FEATURES OF CHINA AND COMPARISONS MAINLY WITH INDIA

To see China in international perspective it is useful to compare a number of its economic and related features with those of India. (Some additional comparisons with Asian-Pacific Economies are given in Chapter 12.) China and India are the two most populated countries on earth. China's population was estimated to be 1088 million in 1988 and India's 815 million (World Bank, 1990). China's 1990 census indicates a population level for China of 1133 million that year. The land area of China is 9561 thousands of square kilometres and that of India 3288 thousands of square kilometres. Thus China has a land mass almost three times that of India. It is also clear from the above figures that the *average* density of population in China is considerably less than that in India.

The land area of China is exceeded only by those of Russia (almost twice the size of China) and Canada, and is slightly in excess of the area of the United States. Thus the Chinese government has a large area to develop, control and protect, extending across a number of geographical regions and containing a diversity of natural resources.

The World Bank (1990) classifies China and India as low-income countries, that is in the group of countries for which gross national product (GNP) per head was less than $US500 in 1988. In that year the estimated GDP per head of China and India were almost the same being $US330 and $US340 respectively. But GNP per capita in China, starting from a lower base, has increased at a much faster rate than in India. In the period 1965–88 it registered an annual growth rate of 5.4 per cent compared with 1.8 per cent for India. The annual growth rate of aggregate production in China, that is of GDP, in the period 1980–88 was almost twice that of India being 10.3 per cent compared with 5.2 per cent. In the same period the annual growth in population was 1.3 per cent in China and 2.2 per cent in India. In the period 1965–80 the growth rate of GDP was higher in China than in India, but the population growth rates were similar (World Bank, 1990). The slower rate of population growth on average in China, plus the *much* faster rate of growth in its GDP, explains why the rise in GNP per head is proportionately much higher in China than in India. If these disparities in growth rates should be maintained, China will soon outdistance India from an economic point of view.

It is interesting to note that life expectancy in China is 70 years (1988 estimate), which is high by world standards. It compares with a life expectancy for India of 58 years. The average life expectancy for high-income countries is 76 years, and for low-income countries other than China and India it is 54 years. In 1988 the adult literacy rate in China was considerably higher than that in India, being 69 per cent compared with 43 per cent.

Not only did China have a faster annual percentage growth rate of GDP than India in the period 1965–88, but all major sectors of the Chinese economy (agriculture, industry including manufacturing, and the service sector) grew at a faster percentage rate than there counterparts in the Indian economy. It is interesting to compare the production structure of the Chinese economy with those of India and other countries. Table 1.1 sets out the percentage contribution to GDP by major sectors for China and India in 1988 and for selected other countries and groups of countries.

A number of features are apparent from the table. First, while the proportion of GDP accounted for by agriculture is the same in China as in India, the proportion of total GDP accounted for by industry and particularly manufacturing is much higher in China than in India. On the other hand, the relative size of the service sector in China is much smaller than in India. This composition may in fact reflect the heavy past and recent emphasis of Chinese planners in encouraging the growth of industry and manufacturing rather than service industries, which Marxists have traditionally regarded as unproductive. This

Table 1.1   Structure of production of China, India, of selected other
economies and income groupings of economies, 1988.
Percentage distribution of GDP

Country or or grouping	Agriculture	Industry[a] (including manufacturing)	Manufacturing	Services
China	32	46	31	21
India	32	30	16	38
Other low- income economies	33	27		40
Australia	4	34	18	61
Japan	3	41	29	57
United Kingdom	2	42	27	56
United States	2	33	22	65

Note: [a] Industry estimates include value added in mining, manufacturing, construction, electricity, water and gas.

Source: Based on World Bank (1990) Table 3.

Chinese emphasis, which now seems to be undergoing modification, reflects past Soviet emphasis and practice. In relation to other low-income economies apart from India, the proportion of GDP accounted for by industry is much higher in China and the proportion attributable to the service sector is much lower. Thus this pattern is a distinctive feature of the current Chinese economy.

For comparative purposes, the structure of production for some high-income countries is given in Table 1.1. In these countries, the proportion of total GDP accounted for by agriculture is comparatively small, and that accounted for by the service sector is very high, compared with low-income economies including China. This is consistent with Colin Clark's (1957) observation that the percentage of GDP accounted for by agriculture tends to fall and that contributed by the service sector tends to rise with increases in per capita income levels.

Comparative macroeconomic features of China's economy are also interesting. Table 1.2 sets out gross domestic investment and gross domestic savings of selected economies as a proportion of their GDP, their exports of goods and non-factor services as a similar percentage, and net private direct investment in the country concerned in millions of dollars (US). Note that international trade balances account for the differences between investment and savings figures. Countries with higher savings and investment ratios have greater comparative levels of capital accumulation and a priori place a heavier emphasis on economic growth and future economic prosperity rather than current consumption.

In 1988 China's gross domestic investment was 38 per cent of its GDP and its gross domestic savings were 37 per cent, giving it the relative highest rate of capital formation and savings ratio in the group of economies shown in Table 1.2. Both these ratios are, for example, well in excess of those for India. If these disparities are maintained it is likely that China's economy will continue to grow at a much faster rate than that of India. This, combined with a slower rate of population growth in China than in India, suggests that per capita GDP in China will soon exceed that in India and increasingly rise above it. Note that China's savings ratio is also well in excess of that for most high-income economies. Only in Japan among the high-income countries is 33 per cent of GDP saved.

However, it should be noted that some reformers believe that the accumulation rate in China is too high because it depresses the real incomes (consumption levels) and living standards of the workers and

Table 1.2   Gross domestic investment, gross domestic savings and exports of goods and non-factor services as a percentage of GDP and net direct private foreign investment in millions of US dollars for selected economies, 1988

	Gross domestic investment % GDP	Gross domestic savings % of GDP	Exports of goods and non-factor services % of GDP	Net direct private foreign investment $US m
China	38	37	14	2344
India	24	21	7	280
Other low-income economies	18	14	19	
High-income economies	22	22	21	
Australia	24	23	17	−460
United Kingdom	21	17	23	−13 078
United States	15	13	11	40 920
Japan	31	33	13	−34 710

Source: Based on World Bank (1990) Tables 9 and 18.

peasants and thereby reduces incentives. It may also result in some investment being undertaken that has a very low or zero return and in insufficient attention being given to the optimal allocation of scarce capital in the Chinese economy. In the past, and up to the present to some extent, capital has not been allocated in the way that is most productive. Critics believe that somewhat greater relative consumption would provide an even greater stimulation to economic growth.

The second feature apparent from Table 1.2 is the extent to which China has become an open economy. In 1988 exports of goods and non-factor services accounted for 14 per cent of China's GDP, twice the proportion for India. On the basis of this measure, China was a more 'open' economy than the United States, and almost as 'open' as Australia. As a result of China's change of course, with the adoption of open-door policies, there has been a dramatic increase in Chinese trade with the outside world. In 1965, for example, China's exports of goods and non-factor services amounted to only 4 per cent of its GDP.

It is interesting to note that, unlike the majority of other low-income countries, both China and India export mostly manufactures, principally light manufactures. In the case of India, however, the proportion of exports accounted for by machinery and transport equipment is higher than in the case of China. The textile industry is an important source of exports for both countries and accounted for about a quarter of the value of exports of each in 1988. Imports also consist principally of manufactures, with the share of imports of machinery and transport equipment being significantly higher in the Chinese case, reflecting in part its higher rates of capital formation. It might also be mentioned that the direction of China's trade is relatively diversified, but a significant dependence on Japan, Hong Kong and the United States exists both as sources of imports and as destinations for exports (Bucknall, 1989). China has in the recent past been accorded most-favoured-nation treatment by the USA, and regards this of very great importance. Both Japan and the United States are, for instance, very important sources of machinery imports, and it is machines which in many instances embody new technology. But Western European supplies are also important sources of China's imports of equipment.

Another significant feature of the Chinese economy is the extent to which direct foreign investment occurred in the 1980s. While after the political disturbances of May–June 1989 such investment dropped, it continues to be encouraged as a means of helping modernisation. In 1988 foreign private direct investment in China amounted to $US2344m, more than 8 times that in India. Hong Kong, Japan, the

United States and Western Europe were amongst the major investors (Bucknall, 1989). In fact, in 1988, no other low-income economy had such a high level of foreign direct investment. The economies in this group with the next highest levels of such investment were Nigeria ($US836m) and Indonesia ($US542m). It is thus clear that both foreign trade and foreign direct investment have become significant features of China's contemporary economy.

1.4 CHINA'S TRANSFORMATION

China is in a state of economic transformation. This tends to bring with it social transformation and is likely to increase pressures for political change. China's modernisation program, following the Maoist period of isolation from the rest of the world, commenced in the late 1970s and has involved reforms of its economic system (the introduction and extension of markets, market reforms, and new systems of economic incentives) and an opening up to the outside world in the fields of trade, production techniques, marketing, and foreign investment. The reasons for the change of direction in Chinese policy are complex. But undoubtedly the economic success of Japan, South Korea, Taiwan, Hong Kong and Singapore have provided nearby examples for emulation, and given cultural similarities, may have led the People's Republic of China to believe that it can have similar success by modifying its system (Jao *et al.*, 1991). Also, the failure of Soviet-type centralised socialism to fulfil its economic promise in Eastern Europe and in the late Soviet Union provides a further pragmatic reason for China to persist with its economic transformation and greater openness to the outside world (Jackson, forthcoming).

None of the above is meant to suggest that China's transformation path is an easy one. It is a difficult road along which a number of temporary reversals have occurred. However, overall, the trend in China of continued market reforms and growing economic interdependence with the rest of the world has been sustained for over a decade. If the general view of von Hayek (1944) of the relationship between markets, democracy and dictatorship is correct then the market reforms will result in increasing pressure for political reforms and possibly an end to the one-party state. The contacts of Chinese with Western democracies will also reinforce these tendencies. Thus economic reform is likely to spill over into demands for political reform, and the CPC is likely to be increasingly tested in its ability to cope with these.

It is difficult to predict how well such political matters will be resolved. But, assuming that they can be resolved, and that political stability can be maintained in China, there is a very good prospect that the country, on the basis of its current economic policies and plans, will become a middle-income economy in the twenty-first century, and thus fulfil the aim of its present leaders. However, the road will be neither easy nor certain given both the political and the economic issues which must be dealt with. Several of these issues are taken up in the next chapter.

REFERENCES

BUCKNALL, K. (1989) *China and the Open Door Policy*, Allen & Unwin, Sydney and London.
CLARK, C.C. (1957) *The Conditions of Economic Progress*, 3rd edn. Macmillan, London.
GARRATY, J.A. and GAY, P. (1972) *The Columbia History of the World*, Harper & Row, New York.
HAYEK, F.A. von (1944) *The Road to Serfdom*, Routledge, London.
JACKSON, S. (forthcoming) *Chinese Enterprise Management: Reforms in Economic Perspective*, De Gruyter, Berlin and New York.
JAO, Y.C., MOK, VICTOR and HO, LOK-SANG (eds) (1991) *Economic Development in Chinese Societies: Models and Experiences*, Hong Kong University Press, Hong Kong.
KLINTWORTH, G. (1989) *China's Modernisation*, Australian Government Publishing Service, Canberra.
MACKERRAS, C. (1982) *Modern China: A Chronology from 1842 to the Present*, Thames & Hudson, London.
SMITH, ADAM (1910) *Wealth of Nations*, Dent, London (1st edn 1776).
WORLD BANK (1990) *World Development Report 1990*, Oxford University Press, New York.

2 Major Policy Issues, Reforms, Protest and Economic Achievement

2.1 PROTEST AND ECONOMIC CHANGE

One does not want to dwell on the demonstrations in China in 1989, given the tragedies involved but they do illustrate the socioeconomic tensions which have arisen during China's economic transformation phase, which have surfaced before (in a less stark form, but still resulting in the downfall of General Secretary Hu Yaobang), and which could surface again. They also point to the difficulties of bringing about evolutionary economic reform in a one-party system, especially if it is dominated by Marxist evolutionary philosophy (Bucknall, 1989, p. 177). The crisis highlighted economic and political areas which require attention in the Chinese setting. The outcome of the demonstrations makes it clear that the present leadership is not prepared to make political concessions from the bottom up on the basis of illegal demonstrations. The leadership has espoused the policy of 'economic reforms now, political reforms later', i.e. once economic development has proceeded far enough. Just how much later these political reforms will come and what nature they will take remains an open question.

The student demonstrations which occurred in China in April and May 1989 led to the declaration of martial law in Beijing which was intended to be effective from May 20. But the demonstrations continued and this culminated in bloody military action on June 3 and 4 to quell them. These demonstrations had partly a political and partly an economic basis (for an analysis, see Mackerras *et al.*, 1989). While some demonstrators and their supporters were clearly in favour of more democracy and liberalism along Western lines, including a multi-party system, others were merely in favour of more liberalism within the existing political order, greater freedom of the press and more effective means of dealing with corrupt officials and eliminating corruption. It may have also been that some young people wanted

11

greater equality of economic opportunity according to ability. Social and CPC connection and seniority still play a large role in the allocation of economic rewards and opportunities in China, and some youths appeared impatient about this. For example, an undergraduate in management at Nankai University told me in 1989 that former students had said to undergraduates that there was no point in studying hard, because on entering business they would find that they would have little chance to influence decisions, owing to the seniority structure. (Of course, it may be noted that such structures also exist in Japan and other Asian countries.)

Support for the demonstrators was widespread in urban areas, at least prior to 20 May. This was partly because of concern about corruption, inflation and rising economic expectations not being fulfilled as quickly as had been hoped. The media also gave considerable coverage to such issues and the demonstrators. This led to speculation that political factions within the CPC were trying to use the unrest to their own advantage, e.g. that the former General Secretary of the CPC, Zhao Ziyang, and his supporters were using the media and the educational establishments to stir up political unrest to gain advantage in their rivalry with Premier Li Peng and the factions supporting him. In any case, the aftermath was that Zhao Ziyang disappeared from the political scene after June 4, and the position of Li Peng was strengthened.

As far as the rest of the world was concerned, there was a period of uncertainty as to what might be the direction of future Chinese economic policy. Zhao Ziyang had a reputation as an economic liberal, whereas the Russian-educated Li Peng was widely regarded as having centralist economic control tendencies. But soon after the end of the demonstrations, Deng Xiaoping, Chairman of the Advisory Committee of the CPC, announced that China's open-door economic policies would continue. Not only has this happened, but in 1991 market reforms proceeded further than ever before in China.

2.2 ECONOMIC ACHIEVEMENTS

The economic growth of China since 1979 has been outstanding by international comparisons, as was apparent from data in the previous chapter. In the decade beginning in that year, China more than doubled its output and was one of the six economies in the North-Western Pacific to experience an exceptionally high economic growth rate (cf. Garnaut, 1989a, b). Annual rates of growth of national income averaged a little over 9 per cent, and in the period 1979–88 and 1983–8 over 10 per cent. China's increase in real national income in 1988 compared with 1987 was 11.2 per cent. While these rates of growth were much higher than in the period 1952–78, when Maoist principles prevailed, even back then the average rate of growth of real national income in China was high by international comparisons, at around 6 per cent, although possibly this was unsustainable under the Soviet-style centralised system adopted at the time (Dernberger, 1989, p. 54).

Since 1979 the structure of the Chinese economy has changed, principally in the increase of the relative importance of the tertiary sector. This contributed 14.8 per cent of GDP in 1979 and 21 per cent in 1988, increasing at the expense of both industry and agriculture, which in 1988 accounted for 46 and 32 per cent of GDP respectively (World Bank, 1990, Table 3).

China has also had to cope with a large increase in population, more than 100 million in the decade 1980–90, and with a rapid growth in urbanisation. Since 1980 the percentage of Chinese living in urban areas has risen from 20 to over 40 per cent (Lavely, 1989, p. 69). While the bulk of China's population is still engaged in agriculture and related pursuits, the percentage so employed has fallen markedly.

Despite the large increase in China's population, real per capita income and consumption per head rose significantly in the 1980s. Real income per head almost doubled and real consumption per head rose by more than 75 per cent. Consumption per capita of key commodities such as grains, meat, cloth and bicycles rose substantially (Dernberger, 1989, p. 53).

Nevertheless, in recent years and since the market reforms and the greater decentralisation of economic decision-making, the Chinese economy has been strained by demand-pull and wage-push inflation. In 1988 the inflation rate reached 18 per cent and in the first quarter of it appeared to be accelerating. This inflation was fuelled by ambitious development plans, deficit financing by the government, and easy-money conditions in which the rate of interest was less than the rate of inflation. One cannot completely blame the inflation on the economic reforms, because inflation earlier tended to be repressed rather than overt. Nevertheless, there are institutional reasons why China is very susceptible to inflation in its transformation phase (Yang and Tisdell, 1991). By early 1989 there were increasing complaints among workers about money wage rises lagging behind the rate of inflation.

Also, a very important change in the direction of China's policy has been its opening up to the outside world and the increase in its reliance on international trade. More and more, Chinese economic activity has been orientated towards international trade. In 1979 exports plus imports amounted to a sum equivalent to 13.6 per cent of national income, but by 1987 this had increased to 33.1 per cent. According to Dernberger (1989, pp. 59–60)

China has changed from being a developing country with one of the lowest foreign trade dependency ratios in the world to being the largest foreign trader in the developing world with a foreign trade dependency ratio that is exceptionally high for a large continental country at any level of economic development.

As noted in the previous chapter, the Chinese economy is now more 'open' than that of the United States in terms of its trade-to-GDP ratio, and almost as open as the Australian.

It is interesting to note that around 40 per cent of China's trade is with less-developed countries, with which China runs a significant trade surplus. This surplus is important in enabling China to help cover its trade deficits with a number of developed countries. Furthermore, the major portion of its trade is with Asian-Pacific countries. Japan is its major trading partner, closely followed by Hong Kong. But trade with the USA is also important. When the figures for trade with Australia, South-East Asia and Canada are added together, the Asian-Pacific area accounts for around three-quarters of China's trade as judged by statistics in Bucknall (1989). Only around 11 per cent of Chinese trade appears to be with communist bloc (or former communist bloc) countries, judging from the 1984 and 1985 figures (Bucknall, 1989, p. 195), whereas in the 1950s more than half of its trade was with such countries. China is unlikely to return to such a pattern of trade in the foreseeable future, and more likely to become further integrated into international development in the Asian-Pacific region.

2.3 STRUCTURAL CHANGE AND ASSOCIATED LONG-TERM POLICIES

China has given a high priority to policies to control population increase. In 1970 it reversed Maoist policies favouring population increase, and adopted a policy of 'late marriage, child spacing and fewer children' that is, *'Wan, Xi, Shao'*. This policy relied on administrative intervention and tax or cost penalties for those exceeding family quotas and publicity campaigns. In 1979 the authorities went further and moved from a policy of two children per couple to one of one. The fertility rate in China has dropped markedly since these policies have been adopted, partly because of the policies themselves and partly because of other influence on the birth rate such as increased urbanisation.

Nevertheless, the government is still some distance from achieving its goal of one child per couple. In 1987 the fertility rate was 2.6 and in 1988 it was 2.4, whereas in 1965 it was 6.4. It has proven much easier for the government to implement its policy in cities than in the countryside. According to Lavely (1989, p. 69), 'The one-child policy is now largely an urban phenomenon; in most rural areas the actual policy is to maintain the rate at two children per couple.'

In 1989 China's population reached the 1.1 billion mark and it appears as though it could exceed the 1.2 billion upper limit originally set for the year 2000. Still, the current fertility rate is far below the norm for a country with China's per capita income and is much lower than a decade ago. From this point of view, China's population policies have been relatively successful. In 1988 China had the lowest fertility rate of any country in the World Bank's low-income group (World Bank, 1990, p. 230). China's population, according to World Bank estimates, is likely to become stationary from around 2000 onwards.

Since 1980 China's rising population has been increasingly accommodated by greater urbanisation. According to World Bank (1990) estimates, China's urban population as a percentage of its total population was 18 per cent in 1965 and 50 per cent 1988. Until 1980, strict policies were adopted to retain rural dwellers in the countryside. But, beginning in 1980, this policy was relaxed and now the percentage of China's population living in urban areas has more than doubled compared with 1979. This change has necessitated a large investment in urban infrastructure and has led to considerable pollution in urban areas, thus creating new difficulties. But population movement to cities as compared with local townships is still impeded, for example, those working in cities on temporary permits suffer economic disadvantages compared with those with permits for permanent urban residence.

To counteract the demand of rural dwellers to migrate to large cities, the government has encouraged the growth of manufacturing in the countryside and in small urban areas. China's township enterprises produced about 30 per cent of the national industrial output in 1990 and this proportion has been increasing (*China Daily*, 11 April 1991). At the end of 1990, rural industrial enterprises in China employed 92 million ex-farmers and thus had made a significant contribution to the absorption of China's surplus agricultural labour force. Nevertheless, a sizeable surplus agricultural workforce remains and even after the planned expansion of rural industry it is estimated that there will still be over 60 million surplus labourers in country areas at the end of this century (*China Daily*, 30 March 1991).

The government has also adopted policies to channel the direction of the population drift to the cities and to shape the pattern of regional development. Its emphasis is on developing the coastal areas and their cities first. The east coast area is regarded as China's window onto the world. It is hoped that once development proceeds sufficiently far in the east it will spread to inland. However, this policy is causing some internal political tension as income disparities between the east and the west of China increase and the 'trickle-down' benefits of this policy fail to be apparent to those in the west (cf. Cheng Fuhu, 1987). Some modification of this uneven regional development policy may become necessary for political reasons.

As indicated in the previous chapter, the Chinese economy is characterised by high rates of investment and capital formation. Investment in fixed assets as a proportion of national income has increased steadily. It rose from 23 per cent in the period 1966–78 to 28 per cent in 1987. To some extent, this high rate of capital formation has counteracted inefficiencies in resource allocation and management. However, there are limits to the extent to which productivity increases can be sustained merely by increasing the quantity of capital. With economic growth it is soon found that the major avenue for increasing productivity is an increase in the quality of factors of production, especially capital (cf. Denison, 1962; Dean, 1955). Capital needs to embody new technologies, the quality of the workforce needs to be improved by training and education, and so on. The Chinese government in adopting its modernisation program and its policy of opening up to the outside world, seems to have had these considerations in mind.

Opening up to the outside world has provided opportunities for the introduction to China of foreign technology and production methods. It has also provided Chinese industry with more competition, because of the increased dependence on foreign trade, which means that

Chinese firms are being forced more and more to sell on the international market. In addition, the government has encouraged direct foreign investment, both in joint venture arrangements and in solely foreign-owned enterprises.

In April 1989 there were 15000 enterprises in China involving foreign direct investment. Of these, 7800 were joint ventures, which, according to the *China Daily* (11 April 1989, p. 2), have played 'an important role in easing fund shortages, introducing advanced technology and management methods, training personnel and increasing exports'. In addition, China had direct investment in 558 enterprises abroad, mainly in Australia, Canada, Hong Kong, the Federal Republic of Germany, Japan, Thailand and the United States. In fact, China's foreign investment abroad is largest in Australia, standing at US$280 million in April 1989 (*China Daily*, 18 April 1989, p. 23) while at the same time Australia's investment in China exceeded US$210 million. As pointed out in the previous chapter, direct foreign investment in China in 1988 exceeded US$2000 million, and was by far the highest level of direct investment in any low-income country (World Bank, 1990).

However, after June 1989 the flow of foreign investment to China fell as a reaction to the political demonstrations and the way in which they were quelled in Beijing. But by May 1991 it was reported that foreign private direct investment in China was again flowing strongly, with Taiwan, Hong Kong, Japan, Western Europe and the United States being important sources, making China once again a major recipient among developing countries of such funds (*China Daily: Business Weekly*, 19 May 1991, p. 1).

2.4 PRIVATE ENTERPRISES, THE MARKET AND INSTITUTIONAL REFORMS

Three types of ownership of business enterprises exist in China – private, co-operative (collective) and state. Private enterprises (mostly family-operated) are now widespread and dominant in agriculture, and important in urban retailing. But state-owned enterprises still preponderate in the industrial sector and remain important in the tertiary. Despite the continuing dominance of state-owned enterprises in manufacturing industry, their share of industrial output fell from 80.8 per cent in 1978 to 69.7 per cent in 1987. At the same time the share of the collective sector increased from 19.2 to 27.1 per cent and the contribution of the private sector (inclusive of foreign-owned enterprises) increased from virtually zero to 2.4 per cent (Liu Guoguang, 1989, pp. 18–19). Outside agriculture, public ownership (either state or collective) of enterprises remains dominant.

The role of the market mechanism in China has steadily increased. Liu Guoguang (1989, p. 19) reports that about half all commodities on sale in China are subject to the market to some degree. This includes about 65 per cent of all farm and sideline products, 55 per cent of all consumer goods and 40 per cent of all industrial materials. Nevertheless, to put this the other way round, about a half of all commodities on sale in China are *not* subject to the market, and many that are subject to the market are so only in a constrained way, for example through the 'double-track' price system whereby a quota is traded at a regulated price and supplies beyond the quota are traded at market prices. Furthermore, many commodities are subsidized, and this puts a heavy strain on the state budget. As Clark (1989, p. 79) points out, 'China's economy suffers from imbalances in resource allocation because of an extensive but shrinking system of state-controlled prices and subsidies.' Regulated energy prices in particular seem to have been a serious contributor to economic inefficiency.

As Liu Guoguang (1989, p. 21), vice-president of the Chinese Academy of Sciences, pointed out

> China has proceeded with economic reform in a piecemeal fashion, so at present the old and the new systems co-exist alongside each other. The aim of introducing reforms gradually was to avoid massive social and economic upheaval. However, this blending of the two systems has undoubtedly generated a series of thorny problems. For example, with neither the old mandatory system nor the new market system dominating the distribution of resources, the defects of both systems have been magnified. Confusion has arisen in production, circulation and management, creating much leeway for speculation and racketeering.

According to Dernberger (1989, p. 62),

> the Chinese have tried to introduce price reform on a marginal basis with small changes for a few items, giving subsidies to those who would be hurt. Although the Chinese leadership admits the need to reform the price system, it has continually stalled, postponed, temporised, and largely avoided the major step necessary for the creation of a new and efficient economic system.

The Chinese government continues, however, to expand the operation of the market system. Subsidies on grain, which have mostly benefited urban residents, were reduced in 1991 and state purchase prices for many commodities were adjusted so as to be closer to market prices. Nevertheless, a major goal of China's reforms has been to work towards an economic system in which 'the state regulates the market, the market guides the enterprise' (Wang Jiye, 1989, p. 16). However, this system is as yet weakly developed. The Chinese government has been unable to restrict aggregate demand to keep it in balance with aggregate supply, and readjustment in the structure of industry has been hampered by subsidies and by the use of non-market and market-constrained prices to allocate capital, labour services and real estate – important factors of production. For example, interest rates have been held below the rate of inflation, credit has been available comparatively readily to state and collective enterprises, and in general state and collective enterprises have not been disciplined for failure to repay loans on time, to make a profit or to maximize economic returns. The fate of such enterprises appears to revolve more around political considerations than economic realities. Economic discipline is therefore weak for most industrial enterprises and possibly for most involved in construction, transportation and commerce (see Chapter 10).

Liu Guoguang (1989, p. 22) points out that in the urban economy increased incentives and an absence of penalties has been the rule for state-owned enterprises, unlike in the collective sector. State-owned enterprises have had their taxes reduced, so they are able to retain more profits, but management structures have not changed, and much of the increased money has been paid out in bonuses and wage increases. He says

> In short, the undue stress on stimulation of interests has not only made no difference in the state-enterprise relations of interests, but has put enterprises in the position of demanding more from the state while contributing less. Such reform has made enterprises short-sighted in production and management, caused a surge in demand and destabilised the economy. (Liu Guoguang, 1989, p. 22)

To overcome this difficulty, increasing consideration is being given to the strategy of separating the ownership and management of state and collective enterprises. But this will not be effective unless appropriate mechanisms exist for markets to discipline enterprises that fail to maximize returns. For example, a capital market may be required, with the possibility of the takeover of companies that do not maximise returns. Such markets can if desired be combined with the state or collective ownership of resources or shares. Separation of ownership and management purely in name is not enough. For example, where a local government body owns all the assets in a local enterprise, there is a temptation to interfere, often on political grounds, in the management of the enterprise and to obtain special economic favours for it, e.g. by putting pressure on local banks to extend loans to it.

Lack of satisfactory economic control and discipline of urban enterprises remains a weak link in the current Chinese economic system, and without further economic reforms this shortcoming is likely to be a serious obstacle to the maintenance of the current rate of economic growth (see Chapter 10).

It may also be noted that economic growth in China, including especially urbanisation, has brought with it increasing environmental and pollution problems, effective policies have not been devised and enforced to deal with these. In general, state and collective enterprises are not forced to pay for the spillover costs imposed by their pollution. For example, in 1989 Sashi City in Hubei Province was ordered to pay compensation to a nearby county for environmental damage caused by the emission of pollutants from a factory. The city said it did not have the money to pay the compensation and has not paid. Furthermore, the pollutants continue to be emitted. Greater attention needs to be given by the Chinese government to developing effective policies to deal with environmental externalities.

2.5 ECONOMIC FACTORS AS A SOURCE OF POLITICAL TENSION

Substantial economic change, especially when it affects the social structure of a country, very often gives rise to political discontent. The economic reforms which have occurred and continue to be made in China involve substantial institutional change and China is, therefore, vulnerable to political dissatisfaction and unrest. Because of the double-track system, the economic transformation phase of the Chinese economy provides scope for corruption. Again, there is a constant risk of inflation being generated and periodically requiring severe centralist measures for its control (Yang and Tisdell, 1991). Increases in income inequality, alterations in determinants of social status and changes in economic security all add to stress on individuals even when there is considerable economic growth. Such factors may very well be a recurring feature of China while it remains in its transformation phase. From that point of view, it is useful to consider the economic issues which were important in China in the period leading up to and during the student demonstrations in 1989. In the early period of the demonstrations at least, there appeared to be widespread sympathy on the part of the urban Chinese for the grievances being aired by the students, and economic factors could well go a considerable way to explain this.

In that period the immediate major economic concerns in China were inflation (both overt and suppressed) (Zhao and Wu, 1988; Hans, 1989), the failure of wages to keep up with inflation in the non-business sector, e.g. among teachers, soldiers and similar public servants, a growing and continuing trade deficit, a rising external debt and growing inequality of income, both between regions and between persons. Apart from rising prices, the economy faced bottlenecks in transport, construction materials and energy. The expansion of electricity production had failed in many areas to keep pace with the growth of industrial production and blackouts and brownouts were not uncommon. Electricity rationing was necessary in a number of areas.

A further problem was rising consumer expectations. Consumption levels and availability of consumer goods had expanded rapidly in the 1980s, and the population was keen to purchase consumer durables, spurred on by advertising on television and elsewhere. But many groups found that their ability to purchase such goods was lagging considerably behind their expectations. This was a source of increasing dissatisfaction. For example, as reported in the *China Daily*, a young soldier committed suicide in early 1989 because his pay was, in his view, inadequate to purchase socially necessary luxuries or extras.

Some of the support for the student demonstrations in April and May 1989 possibly stemmed from economic factors such as the above, as well as general concern about corruption involving state officials. These matters may have been more important than an interest in democracy *per se*. A further widespread grievance was the lack of scope in society for decision-making by younger people of ability, not only in politics but in the economic system and society generally. Scope for corruption was increased by the piecemeal nature of the reforms and the hierarchical power system, and facilitated by inadequate or non-existent accounting systems.

An important issue at the time was whether political reforms should await the completion of economic reforms and substantial rises in income per head. On 4 May 1989 Zhao Ziyang, the then General-Secretary of the CPC, stated on Chinese television what appeared to be the official Party line, namely that political reforms must await the full implementation of economic reforms and the greater economic development of China. He pointed out that China was in midstream as far as its economic reforms were concerned, and that continuing progress could be endangered by lack of patience with the reforms at this time.

The visit of Gorbachev to China in May 1989 added fuel to the issue of whether political reforms should proceed now or be deferred. The *China Daily* reported that Gorbachev said at a news conference in Beijing that in the Soviet Union

> Without political restructuring the economic reform could not make headway. . . . He said that political reform in his country proceeded faster than the economic reform. He stressed the importance of democratisation and openness in political restructuring. He said public opinion is a forceful tool to promote the process of democratisation and openness. But he declined to pass judgement on China's student demonstrations. (*China Daily*, Friday, 19 May 1989, p. 4)

It is true that up until its banning in August 1991 the Soviet Communist Party had proved incapable of bringing about major economic reform in what was then still the Soviet Union, unlike the Communist Party of China. This failure has led to the belief in what was the Soviet Union that only through new political parties will genuine economic reform make progress. So while the Soviet approach has been 'political reforms now and economic reforms later (or as a result of the political reforms)', the Chinese approach is 'economic reforms now and political reforms later'. Which approach is likely to result in greater social and political stability is difficult to judge. Both involve major changes in society and can be expected to generate social tensions and at times political protests.

Of course, what is appropriate to the Soviet Union at its stage in economic development may not be appropriate to China. Indeed, the former Australian ambassador to China, an economist, Dr Ross Garnaut, has suggested that it is difficult to make out a case for other than democratic centralism, i.e. decisive leadership and even authoritarianism at this early stage of Chinese development (Garnaut, 1989a, p. 20). He points out that authoritarian, centralised government proved to be compatible with high growth rates for long periods earlier in South Korea and Taiwan. He goes on to claim, however, that 'heavily authoritarian government becomes more difficult to reconcile with rapid growth the further economic development proceeds' (Garnaut, 1989a, p. 20). He suggests that unless the Communist Party of China itself becomes less authoritarian internally, the political barrier to economic development may be encountered earlier than otherwise.

On the political scene, a continuing question for China is how to permit dissent and its expression in socially acceptable ways. In April 1989, according to reports in the *China Daily*, consideration was being given to the framing of laws to permit public demonstrations under particular conditions. This may, however, have been propaganda for the benefit of readers in the West. Whether or not the government will proceed in that matter in the future remains to be seen. Yet it is unlikely that the democratic parties will be annihilated in China. For example, an Associated Press-Reuter report in *The Courier Mail* (19 June 1989) says: 'The small and powerless democratic parties, made up mainly of intellectuals, voiced some support for students before the military crackdown, but have since come out behind the party's campaign to stifle counterrevolutionary dissent.' We can expect, however, redoubled efforts to be made for some time to prevent dissent from becoming a serious challenge to the leadership of the Communist Party and a source of economic disruption in China.

The extent of popular support for the student demonstrations in April and May 1989, especially before declaration of martial law, may reside more in the economic exigencies of the time. China, despite its high economic growth rate, was facing mounting economic difficulties. An important reason for this was that economic reforms had not proceeded far enough and effectively enough in relation to urban enterprises mostly owned by the state and public co-operatives. Because of political factors they were without effective economic discipline, and this added to inflation and inequality of incomes. The greatest challenge for the Chinese economy is to discipline such enterprises through the effective separation of ownership and management, the possibility of takeovers and effective capital markets (see

Chapter 10). This requires further market-type reforms, but not necessarily the ownership of shares in such enterprises by private individuals – it is possible for shares to be held by state corporations, superannuation or finance companies. The alternative is to return to a rigid, Soviet-style Stalinist era of central direction. This is very unlikely now, because Soviet-style centralisation is out of favour world wide in the 1990s. Furthermore, given the growing complexity of industries and the flexibility and improvements in quality required for economic growth, in China such a move is likely to be retrogressive from an economic viewpoint. The choice of going forward or backward with economic reforms is a constant dilemma facing China, but it is unlikely to be able to stop its reforms in midstream, because of the economic discontent which this would generate. Maybe China is on a tiger's back after all, even if it is a tiger of its own choosing.

Soon after 4 June 1989, Deng Xiaoping appeared on Chinese television to promise that the Government would press forward with its policies of economic reform and continue with its opening up to the outside world. He also emphasised that he was the architect behind China's economic reforms. In so doing, he indicated that the economic reforms and their continuation were not dependent upon the continued presence of Zhao Ziyang as General Secretary of the CPC. China has continued with its market reforms and the general development agenda of China seems to have been basically unchanged since Jiang Zemin became General Secretary (*China Daily*, 25 March 1991, p. 4; and 20 May 1991, p. 4).

2.6 CONCLUDING COMMENT – ECONOMIC DEVELOPMENT AND POLITICAL CHANGE

At a time when most other communist countries have abandoned or are abandoning the one-party system of government, China appears to be out of step in 1991 by retaining it. In particular, its position contrasts with that of East European countries and the Soviet Union. The reasons for this are complex. Bucknall (1989, p. 177) suggests that it is because most Chinese leaders are basically orthodox Marxists in terms of evolutionary thought. Orthodox Marxists believe that society passes through six distinct stages of evolution from primitive (tribal) communism, through slavery, to feudalism, capitalism, socialism and finally full communism, a stage which has not yet been reached by any society. But China is in the socialism phase and the CPC has, in its view, a mandate from the people to guide China to the final phase in a 'democratic' fashion. This can, it is believed, be most effectively achieved in a one-party state. To introduce a multi-party system would be retrogressive and would indicate that the CPC is unable to fulfil its mandate as set out in the constitution of the People's Republic. As emphasised by General Secretary Jiang Zemin, 'the leading position of the Communist Party was established in the course of (China's) historical development and is enshrined in the constitution' (*China Daily*, 20 May 1991, p. 4). Bucknall (1989, p. 177) claims that China's leaders see basic political freedoms, civil rights, and, presumably, a multi-party system as belonging to the stage of capitalism and as a part of bourgeois liberalism. To return to a situation involving these elements would be retrogressive and there-fore supporters of such ideas (such as some supporters of the student demonstrations of 1989) are seen as counter-revolutionary.

Nevertheless, increased pluralism is likely to be encouraged in China by increased freedom of individuals to operate in markets, by more scope for individuals to make their own economic decisions, by greater decentralisation of government decision-making and by further con-tact with Western democracies. In the past China has encouraged *conformity* of thought and action, first through the dominance of Confucianism and then subsequently through Marxism (Schurmann and Schell, 1968). It may however be that diversity rather than conformity is the necessary ingredient of successful economic advance in societies which become increasingly dependent on economic innova-tion and technological progress for continued economic progress, and that diversity becomes more important as economic systems 'advance' and become more complex. While misallocation of resources has been a commonly criticised feature of centralised socialist planning systems, an even more unsatisfactory feature may be their stifling of individual spontaneity and capacity to innovate, thereby retarding technological progress. It may well be true, as John Stuart Mill (1963, p. 240) suggested, that a state which substitutes its own decision-making for that of individuals produces 'little men' and that with little men little can be achieved.

Sometimes it is suggested in the West that because of its *conformist* Confucian legacy China is incapable of introducing a stable political system allowing diversity. But this seems to be too negative. It should be remembered that in the Middle Ages Europe had a feudal system based on obligations and the divine right of Kings. This 'theocratic' system had many parallels with that in China in which the emperors were believed to have the mandate of Heaven. In both cases, rulers could lose their right to govern by not satisfactorily carrying out their mandate, e.g. by abusing their subjects, and this could legitimise their overthrow in certain circumstances. In both cases a well structured social hierarchy existed, with the family being an important unit in society. But this did not prevent social change in the European case.

The mercantilist system of the Middle Ages in Europe (which also had its parallel in China), involving restrictions on trade and central controls, disappeared in Europe as a result of the rise of new technologies, enterprises and entrepreneurs, especially in the area of manufacturing. Eventually this led to the demise of the medieval system of government and the establishment of democracies in most European countries involving multiple parties. In the late eighteenth century, Adam Smith (1910) saw economic liberalism as being necessary at his stage in history to the growth of the wealth of nations. But he also believed, as did many subsequent British liberals, that political liberalism would be conducive to this goal.

However, even in Adam Smith's schema, political liberalism is compatible with the achievement of national economic wealth only if political stability can be sustained. The problem therefore becomes one, in the Chinese case, of how to retain political stability and national cohesion and at the same time to bring about reforms and allow scope for pluralism. Such an issue will not be solved by keeping to past dogmas, because societies develop and change and new social tensions arise which often require new responses for their resolution.

In the above respect, conservative politicians often face the problem of not being able to avoid political instability. In a period of socio-economic change, their failure to make reform may result in violent political upheaval, leading to chronic instability, given the inexperience of reformers and the absence of cohesive social structures in society to accommodate the new political order. This is not to say that a society cannot transform itself without political upheaval, but there is always a risk of such upheaval to a smaller or lesser degree. Caught in the above dilemma, the best a politician might do is to choose the least damaging path, always assuming that he has the ability to choose and has some knowledge of what this path might be.

The leaders of China seem to be well aware of the above issues, as is clear from an excerpt from the speech of Jiang Zemin, General Secretary of the CPC to the Soviet Academic Society entitled 'China on its March Towards the Twenty-First Century'. Although he linked his comments to the reunification of Hong Kong, Macao and Taiwan with the People's Republic, his comment is capable of wider interpretation. He said:

Experience over the past forty years and more tells us that the development of the economy requires, first of all, a political situation of stability and unity. Stability and unity are the prerequisites as well as the guarantee for economic development and reform, while economic development will, in return, promote and further develop a political situation of stability and unity. (*China Daily*, 20 May 1991)

But whether or not economic development will result in political stability and unity in China may depend on the presence of an appropriate degree of flexibility in the political system.

REFERENCES

BUCKNALL, K. B. (1989) *China and the Open Door Policy*, Allen & Unwin, Sydney and London.

CHENG FUHU (1987) *Study on the Poor Areas of China*, Institute of Economics, Chinese Academy of Social Sciences, Beijing.

CLARK, A. L. (1989) 'Problems and prospects for China's mineral and energy industries', pp. 75–82 in C. E. Morrison and R. F. Dernberger (eds) *Asia-Pacific Report 1989. Focus: China in the Reform Era*, East-West Center, Honolulu, Hawaii.

DEAN, P. (1955) 'The implications of early national income estimates for the measurement of long term economic growth in the United Kingdom', *Economic Development and Cultural Change*, 4 (1), pp. 3–38.

DENISON, E. F. (1962) *Sources of Economic Growth and the Alternatives Before Us*, Committee on Economic Development, New York.

DERNBERGER, R. F. (1989) 'China's economic reforms', pp. 53–64 in C. E. Morrison and R. F. Dernberger (eds) *Asia-Pacific Report 1989. Focus: China in the Reform Era*, East-West Center, Honolulu, Hawaii.

GARNAUT, R. (1989a) *China's Growth in a Northeast Asian Perspective*, Pacific Economic Papers No. 167, Australia-Japan Research Centre, Australian National University, Canberra.

GARNAUT, R. (1989b) *Australia and the Northeast Asian Ascendancy*, Australian Government Publishing Service, Canberra.

HANS BAOCHENG (1989) 'Does China face stagflation?', *Beijing Review*, 17–23 April pp. 4–5.

LAVELY, W. (1989) 'Demographic and Social Change in China', pp. 65–73 in C. E. Morrison and R. F. Dernberger (eds), *Asia-Pacific Report 1989. Focus: China in the Reform Era*, East-West Center, Honolulu, Hawaii.

LIU GUOGUANG (1989) 'Economic Reform: A Sweet and Sour Decade', *Beijing Review*, 2–9 January pp. 18–24.

MACKERRAS, D., BUCKNALL, K. and TROOD, R. (1989) *The Beijing Tragedy: Implications for China and Australia*, Australia-Asia Papers No. 51, Griffith University, Nathan, Brisbane.

MILL, J. S. (1963) 'On Liberty', pp. 127–240 in A.W. Levi (ed.), *The Six Great Humanistic Essays of John Stuart Mill*, Washington Square Press, New York.

MORRISON, C. E. and DERNBERGER, R. F. (1989) (eds), *Asia-Pacific Report 1989. Focus: China in the Reform Era*, East-West Center, Honolulu, Hawaii.

SCHURMANN, F. and SCHELL, O. (1968) *Imperial China*, Penguin, Harmondsworth.

SMITH, A. (1910) *Wealth of Nations*, Dent, London (1st edn 1776).

WANG JIYE (1989) 'The state, the market and the enterprise', *Beijing Review*, 10–16 April pp. 16–21.

WORLD BANK (1990) *World Development Report 1990*, Oxford University Press, New York.

YANG RUILONG and TISDELL, C. (1991) *Inflation in the Transformation Phase of the Chinese Economic System: its Occurrence, Causes and Effects*, Discussion Paper in Economics No. 61, Department of Economics, University of Queensland, St Lucia, Brisbane.

ZHAO AI and WU, MING (1988) 'Ten Theoretical Questions Facing Reform', *Beijing Review*, 22–8 August pp. 20–4.

3 New Technology and Development: Policy Issues and Effects

3.1 INTRODUCTION – PAST AND PRESENT FOCUS ON SCIENCE AND TECHNOLOGY IN CHINA

Jiang Zemin, the General Secretary of the CPC, urged in 1991 that more emphasis should be placed on science and new technology as a factor in China's economic development rather than on the mere expansion of production using current techniques and involving the greater production of existing commodities. He proposed to put more reliance for economic progress on the development of science and technology and on improvements in the quality of the workforce (*China Daily*, 24 May 1991, p. 1; 28 May 1991, p. 1). In doing so he was favouring a policy supported by his predecessor Zhao Ziyang and endorsed by the Thirteenth National Congress of the CPC in 1987.

Greater application of science and new technology to Chinese industry is expected to result not only in the introduction of cost-saving and quality-improving new techniques but also in considerable product innovation.

Since the Communist Party came to power in China, it has placed considerable emphasis on science and engineering as a means for economic advancement. In the beginning, Communist China was able to rely on the Soviet Union for assistance in science and technology. But, as a result of disagreement between China and the USSR over ideological issues in 1957 and during the Great Leap Forward (1958–60), Soviet assistance was stopped in 1960 and China entered a period of relative technological isolation from the rest of the world which was substantially reversed only in the 1980s by the policies of Deng Xiaoping of opening up to the outside world – a trend made possible by agreement reached between Zhou Enlai and President Nixon of the United States in 1972.

During the 1960s and most of the 1970s, Chinese leaders held the view that a combination of foreign aid and dependence on foreign technology would hold back the economic development of the recipient by placing the recipient country in a neo-colonial position. This neo-colonial relationship was believed to lead to permanent dependence of the recipient country on other countries and thereby keep recipient countries in an economically backward state. 'During this period, China boasted about being self-reliant and recommended this to all the developing world, explaining that the acceptance of foreign aid weakened the recipient' (Bucknall, 1989, p. 106). Essentially, this outlook is similar to the neo-Marxian position expounded by Frank (1978; Tisdell, 1987). But since this period, China has looked to the outside world, mainly non-communist countries, as possible sources of new technology.

In its imperial past, the lack of technological change appears to have been an important barrier to China's economic development. While in its early history China made important technological advances, for example, in the period of the Tang Dynasty, by the period of the Qing Dynasty its capacity in that respect seems to have been exhausted.

Schurmann and Schell (1968) attributed this mainly to 'centuries of Confucian education and unchallenged preeminence [of China which] imbued the Chinese scholar-official class with a way of thinking that precluded new ideas . . . . [They believed that they] already knew truth and continued to allow the cumulative experience of the past to dictate action.'

The Confucian system in China did not encourage technological inventions and their *economic* application, and this proved to be an inherent weakness in the traditional Chinese economy. 'It [China] was capable of small gains but incapable of innovation in either the institutional or the technological sense' (Ping-ti Ho, 1968, p. 72). Therefore the Chinese social system contrasted with the European socioeconomic system of the seventeenth and eighteenth centuries, which resulted in considerable technological progress and economic development.

While Japan sealed itself off almost completely from the outside world for over two centuries in the Edo or Tokugawa era (1603–1867), it was forced by the US Navy under Commodore Perry in 1853 to open a number of its ports. Further conflict soon after with European powers and the United States indicated that Japan had to modernise to protect itself against foreign aggression. The Tokugawa shogunate had failed to modernise Japan and fighting broke out to bring its power to an end. The Shogun stepped down and the Emperor was returned to full power in 1868. Emperor Meiji made every possible effort to modernise Japan and it modernised at a rapid pace.

By contrast, China had failed to adopt a sustained modernisation policy prior to the establishment of the first Republic in 1912, and then, after that was faced with political turmoil for almost forty years, that is, with political conditions which made it impossible for it to pursue resolutely any policy of economic development (cf. Garratty and Gay, 1972, pp. 938–44). It was not until the establishment of the People's Republic by the Communist Party in 1949 that China had sufficient political stability to pursue steadfastly a modernisation program, requiring in part the introduction of new technologies. Since the late 1970s new international relationships have been conducive to China's bid to modernise and adopt, where appropriate, technology from abroad, especially from non-communist countries.

Why is there so much interest in new technology in China? It is not merely (or principally) that superior technology can be a source of international power or standing, or that the possession of adequate technology ensures that China's past humiliations by foreign powers will not be repeated (Thornton, 1977, p. 177) because of its enhanced ability to protect itself. The fact is that Chinese leaders believe that new technology is an important means for increasing the economic welfare of the Chinese people.

3.2 NEW TECHNOLOGY AS A SOURCE OF ECONOMIC GROWTH

The ability of humans to use and develop technology has been a major factor in the ascent of mankind over nature. It is a hallmark of modern societies that they are less at the mercy of nature than technologically more backward ones. In the long sweep of prehistory and history, new technology has been a major contributor to the economic improvement of mankind. Today technological progress makes a large contribution to the continuing economic growth of advanced economies (Denison, 1962). Therefore, many less-developed countries (LDCs), including China, look to new technologies as a means to assist their economic development. The major part of these technologies often has to be imported from abroad by LDCs, something that is not unusual in itself, for in fact, virtually all economies are *net* importers of technology, including advanced economies. Indications are that, in recent times, only the United States has been a net exporter of technology and technological ideas, and it may soon become a net importer, if this has not already happened.

As pointed out previously, China has in comparison to other countries extremely high savings and investment levels in relation to its national income and GDP. Like many other socialist countries in their earlier phases of socialist development, China appears to have given more attention to increasing the quantity of capital and other productive resources as a means of achieving economic growth than to improving the quality and productivity of its resources to achieve this end. Thus it followed the Stalinist strategy of the quantitative (extensive) development of production, rather than its qualitative development. Nevertheless, as indicated by Jiang Zemin's statements noted at the beginning of this chapter, this approach is changing. Increasingly China is concentrating on enhancing the quality and productivity of its resources through improved technology and knowledge. This change partly reflects changes in China's stage of development and partly mirrors variations in economic thought.

In the 1950s and early 1960s both Marxist and Western economists placed major emphasis on capital formation and quantitative increases in productive resources as the main generators of economic growth. Mechanistic models of economic growth very often involving fixed output–capital ratios were common, and typically economic growth models were based on only two factors of production – capital and labour. Rostow (1952) suggested that the most important prerequisite for a country to takeoff into sustained economic growth might be a sufficiently high level of savings and investment (a minimum critical ratio of about 10 per cent according to Rostow) in relation to national income. The higher the savings and investment ratio of an LDC the more likely it was to achieve sustained economic growth, in Rostow's view. Lewis (1954, 1965) argued that if this investment was allocated to industry rather than agriculture, this would be especially favourable for economic growth. Thus industrialisation and capital formation were viewed as the main engines of economic growth. Incidentally, from a policy viewpoint this was a similar emphasis to that favoured by Stalin. But Stalin went further and gave greater priority to heavy industry rather than light industry, possibly in part for military reasons.

But these simplistic views about the sources of economic growth did not go unchallenged. Denison (1962) argued that in modern economies increased education and improved technology are likely to become more important sources of economic growth than increases in the quantity of capital and labour. He estimated that in the period 1909–29 increases in the quantity of labour and capital contributed 65 per cent of the increase in US real GDP, improved education and technology 25 per cent and other factors 10 per cent. But in the period 1929–57 increased labour and capital contributed only 42 per cent of the increase in US real GDP, whereas improved education and technology accounted for 47 per cent of the increase and other factors 11 per cent (Denison, 1962). This suggests that with the economic advance of a country qualitative improvements in labour and capital become increasingly important as sources of economic growth.

In addition, however, a number of economists argued that a large investment ratio is not necessary for sustained economic growth even in an LDC, and that there is little historical support for Rostow's 'magical' 10 per cent ratio, a ratio which incidentally has been greatly exceeded by China for several decades. Blum, Cameron and Barnes (1967) state that historical 'research indicates that almost every country of today entered a phase of sustained growth with investment ratios below the magic figure of 10 per cent; and that the rise in that rate followed, rather than preceded, the adoption of the new technologies'. Phyllis Dean (1955) argued that it was qualitative improvements in factors of production in Great Britain (application of new technologies and improved education systems) which enabled Great Britain to begin its economic growth and sustain it in the eighteenth century.

These observations indicate that Chinese leaders (consider the statement by Jiang Zemin mentioned earlier) are wise to place increasing emphasis on qualitative factors as a source of economic growth, and more so as the Chinese economy develops. High investment ratios do not ensure sustained economic growth, and poorly directed investment can result in little or in extreme cases even zero or negative economic growth. Chinese experience during the Great Leap Forward and the Cultural Revolution underline this point. During this period labour productivity declined, even though accumulation rates were very high. In any case, poor direction of investment can result in much smaller economic returns and slower economic growth than is possible. China needs to improve mechanisms for directing and allocating its investment, not only in physical capital but also in human capital.

But economic development is not reliant purely on a mechanical allocative process. The scope for such a process to bring about real economic development seems to be extremely limited. As far as the development of new technology is concerned, forces favourable to innovation, individual spontaneity and entrepreneurship are needed (Schumpeter, 1942). The economic motivation of managers is also important, and given reduced structures this is often lacking in social systems, as is pointed out by Berliner (1976). These are the forces which have played a large role in economic growth under capitalism. They tend to be fettered by state bureaucratic systems. While state bureaucratic control systems *may* overcome the problem of malallocation of economic resources, it is doubtful whether economic enterprise (entrepreneurship) can flourish in the shadow of such systems (Schumpeter, 1962). It is clear that the question of how best to encourage enterprise has to be an important item on China's agenda of devising appropriate policies for its economic development.

Although it is clear that new technologies can make a significant contribution to the economic development of LDCs, they raise many difficult issues for policy-makers in LDCs. These include: What type of technology to import? For example, should low, medium or high technology be imported? How best to obtain new technology? How to most economically import technology from abroad and use it without losing a substantial degree of national independence? How much technology to develop indigenously and how much to import? To what extent should research be undertaken to adapt foreign technology to local conditions? (cf. Tisdell, 1981, Chapters 2, 3.)

But even wider social issues are raised by the introduction of new technology. New technology, as Marx suggested, influences the social structure and nature of societies. Many modern technologies, for example, require the specialisation of labour for their efficient use and cannot be used productively by families or small groups. Their optimal use is often in large urban centres and in factories. Thus work and living patterns are likely to change. In *some* circumstances, it may even be that economic efficiency of the use of new technology is enhanced by the more widespread use of the market system. Use of the market system has further *social* consequences for the community e.g. a greater mobility of labour leads to a reduction in bonds and loyalties to the family and to the local community.

3.3 NEW TECHNOLOGY AND THE REDUCTION OF ECONOMIC SCARCITY

As pointed out above, new technology provides a means for reducing scarcity, that is a means to satisfy human wants more fully using the limited resources available. To appreciate the possible significance of technological progress for economic scarcity, it is useful to recount aspects of the theories of the English economists Malthus (1798) and Ricardo (1817) and the debate about economic development which these theories raised. As is well known, Malthus warned that the rate of increase of human population tends to outstrip expansion of production, that is the means of production, and suggested a number of measures to restrict the rate of population increase so as to maintain income per head, for example, late marriages. The limited availability of land was seen as the main barrier to expanding production. The theoretical foundations of limits posed by shortages of land for economic development were specified rather precisely and comprehensively by Ricardo.

Ricardo argued that land is a relatively fixed factor of production (a gift of God) and that as increasing labour (or capital) is applied to its cultivation, its output will increase but at a diminishing rate. Ricardo believed that diminishing marginal productivity in agriculture and the tendency for population to grow when incomes exceed subsistence level could prevent incomes per head remaining above subsistence level for a lengthy period of time. However, he also suggested that technological progress could offset this tendency. It could result in rising incomes even with an increase in population. The essentials of his theory can be appreciated from Figure 3.1.

Assume that, given other available resources, the aggregate output, Y, of an economy is a function of its population. Given the available technology, this relationship might be represented by the production function $Y = f_1(N)$ as indicated by the curve OBC in Figure 3.1. This curve shows decreasing returns to population size, the labour force being assumed to rise with the level of population. If the subsistence level of per capita income is as shown by the slope of the line OBF then the economy may initially be in equilibrium at point B with a population level of N_1. However, if technological progress shifts the production function upwards so that the curve ODF applies, that is the production function becomes $Y = f_2(N)$, income per capita rises to an amount equivalent to the slope of line OD if the population level remains constant at N_1. *If population* levels can be held at N_1 this higher level of income can be maintained. But if population cannot be prevented from rising then the productivity gains of technological change may be frittered away by population increases and eventually equilibrium may be established at point F. This would involve a higher level of population being supported at subsistence level.

The Ricardian theory *suggests* that there are two important policy means to reduce scarcity or increase per capita income – (1) limit population growth and (2) promote technological progress. These are in fact important policies in China today, even though Chinese policies are not necessarily based on Ricardo's theory.

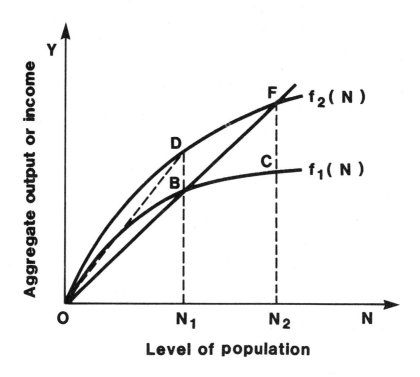

Figure 3.1 A simple Ricardian growth model

Zhao Ziyang (1987, p. 20), in an important report delivered at the Thirteenth National Congress of the Communist Party of China, stated that China should 'give first priority to the expansion of scientific, technological and educational undertakings, so as to push forward economic development through advances in science and technology and improved quality of the workforce'. But, as Zhao Ziyang recognised, scientific and technological progress does not occur automatically. It requires effort on the part of the population and the adoption of appropriate public policies. It may also require some restructuring of social organisation, for example, greater use of market mechanisms and improved two-way communication of information between the masses and the leaders. Concern must be with the substance of science and technology rather than with appearances, and it is important that the substance be translated into practice if productivity is to be increased and economic scarcity reduced. Some writers take a particularly optimistic view of the ability of science to reduce scarcity. Engels, for example, rejected the over-population thesis of Malthus on the following grounds:

science increases at least as much as population. The latter increases in proportion to the size of the previous generation, science advances in proportion to the knowledge bequeathed to it by the previous generation, and thus under the most ordinary conditions also in geometrical progression. And what is impossible to science? (Engels, 1959, p. 204).

More recently, Julian Simon (1981) has adopted a similar view to argue against the danger of the world becoming overpopulated and natural resources being seriously depleted. However, his view seems too optimistic (Tisdell, 1990). While scientific and technological advance can reduce scarcity substantially, we must be careful to avoid going to the extreme of *assuming* that science will automatically and, as if by magic, easily overcome all economic difficulties. The economic results from scientific and technological effort will depend on the *capability* of science, the institutional and social framework in which scientists, technologists and academics must work and the presence of mechanisms to ensure its appropriate *application* to production. We must distinguish clearly between pretence and reality in this regard.

3.4 NEW TECHNOLOGY, GROWTH, RESOURCES AND THE ENVIRONMENT

Questions are being increasingly raised about whether economic growth is always an effective means for reducing economic scarcity, increasing human welfare and ensuring economic development. E. J. Mishan (1967) pointed out that because of environmental spillovers and pollution arising from greater quantities of production, economic growth can impose social costs. Planners need to be aware of this possibility. Environmental costs need to be taken into account, and policy measures should be adopted to ensure that adverse environmental spillovers of economic growth and change are held to economic and acceptable levels. Note that economic growth is not bad in itself (in fact, it is a powerful means to increase welfare and improve environmental conditions), but unfettered, unplanned growth without regard to its wider social consequences can be. On the other hand, one should be clear that from an economic point of view it can be optimal *up to a point* to permit adverse environmental effects from increased economic activity. Indeed, it is rarely economic to eliminate all environmental pollution. This can be illustrated by Figure 3.2.

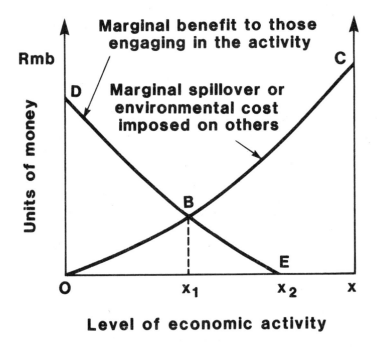

Figure 3.2   An optimal level of pollution

In Figure 3.2, the curve *DBE* represents the marginal benefits appropriated by those engaging in an economic activity. They maximise their gains by expanding their economic activity to level x_2. However, in carrying out this activity, they may impose environmental costs or damages on others through externalities or spillovers. The marginal costs imposed on others might be as indicated by the curve *OBC*. In the absence of regulation, those engaging in the activity in question will, if they follow their own self-interest, expand their activity to level x_2. But this is not socially optimal if the Kaldor–Hicks criterion of welfare is used. This criterion (sometimes called the potential Pareto-improvement criterion) supposes that an economic change is socially beneficial if the gainers from it could compensate the losers for any loss incurred and still be better off then before the change. Using this criterion, the optimal level of activity is x_1; that is, the level for which extra benefits from the activity equal the extra environmental costs imposed on others. This implies that in this case the activity should be curtailed in view of environmental costs, but not entirely prevented. Given its continuing economic growth, China will need to give increasing attention to such issues.

Concern has also been expressed that economic growth may prove to be unsustainable in the longterm. There is widespread fear that unsustainable development may occur because economic growth depletes non-renewable resources and can give rise to environmental degradation and pollution (World Commission on Environment and Development, 1987; Tisdell, 1990). For example, economic growth may result in increased income in the shortterm, but at the expense of a collapse in per capita incomes in the longterm because of depletion of non-renewable resources such as oil. The rate and extent of depletion of such resources depends to a large extent on the level of human population and per capita incomes. One implication of this view is that by restraining population increases, a higher per capita income level in society can be sustained for a longer period of time. Discussion has centred around just how long the world's stocks of non-renewable resources such as various energy resources might be expected to last; that is, on just how long it might be before absolute scarcity of non-renewable resources becomes an acute economic problem. Factors such as the rate of depletion, the size of resource stocks and the nature and speed of technological progress clearly have an important bearing on this matter.

The implications of the resource-depletion controversy for China appear to be mixed. It adds support for current population policy in China. On the other hand, it should be observed that China has barely touched its large reserves of non-renewable minerals. Although China has been held back from developing its mines by lack of modern equipment, there seems no good reason on equity grounds why it should not develop them and increase its use of minerals. However, control of environmental pollution and ecological conservation (conservation of nature) deserve greater public attention in China. On a world scale, there are additional fears about continuing economic growth and introduction of new technologies. The main concern is *global* pollution. For example, fears are being expressed by scientists that the continued burning of fossil fuels such as coal and oil is leading to a rise in the level of carbon dioxide (CO_2) in the air and to a 'greenhouse effect' which may trigger the melting of the polar ice caps. This would lead to a substantial rise in sea level and the inundation of valuable land, for example, large parts of eastern China. To the extent that this is a real problem, international co-operation is needed. Planned expansion of industrial production in China, which is likely to depend heavily on the use of fossil fuels, can be expected to contribute significantly to greenhouse gases and already this is a cause for international concern, as discussed in a later chapter (Myers *et al.*, 1990; Oppenheimer and Boyle, 1990).

Indeed, we live increasingly in an environmentally interdependent world as a result of new technologies and the enhanced power of man over nature (cf. World Commission on Environment and Development, 1987). However, we also live in a world with new risks.

In this respect, the disappearance of species and the reduction in genetic and ecological diversity mainly as a result of continuing economic growth (especially growing human populations) is a concern. This is so mainly from an ethical point of view, if it is accepted that nature has an appropriate place in our universe which on occasions requires humans to forgo the complete gratification of their own selfish desires. But apart from this, there are sound economic reasons for maintaining genetic and ecological diversity. As pointed out in the World Conservation Strategy (IUCN, 1980), sustainable economic development may depend on the preservation of genetic diversity. For instance, to maintain the productivity of important crops such as wheat, rice and sorghum it may be important to have a stock of wild cultivars to draw on for breeding purposes.

Chinese leaders recognise the importance of such issues. For example, Zhao Ziyang in a significant report delivered to and approved by the Thirteenth National Congress of the Communist Party of China declared:

Comrades, I have to emphasise here that population control and protection of the environment and ecological balance have a vital bearing on the growth of our economy and of society as a whole. There have been marked achievements in population control in China. . . . However, we must realise that with so big a population base and so high a number of births, we cannot afford to relax in the least our efforts in family planning. . . . While advancing economic development, we should energetically protect and rationally utilise natural resources, bring environmental pollution under comprehensive control, do a better job of protecting the ecological balance and integrate achievement of economic and social results with improvement of the environment. (Zhao Ziyang, 1987, pp. 31–2)

The importance of environmental issues continues to be recognised by the current leadership of the CPC. But further progress is needed in translating aims into policies and practice.

3.5 IMPORT OF TECHNOLOGY AND ECONOMIC INTERDEPENDENCE WITH THE OUTSIDE WORLD

As mentioned earlier, most countries are net importers of foreign technology. If an economic gain can be made by importing foreign technology and the import does not lead to loss of political independence then there seems to be no good reason for a country not to import it. Indeed, a solid argument exists for the import of such technology. Seemingly only crass nationalism would support technological isolation in such a case.

Current Chinese policy favours of imports of appropriate technology. In 1987, Zhao Ziyang (1987, pp. 21–2) said

We must continue to import advanced technologies from abroad, and integrate them closely with scientific and technological research at home, and we should intensify our efforts to master and assimilate imported technologies and to improve upon them. It is proposed that the State Council work out a medium- and long-range programme for the development of science and technology and launch it as soon as possible by organising the scientific and technological forces for the whole country for this purpose.

This policy is to continue in the 1990s. China's Ten-year Programme for National Economic and Social Development (1991–2000), as approved by the National People's Congress in 1991, states that

China will persist in the basic state policy of opening up to the outside world and in further expanding economic and technical exchange and co-operation with foreign countries (*China Daily*, 12 April 1991).

Technological and scientific know-how and intellectual property are extremely diverse and sometimes complex commodities to trade, especially internationally. Frequently, companies possessing the required technological knowledge have a monopoly on it either at law (e.g. through the patent system) or *de facto* (e.g. through secrecy). It is, therefore, often important from the point of view of maximising national gains for a country importing such knowledge to have a collective policy which limits competition between domestic producers in bidding for the technology. The effect of this is to make sure that the monopolist is faced by a monopsony (a single buyer) rather than many competitive buyers. Under those circumstances, the technology is liable to be transferred at a price more favourable to the importer.

However, there are some circumstances in which technological know-how can be transferred only by joint ventures. For these to be successful, agreements must permit adequate returns to both parties. China is actively pursuing joint ventures where these are likely to be in China's interest.

By having an appropriate policy for international economic co-operation and technology transfer, it should be possible for China to develop rather than 'de-develop' – that is, to avoid becoming trapped in a centre–periphery situation, meaning one in which it is on the periphery with economic backwardness increasing. Japan was able to import foreign technology and develop and catch up with other advanced economies without losing control of its own affairs. There is no good reason to suppose that China cannot advance similarly by adopting appropriate policies. The challenge is, as discussed in the next chapter, to specify appropriate policies in more detail.

3.6   DISTRIBUTION CONSEQUENCES OF NEW TECHNOLOGY

Policies designed to promote technological advance can have far-reaching social implications. They need also to be complemented by improvements in the education system and the quality of the labour force, as is being done in China (Tisdell, 1981, Chapter 1). Furthermore, incentive systems to encourage efficiency and the introduction of new technology are required, and this China's leaders recognise.

In addition, technological change may alter the distribution of incomes. For example, Kuznets (1973) has suggested that with economic development and the introduction of new technology the distribution of income in society at first becomes more uneven. *In the long term*, however, as development proceeds, income distribution may become more even. Whether or not China will experience this type of change in its distribution of income as the economy advances remains to be seen, and the issue will be discussed in Chapter 6. Possibly incentive systems will result in some increased inequality in income distribution. Up to a point this may be socially acceptable, but special care has to be taken to ensure that severe poverty does not emerge for particular individuals or groups in society as structural change proceeds. A socialist economy should, however, be in a good position given that sharing is basic to socialism to deal with such side-effects by providing special economic assistance to those affected.

3.7 CONCLUSION

China's new emphasis on scientific and technological progress can do much to bring about economic development, reduce economic scarcity and improve the quality of life of the people. Nevertheless, it will involve a large and continuing challenge for the economy, for policy-makers and for the people for many years to come if it is to meet with success. This has been recognised by Chinese leaders. In 1987 Zhao Ziyang (1987, pp. 8–9) said

We must be soberly aware that we have a much longer way to go and even more arduous tasks to perform. We are still at a quite backward stage, because our economic foundation was very weak to begin with, and because we lost too much time addressing the problem. Today's world is characterised by a rapidly growing revolution in technology, increasingly intense market competition and a volatile political situation. We are faced with formidable and pressing challenges. If we do not recognise this and redouble our efforts, our country and our people may fall further behind, and China will not be able to take its rightful place in the world.

Top CPC leaders, such as Premier Li Peng and Jiang Zemin, and government officials continue to make speeches and to write articles pointing out that 'the world has been in an accelerating technological revolution. Unless China can catch up with the latest developments in this area, the country can never become strong and its people prosperous'. (*China Daily*, 15 June 1991, p. 4) On this, an editorial in the *China Daily* comments that

> Few people will challenge the truth of this message, or doubt that it is needed. But much work remains to be done before it is fully understood and acknowledged by the general public and translated into concrete action. . . . [The editor continues after outlining some obstacles] that the task ahead is enormous. While prompt action must be started now, we must bear in mind that success will only come in the long term, after strenuous and sustained efforts. (*China Daily*, 15 June 1991, p. 4)

To recognise a problem, and take the first steps towards solving it, is essential for success. China has started on that path but needs to become increasingly aware of obstacles to be avoided on the way and to adopt means to circumvent them.

REFERENCES

BERLINER, J.S. (1976) *The Innovation Decision in Soviet Industry*, MIT Press, Cambridge, Mass.
BLUM, J., CAMERON, R. and BARNES, T.G. (1967) *The Emergence of the European World*, Routledge and Kegan Paul, London.
BUCKNALL, K.B. (1989) *China and the Open Door Policy*, Allen & Unwin, Sydney and London.
DEAN, P. (1955) 'The implications of the early National Income estimates for the measurement of long-term economic growth in the United Kingdom', *Economic Development and Cultural Change*, 4 (1), pp. 3–38.
DENISON, E.F. (1962) *Sources of Economic Growth and the Alternatives Before Us*, Committee for Economic Development, New York.
ENGELS, F. (1959) 'Outlines of a critique of political economy', in K. Marx, *Economic and Philosophic Manuscripts of 1844*, Foreign Languages Publishing House, Moscow.
FRANK, A.G. (1978) *Dependent Accumulation and Underdevelopment*, Macmillan, London.
GARRATY, J.A. and GAY, P. (eds) (1972) *The Columbia History of the World*, Harper & Row, New York.
HO PING-TI (1968) 'From the population of China', pp. 65–74 in F. Schurmann and O. Schell (eds), *Imperial China*, Penguin, Harmondsworth.

IUCN (1980) *World Conservation Strategy*, World Conservation Union, Gland, Switzerland.

KUZNETS, S. (1973) 'Modern economic growth: findings and reflections', *American Economic Review*, 63, pp. 247–58.

LEWIS, W. A. (1954), 'Economic development with unlimited supplies of labour', *The Manchester School*, 22, pp. 139–91.

LEWIS, W. A. (1965) *The Theory of Economic Growth*, George Allen & Unwin, London.

MALTHUS, T. R. (1798) *An Essay on the Principle of Population as It affects the Future Improvement of Mankind*. Reprint 1976, Norton, New York.

MISHAN, E. J. (1967) *The Costs of Economic Growth*, Staples, London.

MYERS, N., EHRLICH, P. R. and EHRLICH, A. H. (1990) 'The population problem: as explosive as ever?', paper delivered at the Fourth International Conference on Environmental Future, 'Surviving with the Biosphere', Budapest, Hungary, April.

OPPENHEIMER, M. and BOYLE, R. H. (1990) *Dead Heat: The Race Against the Greenhouse Effect*, Basic Books, New York.

RICARDO, D. (1817) *The Principles of Political Economy and Taxation*, 1st edn. Reprint 1955, Dent, London.

ROSTOW, W. W. (1952) *Process of Economic Growth*, Norton, New York.

SCHUMPETER, J. (1942) *Capitalism, Socialism and Democracy*, 2nd edn, Harper, New York.

SCHURMANN, F. and SCHELL, O. (1968), *Imperial China*, Penguin, Harmondsworth.

SIMON, J. L. (1981) *The Ultimate Resource*, Princeton University Press, Princeton.

THORNTON, A. P. (1977) *Imperialism in the Twentieth Century*, Macmillan, London.

TISDELL, C. A. (1981) *Science and Technology Policy: Priorities of Governments*, Chapman & Hall, London.

TISDELL, C. A. (1987) 'Imperialism, economic dependence and development: a brief review of economic thought and theory', *Humanomics*, 3, pp. 6–29.

TISDELL, C. A. (1990), *Natural Resources, Growth and Development*, Praeger, New York.

WORLD COMMISSION ON ENVIRONMENT AND DEVELOPMENT (1987) *Our Common Future*, Oxford University Press, Oxford.

ZHAO ZIYANG (1987) 'Advance along the road of socialism with Chinese characteristics', report delivered at the Thirteenth National Congress of the Communist Party of China 25 October 1987, pp. 3–80, in *Documents of the Thirteenth National Congress of the Communist Party of China (1987)*, Foreign Language Press, Beijing.

4 International Technology Transfer, Direct Investment and Joint Ventures

4.1 INTRODUCTION – BENEFITS AND MEANS OF INTERNATIONAL TECHNOLOGY TRANSFER

China, as mentioned in the previous chapter, is looking to international technology transfer as an important means of expanding and improving its stock of techniques. The 'self-strengthening' policies which China adopted in the 1980s as a part of its open-door strategy are planned to continue and develop under its Ten-year Programme for National Economic and Social Development (1991–2000). In reporting on the Ten-year Programme and the Eighth Five-Year Plan (1991–5) to the National People's Congress, Premier Li Peng

> pledged continued efforts to implement and improve the policy of opening to the outside world, saying that further efforts should be made to expand economic and technology exchanges with other countries and do a better job in the areas of foreign trade, utilisation of foreign capital and the introduction of technology and intellectual resources. *China Daily*, 26 March, 1991, p. 4)

China is still in its early stages of economic development and, like Japan before it, may well make substantial economic gain from international transfer of technology. Also, it should be remembered that the majority of high income countries continue to obtain substantial economic benefits from international technology transfer. Furthermore virtually all import more technology than they export, as indicated by a variety of crude measures of technology flows. National deficits in international technology trade seem to be the norm rather than the exception. Given the fact that each nation is comparatively small in relation to the rest of the world, it is not surprising that all (with the possible exception of the United States) have an excess of technology imports over technology exports.

One might also expect this relative deficit to be larger for countries in the early stage of economic development, such as China. At that stage the technological gap between the less-developed country and higher-income countries tends to be greatest. During this period, it may be most beneficial to the country to concentrate on imitating and importing foreign techniques (as Japan did), rather than concentrating on the development of indigenous techniques, reinventing foreign techniques independently or rejecting them entirely. This is not to suggest that there is no scope for indigenous independent research effort, but rather that it does not seem rational to make this the main priority. The transfer and adoption of foreign technologies seems a more appropriate emphasis in science and technology policy. However, to be most successful this does require indigenous or domestic scientific or technological effort (local research and development). Up to a point, the benefits from local research and development and the import of technology are *complementary* (Tisdell, 1981; Pazderka, 1991). In any case, the substantial transfer of international technology appears to involve active rather than passive processes. While some methods of transfer may be relatively passive, e.g. technology embodied in machines, most transfers of substance which add to local knowledge involve considerable effort. Furthermore, the selection and adaptation of foreign techniques to local requirements involves such effort.

Science and technology can be transferred between nations in a variety of ways. They may be transferred embodied in traded products, through books and publications, via informal contacts and observations, by means of specifications and blueprints, through formal personnel exchange arrangements and through interchange of individuals in education. However, the transfer of much scientific and technological information is not a simple process. It is increasingly recognised that to be successful it requires considerable effort on the part of both the transferrer and the recipient (Teece, 1977).

Pack (1981, p. 7) says:

The characteristic features of the required knowledge are that it is not easy to specify in blueprints or manuals . . . ; [that] it is difficult to negotiate about, since so much of it is tacit and thus a 'fair' price is difficult to define; and that recipients of technology cannot be passive but must undertake purposive action to increase the ability to identify their needs, to learn about those technologies that might be particularly useful, and, especially to operate them successfully.

He emphasises that technology transfer is not free, but involves hard work and substantial monetary costs both by the transferor and the recipient. Free *availability* of technology or scientific knowledge is not a recipe for its transfer.

A number of alternative institutional possibilities exist for scientific and technological co-operation and transfer. It may be arranged by privately owned companies. It can be via direct investment (as in the case of many multinational enterprises), by licensing to indigenous enterprises, by supply through consulting services, or by arrangement through a joint business venture. Alternatively, it can involve government-to-government arrangements or arrangements through semi-autonomous research bodies of the governments. Other possibilities include transfer or co-operation through private individual contacts, through voluntary organisations and through tertiary educational/ research institutions. Technology transfer and scientific co-operation may be on a bilateral basis, or by joint agreement between countries or parties therein, or arranged through international agencies on a multilateral basis. Australia, for example, contributes funds to the Consultative Group on International Agricultural Research (CGIAR), which supports a number of important agricultural research centres, most of which are located in developing countries, for example the International Rice Research Institute in the Philippines. But as Karunaratne (1981, p. 4) points out, in a global context the importance of commercial technology transfers to developing countries (TTDC) far outweighs non-commercial transfers.

The actual type of institutional arrangement used for technology transfer and scientific co-operation can be expected to influence the success of the venture and the distribution of benefits from it. The fact that research institutes associated with CGIAR are mostly located in LDCs seems advantageous in the agricultural field. Different arrangements may be appropriate for different types of technology and research. In this chapter, the discussion will concentrate on technology transfer in relation to business, especially through direct investment. It is at the business and production unit level that technology needs to be applied in *most* cases to provide economic benefits.

A number of scholars and policy-makers have attempted to generalise about the benefits from increases in the flow of science and technology from more developed to less-developed countries. Two polar views exist:

(1) A number of neo-Marxists, institutionalists and neo-mercantilists argue that science and technology flows from developed countries are to the disadvantage of LDCs. They are variously seen as means of economic exploitation, as means of global political domination, and as giving rise to structural problems in LDCs which hinder their economic development. This group argues that the best policy for LDCs is to dissociate themselves from developed countries or at least to engage in selective de-linking. For a time Mao Zedong during the 1970s, especially under the influence of the Gang of Four (Harding, 1989, p. 132), extolled the *disassociation* policy and urged developing countries to follow a similar policy (Bucknall, 1989). While the disassociation view was given attention at the United Nations Conference on Science and Technology for Development, the selective de-linking view seemed to be most favoured (Rittberger, 1982).

(2) At the other extreme is the view that LDCs are bound to gain as a result of a greater flow of science and technology from more developed countries. The '*integrationist*' school of world development argues that the best way for developing countries to progress is to rely on the benefits of international co-operation. Morehouse (1982, p. 52) claims that:

> Most policy initiatives in recent decades have assumed that the best way to attack inequities within and among nations through the international system has been to increase the flow of technology in the form of skills, knowledge, and hardware from North to South. [President Truman of the United States stated this policy in 1949 in his inaugural presidential address and] . . . it has been the cornerstone of not only US but other industrialised-country development policies as well as those of multilateral institutions, ever since.

Two different policy prescriptions have arisen from the disassociation hypothesis. These fall short of advocating complete disassociation of LDCs from developed countries; so in some respects they could be described as modified integrationist policies. They are:

(1) The recommendation for initial complete disassociation of LDCs from developed countries followed by selective re-linking. The Chinese case has been put forward as an example of this.

(2) Continuing but selective linking. Each LDC should only import science and technology in specific fields, which it nominates after establishing its priorities. Morehouse (1982, p. 54) suggests that:

> Selective de-linking does not, of course, involve technological isolation of the Third World, which would obviously be foolish in view of the overwhelming dominance of industrialised countries in virtually all areas of modern technology. It does mean carefully targeted technology acquisitions on the initiative of developing countries rather than the present system of indiscriminate North-South technology flows. . . .

Some versions of this approach, as indicated by Morehouse (1982), recommend that, to the extent that the LDCs become involved in international co-operation and technology transfer, they should try to depend on one another rather than on developed countries. Incidentally some writers such as Parry (1981) suggest that technology transfer from 'intermediate' countries such as Australia to developing countries is more appropriate for developing countries than transferring technology directly from central developed economies. According to this view, Australia acts as a useful filter and modifier of technology from larger advanced economies. It modifies process and product technologies for its smaller market and these become more appropriate to the economic conditions facing LDCs. Karunaratne (1981) also accepts this thesis, but Hill and Johns (1988) are more critical of it. In any case, there is a wide range of technology in Australia and not all of it is likely to be appropriate to LDCs. Much of Australian agricultural technology, for example, is designed for low labour intensity in use, and much of it is indigenous technology rather than filtered technology from other economies.

Karunaratne is critical of the disassociation strategy for developing countries. He says:

> Some economists, befuddled by the complexity of issues involved in technology transfer to developing countries, maintain an aloofness and others suggest that donor countries would be wise to down-play technology transfer to developing countries. For example, it has been argued that increasing the elasticity of supply of technology by fairer and freer transfers would undermine the capacity of developing countries to build an indigenous technological capability. The argument seems to condemn developing countries to languish in their underdevelopment. (Karunaratne, 1981, p. 9)

He sees technological transfer to developing countries as a positive-sum game in which both the donor or source of the technology, as well as the receiver, benefit.

It seems unwise to generalise to the extent that has occurred on the basis of mixed evidence. Science and technology and its transfer are not homogeneous, even in developed countries. A range of different effects and consequences can follow, depending upon what piece of science and technology is being transferred to a developing country. This suggests that some selectivity is required. An important question then becomes whether existing mechanisms of selection and transfer are adequate. If not, can they be improved *in practice*.

Theoretical evidence tends to suggest that a selective approach to international technology transfer is likely to be optimal from the recipient's point of view. But how should one select, and what conditions should be imposed on the transfer of technology transfer? To what extent is it possible to devise rational and practical policies in this regard, given that 'excessive' bureaucratic control can be costly and may add so much to international technology transfer costs as to seriously impede transfer? In that respect we need to bear in mind that international technology transfer is not a cut-and-dried or static exercise. To consider it in this way would be to ignore the importance of search, experimentation and motivation in human behaviour and endeavour. We often have to discover possibilities, including scientific and technological opportunities, and this calls for a degree of entrepreneurship. The ingredient of enthusiasm is a fragile but important component in our endeavours. Rational, comprehensive models of decision making are useful, but are too mechanical to capture all aspects of human endeavour.

Note that even if one favours *in principle* selective choice of foreign technology and control of its import by government in order for the importing country to maximise its gains, one may be sceptical about the ability of governments and public bureaucrats to make the appropriate choices. Furthermore, bureaucratic controls cause delays and add to exchange transaction costs, thereby deterring international technology transfer, even favourable transfers, as a result of such 'deadweight' imposts. Consequently, *laissez-faire* or near-free international transfer of technology may be favoured *in practice* if it is believed that international technological integration on the whole is beneficial, and bureaucratic intervention is unlikely to increase national gains and may even reduce these. On the other hand, if one basically believes in the strong disassociation hypothesis that free international trade in technology is likely to be disadvantageous to an LDC, but that international technology exchange with some selectivity can be optimal compared with no trade, then incompetence or the transaction costs involved in bureaucratic control or international technology exchange may lead one *in practice* to opt for a policy of no international technology exchange. In any case, the bureaucratic costs involved in any interventionist policy cannot be ignored in assessing the national advantages or disadvantages of a policy.

4.2 CHINA'S INTERESTS IN DIRECT INVESTMENT AND INTERNATIONAL TECHNOLOGY TRANSFER

With its opening up to the outside world and its adoption of modernisation goals, China has encouraged foreign direct investment in its industry and in some sectors of its service industry e.g. hotels and their operation. In 1988, foreign direct investment in China was far in excess of that in any other low-income country (World Bank, 1990), but fell substantially in 1989 after the student demonstrations. By 1991 it was increasing strongly again. China also has substantial direct investment abroad, but this is much smaller than foreign direct investment in China. Because of China's relative shortage of foreign exchange, one would expect its direct investment abroad to be limited.

Direct investment in business may involve the establishment of solely owned enterprises or joint ventures. Both forms of foreign investment occur in China, with equity joint ventures being slightly more common there, according to Chinese statistics. Both types of investment can result in the introduction of new techniques by foreigners. In April 1989, of the 15 000 foreign corporations conducting business operations in China, 7800 were joint venture enterprises. Equity joint ventures are said to have played 'an important role in easing fund shortages, introducing advanced technology and management methods, training personnel and increasing exports' (*China Daily*, 11 April, 1989, p. 2).

China's direct investments abroad are mainly in Australia, Canada, Hong Kong, Germany, Japan, Thailand and the United States. China is said to have three main reasons for investing abroad: (1) to provide the communication channels and contacts to facilitate the sale of its own products, (2) to ensure stable and adequate supplies of raw materials for China's industries, and (3) to obtain advanced technology, especially in industrialised countries (*China Daily*, 31 March 1989).

Given the importance of these issues to China, most of the remainder of this chapter will discuss the benefits and drawbacks, to domestic enterprises and to a country, from international joint business ventures both at home and abroad. Account will be taken of such factors as transfer of (and failure to transfer) technology and know-how, access to markets, cost considerations, provision of capital and foreign exchange. Alternatives to joint ventures as means of international technology transfer are also considered. These include the purchase of know-how or the licensing of its use, solely foreign-owned enterprises, franchising, and symbiotic co-operation between legally independent firms. The impact of profit distribution between partners in a joint venture on knowledge transfer and collective returns is analysed from a viewpoint different from that normally adopted in the literature. This highlights the dangers of viewing the distribution between partners of total profits or payoff from a joint venture as a constant sum game. Practical problems are also raised, such as the gathering of information about potential business partners and the revelation of information about joint venture behaviour which is anti-social, such as 'cheating' of various types by foreign partners.

4.3 BENEFITS OF INTERNATIONAL JOINT VENTURES

The long-term success of an international joint venture depends upon benefits being received by all the parties to the venture. All must gain more by co-operation than by going it alone, and each should not get less from the joint venture than could be obtained from the next best alternative, namely institutional arrangement or investment. The results of co-operation should ideally be synergetic; that is, the total gain should be greater than in the absence of co-operation. Let us consider some of the possible benefits of joint ventures before we consider costs in the next section. It is most convenient to approach this in two parts: (1) joint ventures in the host country, (2) joint ventures abroad.

Let us examine first the benefits to the host of a joint business venture in the host country, and then the possible benefits to the foreign partner of being involved in a joint venture in the host country, after which joint ventures abroad will be examined. The difficulties or costs of international joint ventures will then be discussed before we consider alternatives to joint ventures as means of technology transfer and industrial development, highlighting issues involved in profit-sharing in joint ventures and discussing some practical issues.

4.4 BENEFITS TO THE HOST OF JOINT VENTURES IN THE HOST COUNTRY

4.4.1 Technology Transfer

International technology transfer can be an important benefit to a host country of joint business ventures at home with foreign partners. Such arrangements have the potential in any enterprise to bring the host country up to date with the latest technology or know-how appropriate to its needs. Much technology and know-how cannot be purchased in the market place (Teece, 1977). Specifications of new technology are often incomplete and normally the best ways to use new technology and maintain it are known only to those who have experience with it. Unless one can draw directly on this experience, one may make many costly mistakes before perfecting the use of technology.

Also, technology and know-now are often 'experience' rather than search goods, as described in the literature (Dunning and McQueen, 1982, pp. 81–2). Once the new technology or know-how is thoroughly inspected it is likely to become known to the potential buyer, who may then not purchase it but instead simply rely on the knowledge revealed by the inspection to replicate it. This creates a problem for transactions in commercial knowledge, especially since the prospective seller's knowledge and that of the prospective buyer are likely to be different (that is, asymmetrical). The seller of technology (often the user or inventor of it) will have detailed knowledge of the technology, whereas the prospective buyer will have only a general view of it. The prospective buyer may, however, have a better appreciation of its potential value in his or her own context. In these circumstances, there is some uncertainty on the side of both parties about the potential value of the technology exchange. One way to reduce this uncertainty is for both parties to share in the potential returns and risks from its use. Joint ventures can provide a means for this sharing of risk. They provide a type of co-insurance.

The costs of transferring technology and the amount of time required to transfer it are often greater than is realised, and direct, continuing contact and commitment on the part of the originator of the technology are frequently required for its effective transfer (Welch, 1983). Joint venture arrangements may be more conducive to such contact and commitment than alternative types of business arrangements.

4.4.2 Access to Markets

It may very well be that the product of the joint venture is to be exported to the country of the foreign joint venturer or to other countries in which the foreign joint venturer has established connections, or it may be that the production will replace imports in the domestic market. This can be of benefit to the host country provided that the negotiated terms are favourable to it. Reasonable access to some foreign markets may only be possible through a joint venture.

4.4.3 Capital and Foreign Exchange

In an equity joint venture the foreign partner may contribute capital in the form of foreign exchange. A host country may consider this of value because it could provide additional foreign exchange. However, much of the foreign exchange contributed to the project may leak away, owing to imports needed for the joint venture project. Furthermore, if foreign exchange receipts are considered to be the main advantage of the joint venture then consideration should be given to whether foreign exchange can be obtained more cheaply, for example by direct loans from overseas.

4.4.4 Adaptation to Local Needs and Customs

In a joint venture, as compared with a solely foreign-owned-and-managed enterprise, the local joint venturer may be in a position to influence the joint venture to take greater account of local needs and customs. This may mean that the activities of the enterprise are better adjusted to the host society.

4.5 BENEFITS TO FOREIGN PARTNERS OF JOINT VENTURES IN THE HOST COUNTRY

The main benefits to the foreign joint venturer from operations in a host country may be one or more of the following:

(1) Transfer of technology with lessened risk.
(2) Access to a larger market for products in the host country.
(3) Assured supplies of commodities in accordance with own specifications and at lower cost of production than is possible elsewhere. This lower cost may, for example, arise partly from 'cheap' labour in the host country. Also, in countries where the power of trade unions is weak greater continuity of production and fewer labour 'on-costs' may be incurred.
(4) Increased and continuing information about additional trading opportunities in the host country.
(5) Special political consideration denied to a sole foreign venturer.

Regarding technology transfer, the same argument as advanced earlier applies. Through a joint venture, the risk of both parties to the technological transfer can be reduced. Also, by transferring technology or know-how under such arrangements the joint venturer reduces the risk that the host might independently learn of the technology or know-how, or buy instead a substitute technology from a competitor.

Another advantage may be better access for the overseas joint venturer to the host country's market. The partner in the host country may, for example, have established distribution channels in the host country or know better how the product should be modified to suit the local market. It may also be agreed that the foreign joint venturer shall be allowed to import some products not in the range produced in the host country so as to fill market 'gaps'. Furthermore, depending upon arrangements, there may be a chance for the foreign joint venturer to promote the brand name of the foreign partner's products or a modified brand name in the host country.

It may be that the main aim of the foreign joint venturer is not so much to gain access to the host's market as to use the host country as a manufacturing base for exporting products either to its home country or to associated countries, where the overseas joint venturer has an established brand name, distribution and marketing networks and so on. The foreign joint venturer's main purpose is to have a cheap (e.g. because of low labour costs) and a reliable (perhaps because labour strikes are absent) source of supply of the manufactured product available for sale outside the host country. However, low-wage labour is not cheap labour if it is relatively unproductive, as Chinese labour is sometimes reputed to be (Bucknall, 1989).

Exports from China may be required, for example, for markets in developed countries. In such a case, it is important that the product be manufactured so as to meet the specifications or requirements of foreign purchasers in, say, the USA, Japan or Australia. In this matter, the overseas parent of the overseas joint venturer is likely to be much better informed than its Chinese partner. As fashions and needs change in overseas markets, the overseas parent of the foreign joint venturer can arrange for the product manufactured in China to be suitably modified and is likely to be in a much better position than a Chinese company located in China to predict changes in foreign tastes and fashions. The overseas partner may also bring the latest technology needed to meet overseas manufacturing standards.

By being involved as a joint partner within a host country, the overseas joint venturer can often gain information about additional business opportunities in the host country, and improved knowledge about the workings of the political and administrative system. Increased knowledge is obtained about possible future business partners and the reputation of the joint venturer can be better established in the host country. Joint venture arrangements have the advantage in the early stages of limiting the overseas partner's exposure to risk. Information gathering can be a very valuable side-benefit for an overseas firm involved in business operations in another country (Jussawalla, 1983).

Many joint venturers believe (maybe correctly) that, because of local equity or sharing in the venture, the host country will treat them more favourably than foreign enterprises which are solely foreign-owned. Furthermore, they may believe that the local partner in the joint venture will be of assistance in dealing with difficulties which may arise in dealing with government administration.

4.6 JOINT VENTURES ABROAD

Basically, the pattern of benefits to a country is reversed in the case where it is involved in joint ventures outside the country. However, some differences in emphasis may exist, which can be illustrated by the case of China. The extent of new technology or products to be transferred to developed countries by China may be small, as is the case with traditional medicines and tonics. So this aspect is not likely to be strong at present, but China will be, or is, in a position to transfer some technologies to less-developed countries through joint ventures. An important benefit in some cases to the foreign host country of being involved in a joint venture with China is access to China's markets on an assured basis, such as Australia has with exports of iron ore to China from the Chinnar mine. Furthermore, information about market opportunities increases on both sides.

As is well known, many developed countries have 'sent' or transferred some of their industries and associated technologies off-shore to less-developed countries to avoid the increasing relative cost of labour at home. In these circumstances it is often more economic to relocate the industry and associated technology in a low-labour-cost less-developed economy. To some extent such a pattern reflects the international product cycle as described by Vernon (1966), but the transfer may not be attributable entirely to that cycle. Thus, increased pollution control in developed countries may contribute to the relocation of 'dirty' industries and technologies offshore in developing countries, some of which may 'drift' to China for example.

4.7 POSSIBLE DIFFICULTIES OR COSTS OF JOINT BUSINESS VENTURES

Joint ventures are of course subject to the difficulties which normally arise from new partners working together. Joint venturers have to learn how best to interact with one another, and this takes time. In some circumstances results may not live up to expectations. For example, the business may be unprofitable, or less profitable than anticipated, or the contribution of the partner may be less than expected. It is necessary to cope with such setbacks and adjust. But apart from such difficulties, there can also be problems of general importance to a society.

In extreme cases the foreign partner may fail to transfer know-how effectively to personnel in the host country. Top managerial positions may be retained by foreigners, and local personnel may be given little opportunity to participate in top management or to become fully aware of techniques. In cases such as this, the foreign partner may get benefits without transferring very much.

Furthermore, if there are arrangements which tend to tie the joint venture into buying inputs from the overseas parent or subsidiaries of the foreign joint venturer, or which require it to sell to these, then transfer pricing may occur. In other words, the price of the imported inputs may be inflated or the price paid for the exported product of the joint venture may be depressed, thereby raising the profit of the parent company of the foreign joint venturer. The joint venture may be left with a low return on capital. This can become a problem when the joint venture is locked into exchange arrangements with the parent company or with subsidiary companies of the overseas joint venturer. In such cases, the foreign joint venturer may skim off the profit of the joint venture. This can also occur where management personnel from the host country are unassertive and not well informed. Effective control will then pass to foreign management (Doulman, 1989).

In some instances, joint venture arrangements may limit exports or restrict these to a particular geographical region. This is usually intended to reduce competition with the overseas parent of the foreign joint venturer or its subsidiaries. This may be a necessary price to pay for co-operation, at least in the medium term, but may be a matter for concern in the longer term.

Furthermore, joint venture arrangements may foster continuing dependence on the foreign partner. This is not certain to happen, but it may occur. For example, the partner's brand name may become so firmly established in the host country that an independent local brand for the same product may be unable to make headway. Furthermore, the joint venture as such may find it impossible to make any independent technological advance. Joint venture arrangements may result in the host country, as a whole, being unable to make independent technological advances (independent, that is of overseas partners) because (1) all domestic experts in the host country may be in international joint venture(s), so that information is directly available to foreign partners, or (2) any independent advance within the country can be observed early by foreign partners, and then initiated or improved on early by them. On the other hand, one should not be too doctrinaire about claiming that it is undesirable to have continuing dependence on foreign know-how through a joint venture or other relationship. In some industries, it may be more economical to rely on continuing dependence than to try to develop independent technology.

Just a few of the many net benefit possibilities for the host country can be illustrated by Figure 4.1. Two possible streams of host-country benefit from joint venture arrangements are indicated by the paths marked (1) and (3). The path marked (2) indicates hypothetical net benefits from having an independent national enterprise. If path (1) applies, then to have a joint venture arrangement is clearly optimal. But if path (3) applies, while the joint venture gives higher returns in the short run than would an independent national enterprise, this is not so in the long run. In this case the decision about whether or not one should engage in the joint venture depends upon how much the future is discounted.

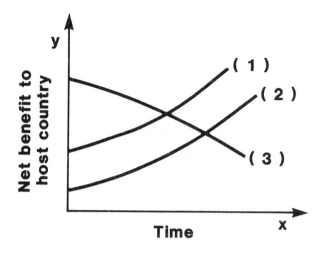

Figure 4.1   Some hypothetical alternative patterns of the net benefits to a host
country of international joint business venture arrangements

In some instances, a host country may enter into a joint venture for a limited time-period, then phase out foreign partners at the end of the period so that domestic operations are then fully owned and managed domestically by the host country. This may be done because it is believed that during the co-operative period all appropriate knowledge skills and technology will have been transferred by the foreign partner and the host will have completed the learning-by-doing phase. However, if the joint venture is limited in duration then foreign partners may be selective in their transfer of know-how or may be unwilling to enter into an arrangement. Furthermore, a continual joint venture may be profitable because foreign partners may be continually developing new technology and know-how which cannot be developed in the host country.

4.8   ALTERNATIVES TO JOINT VENTURES AS MEANS OF TECHNOLOGY TRANSFER AND INDUSTRY DEVELOPMENT

There are a number of alternatives to joint ventures as a means of transferring technology internationally, but they are not always superior. For example, a wholly owned Chinese company may try to buy in technology and know-how from abroad, or send individuals abroad for training and to observe foreign technology and methods in the hope that the Chinese company can imitate these. However, these alternatives are not always satisfactory or possible. If just a few foreign firms possess the desired technology or know-how then they may not reveal the full details and may be reluctant to sell. Furthermore, the Chinese company may not be given a chance to evaluate the technology fully prior to purchase. This is because according to common definitions used in the economic literature, knowledge is like an 'experience good' as contrasted to a 'search good'. The former cannot be inspected in advance and evaluated before its actual transfer, whereas the latter can. Once know-how is fully explained or inspected, it is transferred, or at least partially transferred. The potential purchaser may therefore refuse to pay after inspection, yet may gain the knowledge required as a result of the inspection.

Nevertheless, even where the seller acts in good faith in selling technology specifications, blueprints and so on, it is often found that these contain only part of the information needed for the use of the technology. The experience of the overseas user may have resulted in small but important modifications to the technology in practice, and knowledge about these may come only with personal and continuing contact between a potential or actual Chinese user and an overseas user (Welch, 1983). However, in some cases technology (especially if it is simple) can be transferred successfully without a joint venture. This is also true for other types of know-how, including management and marketing methods.

Where foreign capital (especially foreign exchange) is required by a domestic company, this may be obtained by loans if a joint venture is not otherwise required, or by the issue of shares to foreigners. Loans have the disadvantage that they alter the gearing of the company and the company needs to be sure, in using the loan, earning more than the rate of interest payable on it.

Again, a country may contemplate a solely owned foreign enterprise as an alternative to a joint venture. In this case, most of the business risk is taken by the foreigner. In the host country, employees of such a firm may learn techniques and methods which they may be able to apply elsewhere in the economy to indigenous firms. One cannot safely say in advance that there is never a place for a solely owned foreign enterprise.

In some instances other means of international business contact and transfer of know-how are worth considering, such as franchising and the establishment of symbiotic relationships between firms. A detailed outline of possibilities in the context of China is given by Bucknall (1989, Chapter 6). Let us consider some of these possibilities.

Franchising is quite common in retailing, and some franchisors operate internationally. The franchisor develops a marketing system, a particular product that appeals to consumers, has a trademark, a standard and so on. On payment of a fee, a prospective franchisee can become franchised. But the franchisee must agree to present the product in the standard way recommended by the franchisor, who will continue to promote the product and possibly improve on the system of its supply. Many petroleum companies use this method in retailing their petrol. In the fast food business, McDonald's (hamburgers) and Kentucky Fried Chicken are well-known examples. Franchising has the advantage that economies in product development, management development, presentation and marketing can be obtained, and individual franchisees have an incentive to be efficient since their profit (at least, in the short run) depends to a significant extent on their own effort. However, the possible disadvantage in the long run for franchisees are the inability to become independent and the possibility that fees may be raised if the franchisee makes high profits. Most of the above average profit (or all of it) is appropriated by the franchisor, the owner of the business system.

Another possibility is to develop a symbiotic co-operative relationship between firms which are in fact separate legal entities. The British retailer Marks & Spencer has done just this. It has undertaken research and product development for many of its independent manufacturing suppliers. In some cases, the symbiotic relationship between Marks & Spencer and its suppliers has been maintained for more than a hundred years. Because Marks & Spencer is larger than most of its suppliers and better attuned to market needs, it is more economical for it rather than its suppliers to undertake the necessary product development and research on market needs and some production methods (Tse, 1986). Chinese firms may be able to develop similar symbiotic relationships with foreign companies, and no doubt some have already done so (Tisdell, 1987). But this method is not always an option.

4.9 PROFIT SHARING AND JOINT VENTURES

In joint equity ventures some difficulties may arise in the parties agreeing about what the shares of the partners ought to be in the returns or the profits of the enterprise, or about the amount of capital that each should contribute to earn a particular share. As a rule there is room for bargaining, but no rational party to a joint venture will co-operate for less than it can obtain in the absence of co-operation (Luce and Raiffa, 1957), which sets limits to the bargaining.

This can be formally illustrated by Figure 4.2. There *OA* = *OD* is the amount which the joint venture can earn of, say, profit annually, and this may be divided between the parties in any combination along *AD*. If the foreign venturer can ensure itself of *OK* without being in the joint venture and the domestic venturer can ensure itself of, say, *OM*, then the only relevant area for bargaining is along the line segment *BC*. There is room for agreement in the case illustrated, because the lines marked *KL* and *MN* intersect below line *AD*. Should *OK* and *OM*, that is, the profits of the potential joint venturers in the absence of co-operation, be so large that lines *KL* and *MN* intersect above line *AD*, no co-operation is possible.

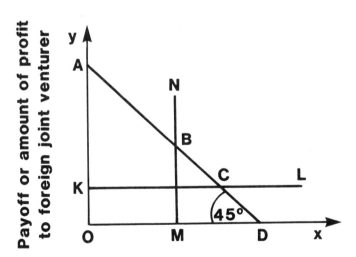

Payoff or amount of profit to domestic (e.g. Chinese) joint venturer

Figure 4.2   Classical problem of profit sharing between joint venturers. In this case, the level of joint profit is assumed to be independent of the sharing arrangements

In Figure 4.2 the total profit available for distribution is assumed to be independent of the relative shares of parties to the joint venture. But this may not be so. The contribution of parties to the joint venture to profit may – up to a point – be influenced by their relative shares. If the contribution of the foreign joint venturer has a large influence on the total level of profit then it may be short-sighted to cut the joint venturer's share to the minimum level necessary to gain participation of the foreign partner.

This can be seen from Figure 4.3. There the curve *ABCDE* represents the total profit available for distribution and is not a straight line as in Figure 4.2, since it is influenced by the relative shares of the parties. In Figure 4.3 the share to the foreign venturer indicated by the slope of *OD* is the minimum share necessary to gain co-operation. But to pay such a share is suboptimal from the point of view of the host partner and the host country. The share indicated by the slope of the line *OC* would result in a greater gain for the host, for instance, because the foreign joint venturer is more co-operative and has a greater incentive to transfer know-how.

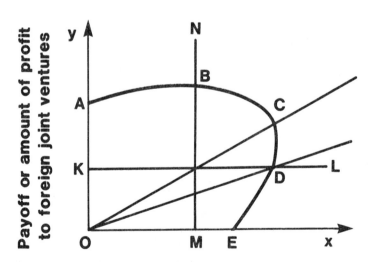

Payoff or amount of profit to domestic (e.g. Chinese) joint venturer

Figure 4.3   Non-traditional analysis of profit sharing between joint venturers. The level of joint profit depends on the sharing arrangements

It might be noted that when joint payoffs are not independent of the relative shares of partners or the distribution of joint payoffs then the solution of the co-operative game cannot be achieved in the dichotomous manner suggested by von Neumann and Morgenstern (1953). Their solution involves maximising the joint payoff independently of the exact distribution of the total payoff.

Another factor that may be subject to bargaining is the phasing out of the foreign joint venturer after some period of operation of the joint venture. Other things being equal, the faster is the phase out, the less is the incentive of the foreign prospective partner to join the joint venture. However, where knowledge is not rapidly developing, or the host country is able, once the joint venture has been established for some time, to keep up with new knowledge on its own, there is a good case for the phasing out of the foreign venturer. But this is not necessarily so when world knowledge in a field is advancing rapidly and the host country is unable to keep up with such advance by relying solely on its own resources. There needs to be some flexibility in relation to the possibility of phasing out foreign partners.

4.10   SOME PRACTICAL MATTERS TO CONSIDER

Some practical matters which may have to be considered in relation to joint ventures are the selection of partners, the nature of agreements, monitoring, the legal system in the host country and the enforcement of agreements. One has to be sure that the partner is capable of delivering what is required by the joint venture on reasonable terms, and that the partner is economically viable. As a rule the financial viability of a potential partner can be checked out through bankers and so on. As for reasonable terms, it is possible to request offers or bids from potential joint venturers. However, one should not necessarily accept the lowest bid, since the party involved may not be able to fulfil joint venture requirements, or may do so poorly. Also, one has to consider how many details must be supplied with expressions of interest. The more detail is required, the greater is the cost, and less likely it is that some potential joint venturers will pursue the matter.

In relation to agreements, opinions differ about how precisely and in how much detail they should be specified. Certainly the substance of the agreement should be given, but it is usually impractical to lay down all details. In this respect, the goodwill of the parties towards one another is important and one often only learns about that by working with a partner for some time.

In some countries, where governments are joint venturers with foreign firms, they sometimes think it enough to set up the agreement and the joint venture, and do not adequately enforce or monitor the agreement (Doulman, 1989). This may be because appointments by the government to the board of directors are political. Such appointees may have little business knowledge, or they may be afraid to cause political embarrassment for the foreign joint venturer and the host government by speaking out against malpractice in the company. Effective management and control then tends to reside with the foreign joint venturer, who may, for example, engage in transfer pricing. It is important that those appointed to the board of directors and managerial positions in joint ventures be competent in business evaluation, and that socially acceptable mechanisms be developed for the detection, reporting and correction of malpractices within joint ventures.

4.11 CONCLUDING COMMENTS ON JOINT VENTURES AND INTERNATIONAL TECHNOLOGY TRANSFER

Joint ventures can have all the virtues commonly attributed to them, including the facilitation of technology transfer, but they are not bound to have such benefits, nor are they always superior to alternative institutional arrangements. It seems that each case has to be evaluated on its merits, and that a pragmatic rather than a doctrinaire approach to joint ventures is required. At the same time, care needs to be exercised that bureaucratic control does not become a *major* barrier to international technology transfer.

It is also clear from this discussion of technology transfer that the core issues revolve around the economics of knowledge and information, transaction and search costs, the problems of asymmetry of information and the difficulties of detecting and revealing information about socially unacceptable behaviour by a partner to a joint venture. Aspects of moral hazard and signalling would also seem relevant (Varian, 1990, Chapter 32). Scope exists for detailed analysis of these issues in the future. There are also practical, cultural and organisational problems which require further attention as pointed out by Shenkar (1988).

4.12   SOME ADDITIONAL POINTS ABOUT DIRECT FOREIGN INVESTMENT IN CHINA AND INTERNATIONAL TECHNOLOGY TRANSFER

According to Bucknall (1989, p. 127), foreign funds accounted for 8.7 per cent of total accumulation in China in 1986, and averaged around 5 per cent of total investment in China in the period 1979–86. Bucknall therefore argues that foreign funds are not an important source of investment in China. In the period January 1979 to September 1985, 69.5 per cent of foreign capital used by China was in the form of loans and 30.5 per cent in the form of direct investment (based on Bucknall, 1989, p. 122). However, the latter component has tended to increase relatively with the passage of time. Nevertheless, given Bucknall's view, direct foreign investment is relatively insignificant as a contributor to total investment in China.

However, it might be argued that direct foreign investment has an economic value which is not reflected in its proportionate contributions to capital accumulation in China because it is a source of new technologies and methods (cf. Liu Jianjun, 1989). But even in that respect Bucknall appears somewhat sceptical, because he states that 'Experience in other countries suggests that spillover [or trickle-down] effects are often small and slow to arrive, and within joint ventures the Chinese managers are not always willing to listen and learn' (Bucknall, 1989, p. 125). In addition, he argues that the technology transferred from abroad is often inappropriate to China's needs and conditions. The most advanced technology is not always suitable for China (Bucknall, 1989, p. 138). Questions are also raised about whether foreign investors in China are able to earn and repatriate sufficient profit to make their investment there worth while. In this respect Bucknall (1989, pp. 140–1) provides some practical advice to would-be foreign investors in China.

One might have expected Bucknall to reach a negative conclusion about the benefits of foreign investment in China, but he does not. He concludes:

Despite these problems, foreign aid and investment have had a stimulatory effect on the economy and led to an increase in output, a higher quality of goods, an improved standard of living and higher levels of employment. The benefits in terms of technology, added dynamism and economic growth easily outweigh the problems. (Bucknall, 1989, p. 142)

Special economic zones, open cities and regions have played a role in China's bid to attract foreign direct investment and technology and develop the country (see, for example, Harding, 1989, pp. 163–70). These aspects have not been discussed in this chapter, but China's regional policies are the focus of the next.

REFERENCES

BUCKNALL, K.B. (1989) *China and the Open Door Policy*, Allen & Unwin, Sydney and London.

DOULMAN, D.J. (1989) 'A critical review of some aspects of fisheries joint ventures', pp. 28–36 in H. Campbell, K. Menz and G. Waugh (eds), *Economics of Fisheries Management in the Pacific Islands Region*, Australian Centre for International Agricultural Research, Canberra.

DUNNING, J.H. and McQUEEN (1982) 'The eclectic theory of multinational enterprise and the international hotel industry', pp. 79–106, in A. Rugman (ed.), *New Theories of the Multinational Enterprise*, Croom Helm, London.

HARDING, H. (1987) *China's Second Revolution: Reform After Mao*, Allen & Unwin, Sydney and Melbourne.

HILL, H. and JOHNS, B. (1983) 'The transfer of technology to western Pacific developing countries', *Prometheus*, 1 (1), pp. 60–83.

JUSSAWALLA, M. (1983) 'Trade, technology transfer and development', pp. 134–154 in S. Macdonald, D. Lamberton and T.D. Mandeville (eds), *The Trouble with Technology: Explorations in the Process of Technological Change*, Pinter, London.

KARUNARATNE, N.D. (1981) 'Australia and technology transfer to developing countries', *Economic Activity*, 27 (2), pp. 2–12.

LIU JIANJUN (1989) 'Decade of successful foreign investment', *Beijing Review*, 6–12 November pp. 14–19.

LUCE, R.D. and RAIFFA (1957) *Games and Decisions*, Wiley, New York.

MOREHOUSE, W. (1982) 'Technological autonomy and disassociation in the international system: An alternative economic and political strategy for national development', in V. Rittberger, *Science and Technology in a Changing International Order: The United Nations Conference on Science and Technology for Development*, Westview, Boulder, Colo.

NEUMANN J. von and MORGENSTERN, O. (1953) *Theory of Games and Economic Behaviour*, 3rd edn, Princeton University Press, Princeton.

PACK, H. (1981) 'Preface', *Annals of the American Academy of Political and Social Sciences*, No.458, p. 7, Philadelphia, USA.

PARRY, T.G. (1981) 'The multinational enterprise and two-stage technology transfer to developing nations', *Research in International and Business Finance*, 2, pp. 175–92.

PAZDERKA, B. (1991) *Adequacy of R & D expenditures in small open economies*, Discussion Paper in Economics No. 65, Department of Economics, University of Queensland, St. Lucia, Brisbane.

RITTBERGER, V. (1982) *Science and Technology in a Changing International Order: The United Nations Conference on Science and Technology for Development*, Westview, Boulder, Colo.

SHENKAR, O. (1988) 'International joint ventures, problems in China: culture, politics or organisational structure', mimeo., Faculty of Management, Tel Aviv University.

TEECE, D. (1977) 'Technology transfer by multinational firms: the resource cost of transferring technological know-how', *Economic Journal*, vol. 87, pp. 242–61.

TISDELL, C. A. (1981) *Science and Technology Policy: Priorities of Government*, Chapman & Hall, London.

TISDELL, C. A. (1987) 'Lessons about technology transfer and economic cooperation for Hong Kong, China and other countries from Dr Tse's study of Marks and Spencer', *The Hongkong Manager*, 23 (1), pp. 38–46.

TSE, K. K. (1986) *Marks and Spencer*, Pergamon Press, Oxford, England.

VARIAN, H. R. (1990) *Intermediate Microeconomics: A Modern Approach*, 2nd edn, Norton, New York.

VERNON, R. (1966) 'International investment and international trade in the product cycle', *Quarterly Journal of Economics*, 80, pp. 190–207.

WELCH, L. S. (1983) 'The technology transfer process in foreign licensing arrangements', in S. Macdonald, D. Lamberton and T. D. Mandeville (eds), *The Trouble with Technology: Explorations in the Process of Technological Change*, Pinter, London.

WORLD BANK (1990) *World Bank Report 1990*, Oxford University Press, New York.

5 Regional and Urban Development: Government Intervention

5.1 INTRODUCTION – CHINA'S BASIC REGIONAL DEVELOPMENT STRATEGY

The view that the government can accelerate national economic development and growth by encouraging the economic growth of selected regions or cities seems to have been accepted by Chinese authorities. In effect, such a policy involves the promotion of uneven or unbalanced regional development – the 'forced' growth of particular areas, very often with the expectation that this growth will radiate out to a wider area at a later stage. Such a policy was enunciated clearly by Zhao Ziyang in 1987 at the Thirteenth National Congress of the Communist Party of China. He said:

> It is necessary to consolidate and develop the pattern of opening to the outside world that has begun to take shape, with the open policy extending progressively from the special economic zones to coastal cities, then to coastal economic regions and finally to interior areas. With the overall interests of the national economy in mind, we should draw up a correct development plan for all these zones, cities and regions. They should focus on development of export-oriented economy and expand their horizontal economic ties with the interior areas, so as to serve more effectively as a base for implementing the open policy and as a window open to the outside world. (Zhao Ziyang, 1987, p. 27)

This uneven regional development policy has concentrated on the development of coastal areas as China's window on the world. Li Peng, in introducing the Ten-year Programme for National Economic and Social Development (1991–2000), promised to continue the basic strategy of developing coastal areas. Policies for this will involve 'better management of the existing special economic zones, consolidating and developing the existing economic and technological zones, open cities and areas and stepping up the development of the new Pudong area in Shanghai' (*China Daily*, 12 April 1991). But, in addition, some inland cities and areas along the national borders with other countries such as the former Soviet Union will be selected to promote the growth in the volume of foreign trade and technological exchange (*China Daily*, 12 April 1991).

China, in order to increase its rate of economic growth and to help modernise, set up four Special Economic Zones on its coastline (see Harding, 1989, pp. 163–70). Foreign industries establishing in these zones have been given special concessions such as lower taxation and subsidised availability of business sites. The zones are designed to attract foreign investment and technology, to encourage the introduction of foreign management methods and business practices and to train Chinese workers in the use of new technology and equip them with skills likely to be of value in modern industry. In addition, Chinese firms in the zones are encouraged to improve on imported technology, and where practical to engage in reverse engineering, that is after inspecting foreign products embodying new technology, to find engineering methods of producing these thus avoiding purchases of the knowledge involved.

The economic success of the zones seems to be mixed. Shenzhen (near Hong Kong) appears to have done best (Bucknall, 1989, Chapter 7). Furthermore, with the extension of economic concessions to foreign businesses by several cities and other areas in China, the zones are now less attractive to foreign businesses than they were. Bucknall (1989, p. 156) suggests that it may indeed be more profitable for a foreign enterprise to establish itself in a city such as Tianjin than in one of the zones, despite the government concessions available in the latter.

The selection of appropriate growth centres or regions by governments is a difficult and risky task. Ideal areas may not be selected for 'forced' or favoured growth. Not all the Special Economic Zones selected by the Chinese government may have been ideal. In some cases, it may be better to build on existing regional strengths, and the Pudong development in Shanghai, for instance, seems to do this.

The productive potential and scope for economic development of different regions of a country varies considerably, and the maximisation of economic growth and of production in relation to the scarce resources of a country requires that this be taken into account. Natural and social circumstances may favour some regions for development in comparison with others. In general, with economic development, productivity and incomes are likely to grow in some regions at a faster rate than in others and interregional income disparities may widen. Thus there may be political pressure for more even economic development throughout a country, and/or for measures to make internal migration easier, so that individuals can leave relatively backward regions and earn larger incomes in developing regions and cities.

Many different views exist about ideal patterns of regional and urban development and about the value of the free movement of resources (labour and capital) between regions as a means to maximise national output and prevent larger per capita income disparities occurring between regions. Let us consider some of those theories, such as the neo-classical economic theory, the centre–periphery theory and some 'market failure' theories, and relate these to the Chinese situation.

5.2 NEO-CLASSICAL ECONOMIC THEORY, REGIONAL AND URBAN DEVELOPMENT

Neo-classical economic theory suggests that in many circumstances uneven regional and urban development is necessary to maximise national production. It argues that if the value of national production is to be maximised then resources (labour and capital) should be allocated to those areas where the value of their addition to total production is greatest. The *ideal* situation from the point of view of maximising national production is that a resource (e.g. capital or labour) be allocated between regions, so that the value of its marginal product is equal for all regions. This can be illustrated by Figure 5.1.

Suppose that the country is divided into region 1 and region 2, and for simplicity assume that productivity in each of these depends on a single resource, labour. The value of the marginal productivity of labour in region 1 is higher than in region 2. In Figure 5.1 the former is shown by curve ABC and the latter by line DEF. Suppose that the total supply of labour is the country is L^*. Initially this is allocated so that $\hat{L}_1$ is employed in region 1 and $\hat{L}_2$ in region 2. The value of the marginal productivity of labour in region 1 then is w_3 and in region 2 it is w_1. Thus equality in the value of the marginal product has not been achieved.

Production in region 1 should be expanded and that in region 2 should be reduced by transferring some labour from region 2 to region 1 in order to increase national production. Maximum national output is achieved when $\bar{L}_1$ of labour is allocated to region 1 and $\bar{L}_2$ is allocated to region 2. Moving $\hat{L}_2 - \bar{L}_2 = \bar{L}_1 - \hat{L}_1$ of labour from region 2 to region 1 reduces the value of output in region 2 by the equivalent of the hatched area, and increases the value of output in region 1 by the equivalent of the dotted area. Since the dotted area exceeds the hatched area, total production goes up as a result of the resource movement.

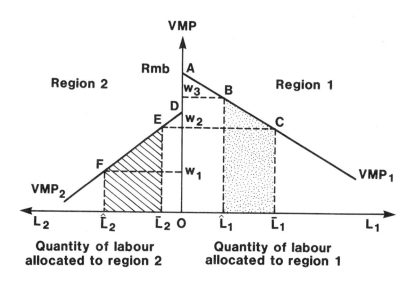

Figure 5.1   Neo-classical economics model of the optimal allocation of labour between regions

If labour is paid the value of its marginal product then initially the wage rate in region 1 is w_3 and exceeds that in region 2, where the wage rate is initially w_1. After the labour migration to region 1, the wage rate becomes equal in both areas and is w_2. The wage rate rises in the region which had the lower wage rate and falls in that with the higher. Thus the less-well-off workers gain.

It has been argued by neo-classical economists that if perfectly competitive markets exist, if wage-earners are free to move wherever they wish, and if their aim is to maximise their income then this will automatically ensure the allocation of resources which maximises the value of national production. In terms of its *assumptions*, the theory seems to be correct. But it does require special assumptions, which may not be satisfied in practice. For example, there may be economies of agglomeration or of regional scale of activities, and environmental externalities or spillovers (such as may occur from pollution). Furthermore the residents of cities or of some regions may participate in some benefits on an average or common basis rather than a marginal basis (Tisdell, 1975). In all such cases, perfect competition and the free movement of resources does not lead to an optimal allocation of resources between regions and urban centres. Such circumstances, in terms commonly used by Western economists, are a source of market failure. Argument about the matter then tends to revolve about how significant the factors are in practice. For instance, it may be argued that while the free market approach in such cases may be imperfect, it is not very imperfect or not as imperfect as direct control. Such an argument can be resolved only by examining the empirical evidence carefully. I shall return to the market failure aspect later.

Liberal or pro-market reform economists in China sometimes base their argument at least implicitly on neo-classical economic theory. For example, those arguing in favour of the free movement of labour between regions and between rural areas and cities (as well as free choice of occupation) often do so. Under the conditions assumed in neo-classical theory such freedom will increase national product in the Chinese case, because there appear to be large regional and urban-rural differences in the marginal product of labour. It is believed, for example, that the marginal productivity of labour in China is lower in agriculture than in the cities and liberal economists argue that if there were fewer restrictions on labour movement then this would raise China's national income. But this argument is based on a greatly simplified picture of the world.

The argument, among other things, ignores externalities. It also ignores the dynamics or the process of adjustment, because its theoretical basis is comparative statics. For example, in a situation of free movement labour may not migrate in a smooth fashion, so the new equilibria are not gradually approached, but migration *may* fluctuate somewhat erratically before stabilising. This is not to say that greater freedom of human migration in China than existed in the past is undesirable from an economic point of view, but to point out that neo-classical theory is a simplification. In some cases it is even a gross simplification and misleading. This may be especially so in relation to regional development and human migration.

5.3 CENTRE–PERIPHERY THEORIES OF REGIONAL DEVELOPMENT

While neo-classical economists are as a rule convinced of the virtues of free trade both within a country and internationally, centre–periphery theorists are not. Indeed, the most optimistic free trade economists believe that free trade is bound to benefit *all* participants. By contrast, the centre–periphery theorists argue that the economic contact of a more developed region and the establishment of free trade between the regions tends to be to the economic disadvantage of the less-developed region. In its extreme form, it leads to the policy conclusion that the economic development of a backward region or country is best served by economic autarky or independence. (Under Mao Zedong, China adopted such a policy for a time; see the previous chapter and Chapter 3.) This conclusion is therefore diametrically opposed to that of the most optimistic free trade economists.

However, there are grounds for rejecting *both* extreme views (Tisdell, 1981, Chapter 18). Even under relatively ideal conditions, free trade does not *necessarily* benefit *all* persons and *all* regions given the neo-classical theory. Take the previous example discussed using Figure 5.1. Introduction of free labour mobility led to a reduction in total production in region 2 and to an expansion of production in region 1. Region 2 'de-developed' as a result of the removal of restrictions on the movement of labour. While the income of wage earners in region 2 rose, that in region 1 fell. So everyone did not gain. Nevertheless, total production increased and (in principle) a *potential* Paretian improvement was possible, that is everyone could have been made better off.

Nevertheless, free trade and resource movement does not necessarily lead to complete 'de-development' of a less developed region. In some circumstances, capital will flow to an underdeveloped region and its economic expansion will occur, given the assumptions of neo-classical theory.

The centre–periphery theory raises several aspects of a dynamic and social nature which require particular consideration. As is well known, some writers connect the theory with the concept of neo-imperialism and neo-colonialism (Frank, 1978; Tisdell, 1987). For instance, with the inflow of foreign capital and the opening up of trade, it is suggested that the ruling élite or group of a country may be 'captured' by foreign interests, domestic technology fail to develop and the economy become backward and lacking in vitality. Those who favour opening up to the outside world and encouraging the inflow of modern technology and direct investment reach the opposite conclusion. They suggest that it will result in a dynamic, growing economy in which technological progress will be encouraged.

The observations of the centre–peripherists do not in themselves establish a case for economic autarky or for not opening to the outside world. Rather, it is a case for doing so in a selective way, on terms carefully considered by the recipient of foreign capital and of foreign expertise (see Chapters 3 and 4). Terms should be such as to maintain the political independence of the recipient nation. Basically, from a nationalistic point of view, one's policies should be designed so as to encourage all beneficial foreign inflows subject to *minimal* restrictions or conditions designed to maintain national political independence. One seems to need a balance between a very restrictive policy and an absolutely free one. In past times, it appears that Japan opened up to the outside world by using a selective policy for the import of foreign technology and capital. That is not to say that the Japanese model is exactly appropriate to other countries and applies just as much now as in the past. But it is indicative of how it is possible to open up and maintain national independence.

One may, however, wonder about the relevance of this discussion of international economies to interregional economic issues. Up to a point, an international economy can be considered to be an inter-regional economy. The particular focus of international economics arises out of national barriers to trade and factor movement. For instance, the migration of labour is usually much easier within nations than between them. Thus uneven economic development within a nation may pose less of an income inequality problem than between nations because those individuals belonging to economically 'back-ward' or 'dedeveloped' areas may migrate to areas showing economic advance.

However, inequality problems do arise from uneven development when labour migration within a country is restricted as in China. As incomes fall in developed areas, or fail to rise, income inequality becomes magnified and because those from backward areas have no option or only a limited one of moving to advancing areas, political pressure can be expected to grow in the 'backward' regions for participation in economic development. Promises of 'trickle-down' or 'trickle-out' of development from growth centres will not be sufficient as a rule to allay political problems, if the 'trickle-out' is slow, or, worse, if it seems that the growth centres are actually holding back the economic development of peripheral regions.

Even free movement of labour may not solve the political problem completely. In as much as many individuals have an affinity and a loyalty to their own region, they may wish to see it develop economically. They may be appalled by the prospect of outward migration and reduced population in the region. Furthermore, the development of extractive industries to provide raw materials for the centre may not be an attractive option politically to those in peripheral regions, even though the development of rural industries as in China may be a palliative. In the Chinese case, the coastal regions and major cities may be regarded as the centre, with western areas in particular corresponding to the periphery. This is a crude representation, but it is not an entirely irrelevant indicator of Chinese regional development issues in terms of the centre–periphery paradigm.

5.4 MARKET FAILURE IN REGIONAL AND URBAN DEVELOPMENT

However, one does not have to rely on centre–periphery theories to see that, in relation to regional development, there may be a case for interfering in the operation of free markets and in the movements of labour. Even within the type of framework envisaged in neo-classical economic theory, phenomena occur which result in free markets not maximising national production or not ensuring the most efficient allocation of resources. The policy suggestion frequently made as a result by Western economists is that some government intervention is required to modify the operation of market forces, but not usually to the extent that they are entirely supplanted by government regulation.

Externalities and spillovers, particularly those of an environmental nature, may require such intervention. An externality occurs when an economic activity has an effect on others which escapes being priced, for example pollution which damages the production of others but for which they are not compensated by those causing it. If the expansion of a city or if an economic activity in a particular region is likely to have an unfavourable external effect, for example, on production elsewhere via air or water pollution, then this should be taken into account. In fact, air and water pollution from industrial growth is a particularly serious problem in China; for example, the expansion of industrial activity in Beijing has resulted in water pollution which has damaged both farm and industrial production in nearby Hebei Province.

External economies in production (as observed by Marshall, 1961) may occur from the expansion of economic activity in an area, and on a sufficiently large scale this can indeed be economic. However, this expansion may not come about in a market system dependent on myopic (localised) adjustment. This can be illustrated simply by Figure 5.2. There, *DD* represents the demand for a particular product of a region. *SS* identifies the supply curve and represents the supply price of production in the region. The supply curve (which also indicates per unit cost) is downward-sloping, indicating economies of agglomeration in a region. Per unit costs of production fall as economic activity in the region expands, but the economies are *external* to individuals and

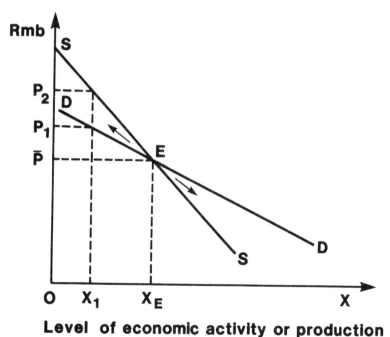

Figure 5.2   Possible failure in regional development due to dynamic elements and external economies. The single equilibrium is unstable given the Marshallian reaction assumption

individual productive units or firms. An equilibrium level of economic activity (production) in the region exists for an output of X_E. But will this market equilibrium be achieved? No, not necessarily. The equilibrium corresponding to E may not be achieved in a free market situation. Given localised or myopic reactions by firms and individuals, insufficient economic activity may be generated in a region to sustain productive activity which could be economic if it happened to be of sufficient magnitude in the region. Suppose that in Figure 5.2 the production of commodity X in the region is initially X_1. The price the market is willing to pay for this output is P_1 and is less than the per unit cost of producing it, P_2. Marshall assumed that producers would react to an excess of supply price over demand price by reducing their quantity of production and supply to the market, and would react in the opposite way to an excess of demand price over supply price. Hence (given the market adjustment assumptions made by Marshall) producers can be expected to reduce their output. But this leads only to a greater excess of costs of production over market price. Eventually production of commodity X in the region ceases. The equilibrium corresponding to point E is unstable given Marshallian market adjustment assumptions rather than those of Walras (Samuelson, 1947, Chapter 9; Tisdell, 1972, Chapter 5). However, if initial production is on the scale X_E then it is economic and can be sustained by market forces.

It is clear that in this case production of commodity X in the region will be economic only if it is on a sufficiently large scale. But market and related mechanisms involving freedom of individual action may fail to ensure that the necessary critical mass in regional activity is achieved. Government action and co-ordination is needed to ensure that this threshold is reached.

Theoretically, a number of *possibilities* can be imagined along the above lines. For example, the situation depicted in Figure 5.3 may be more realistic than that shown in Figure 5.2, because the system illustrated in Figure 5.2 is completely unstable for Marshallian market reaction assumptions, although it is stable for those of Walras. In Figure 5.3, the straight line marked DD represents the demand for the region's product and the wavy curve marked SS represents the supply curve for this product. Three possible equilibria exist which are marked E_1, E_2 and E_3. Equilibria E_1 and E_3 are stable, given Marshallian assumptions, but E_2 is unstable. This region may be in economic equilibrium initially, with production corresponding to X_1. Equilibrium E_1 is relatively stable. The system is likely to return to it unless a disturbance pushes production in the region above X_2. If this happens then the system will gravitate to equilibrium E_3. Given this situation, if a region's production is relatively stagnant at a level corresponding to E_1 then the government by providing incentives which push the level of production above the threshold X_2 releases forces which will result in a new equilibrium being established at E_3. The government thereby permanently develops the level of production in the region by providing a big economic push.

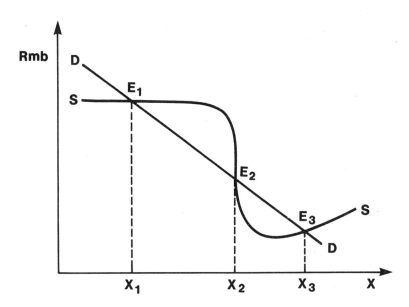

**Level of economic activity or production
in a region**

Figure 5.3   Multiple equilibria resulting in failure in regional development and possible optimality of a 'big push' to escape a low-level equilibrium

The Chinese government may have a model or models of the above type in mind in pursuing its policies of selective regional development, but this is unclear. A big push may be economically beneficial in some areas, but not in all. In each case it will depend upon the fundamental economic structure of the region.

But there are also other possible models of the economic world. In some cases, it might be reasonable to assume that individuals resident in a region or city share collectively in the income or benefit obtained there. The theory of common property or common access to resources may apply. To the extent that this is so, excessive levels of population and economic activity from the point of view of maximising national production will occur in the most productive regions and cities. Fewer urban centres and larger ones than would be optimal for maximising national production may come into existence.

Given the above view (see Tisdell, 1975, 1981, Chapter 15) a case may exist for governments curbing the growth of large cities and encouraging the development of smaller urban centres. China's policy of restricting population migration to very large cities, and of encouraging the growth of urban centres in the countryside so as to give rural dwellers opportunities to participate in manufacturing activities, would be consistent with this. However, I am not arguing that all urban centres should be small or of equal size.

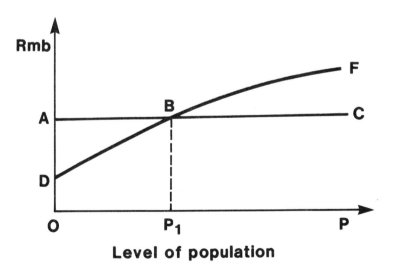

Figure 5.4   Case in which the myopic reactions to income differences result in a non-optimal pattern of regional development

The possibility also exists that one particular region or city may develop rather than another, because of myopic or localised reactions, when the development of that region or city is not optimal from the point of view of maximising national production. For example, in Figure 5.4 income per head at site 1 as a function of population there might be as indicated by the line ABC. At site 2, income per head as a function of population might be as illustrated by curve DBF. At a population less than P_1, income per head at site 1 is higher than at site 2. At low levels of population, site 1 is likely to develop. Once it has developed and population has expanded beyond P_1 there is no simple way to ensure that site 2 develops. However, for a population greater than P_1, site 2 is more productive than site 1. A large adjustment, and one that is unlikely to come about by localised reactions, is needed to make sure that site 2 develops when population exceeds P_1. (For further discussion of related matters see for example, Tisdell 1990, Chapter 9.)

5.5 CONCLUDING COMMENTS

Under some theoretical conditions, perfectly competitive markets and resource mobility can result in a pattern of regional development that maximises national production. However, effects such as externalities can arise in practice which prevent this from happening and which may require government intervention in the development of regions and cities so as to increase national production. Many complex issues are involved, and we should be wary of hasty generalisations about this subject such as those made by extreme advocates of free trade or by extreme centre–periphery theorists. More research and collection of empirical evidence is needed to determine optimal patterns of regional and urban development. To date it seems likely that Chinese regional development policy has been built more around economic hunches than solid empirical evidence and analysis, even though before establishing its Special Economic Zones China 'did its homework', according to Bucknall (1989, Chapter 6).

In the world as a whole, a country may be regarded as a region. I have argued that an open-door policy will not inevitably lead to the dedevelopment or backwardness of a less developed country especially if it is a selective open-door policy. The economic growth of Japan, Hong Kong, Singapore and South Korea provide examples where an open policy has led to considerable economic growth. There seem to be no cases where a country has remained virtually isolated from the rest of the world and experienced substantial economic growth. For example, in the case of Burma, which followed a closed-door policy, there was no economic growth. In the case of some of the Latin American and African countries, however, the extent to which they have been assisted by foreign contact is debatable. But societies are very complex. Foreign contact and trade is only one influence on them. It is always easy politically to blame the foreigner for one's own failings. In China's case, an open-door policy is appropriate to its need. However, to take full advantage of it will require continuing and consistent effort, application, patience and wisdom on the part of the Chinese people.

REFERENCES

BUCKNALL, K.B. (1989) *China and the Open Door Policy*, Allen & Unwin, Sydney and London.
FRANK, A.G. (1978) *Dependent Accumulation and Underdevelopment*, Macmillan, London.
HARDING, H. (1989) *China's Second Revolution: Reform After Mao*, Allen & Unwin, Sydney and London.
MARSHALL, A. (1961) *Principles of Economics*, 9th (variorum) edn, Macmillan, London.
SAMUELSON, P.A. (1947) *Foundation of Economic Analysis*, Harvard University Press, Cambridge, Mass.
TISDELL, C.A. (1972) *Microeconomics: The Theory of Economic Allocation*, Wiley, Sydney and New York.
TISDELL, C.A. (1975) 'The theory of optimal city-sizes: elementary speculation about analysis and policy', *Urban Studies*, 12, pp. 61–70.
TISDELL, C.A. (1981) *Microeconomics of Markets*, Wiley, Brisbane, New York.
TISDELL, C.A. (1987) 'Imperialism, economic dependence and development: a brief review of economic thought and theory', *Humanomics*, 3, pp. 6–29.
TISDELL, C.A. (1990) *Natural Resources, Growth and Development*, Praeger, New York.
ZHAO ZIYANG (1987) 'Advance along the road of socialism with Chinese characteristics', report delivered at the Thirteenth National Congress of the Communist Party of China 25 October 1987, pp. 3–80 in *Documents of the Thirteenth National Congress of the Communist Party of China (1987)*, Foreign Languages Press, Beijing.

6 Poverty, Income Inequality and Development

6.1 INTRODUCTION – POVERTY AND CHINA'S INCOME POLICIES

Poverty and income inequality exist in all countries. While poverty does occur amongst plenty in more developed countries because incomes, resources and opportunities are unevenly distributed, the incidence of poverty tends to be higher in underdeveloped countries, that is, in countries where average income per head is low. While the saying that 'the poor are always with us' has some value in that it reminds us of the poor, it can become an excuse for lack of concern and action in as much as it suggests that the existence of poverty is a fact of life and little can be done about it. In fact much poverty can be eliminated by appropriate economic policies, even though they often require time to become effective.

Economic poverty reflects economic scarcity and is frequently accompanied by other forms of poverty such as cultural poverty. Economists have suggested two main means for dealing with poverty: (1) the redistribution of income and (2) the promotion of overall economic growth. Most economists (but not all) recommend that the latter policy be combined with policies to limit the rate of population growth.

The redistribution of income may take the form of (1) direct redistribution of income or (2) redistribution of opportunities to earn income, such as *may* be made possible by market reforms, by the redistribution of property or by more equal access to education. Economic growth may come about as a result of the introduction of new technology, capital accumulation and improvements in the quality of the workforce, and as a consequence of improvements in the allocation of resources. While an economic growth strategy may do much to relieve poverty, a broad-based economic growth strategy is not sufficient in itself to address poverty everywhere. Specific policies targeted to particular groups in poverty and particular areas or regions with a high incidence of poverty are also needed. It is not enough to rely on broad, trickle-down policies.

Since the coming to power of the Communist Party in China in 1949 the incidence of poverty in China has been much reduced, possibly to a large extent because of economic growth and the comparative political stability that China has enjoyed compared with the period to 1949. Whether or not faster economic growth and greater alleviation of poverty would have occurred if the Kuomintang had been in control is a hypothetical question, even though some suggest that they may, on the basis of Taiwan's economic development. But had the Kuomintang been in control of the whole of China and able to sustain political stability, it may not have had the challenges it faced on Taiwan nor the same amount of aid (technological and otherwise) as it had there from the United States. Even the same amount of aid would have been small in relation to the whole of China. Also, it would have been deprived of the opportunity to learn from its negative experiences on the mainland prior to 1949.

Although the policies of Mao Zedong tended to reduce local inequalities of per capita income, they did little to reduce such inequalities interregionally. Furthermore, lack of emphasis on reward according to effort and ability proved to be serious drawbacks of Mao's policies, which resulted in China displaying pathological social and economic symptoms during the period of the Cultural Revolution. It became clear, as a result of this, that political exhortation and capital accumulation are not sufficient to reduce economic scarcity, relieve poverty and build a good society. Nevertheless, despite all these difficulties, the incidence of poverty in China has been much reduced since 1949. Zhao Ziyang was able to say in 1987:

The overwhelming majority of our one billion people have secured a life with enough food and clothing. People in some areas are beginning to become well-off. There are still certain areas where the problem of food and clothing has not yet been solved, but even in those places there has been some improvement. (Zhao Ziyang, 1987, p. 4)

In 1991 Premier Li Peng, in introducing China's Ten-Year Programme for National Economic and Social Development, said that China had already raised its living standard since 1949 to a level where all have enough food and clothing and that the aim of this programme was to enable all to lead a relatively comfortable life by the year 2000

(*China Daily*, 26 March 1991, p. 1.). He indicated further that there was no intention of returning to the 'iron-bowl policy' of the past, a situation in which all share from a common bowl without reference to the contribution of each. Instead the government will continue to use an income distribution system based on the principle of 'to each according to his work' as the main element and gradually improve the personal income distribution system (*China Daily*, 12 April 1991). So the main emphasis will be on reward for work (and presumably ability), thereby providing an incentive to work and economic effort and stimulating economic growth. Possibly once economic growth has resulted in a substantial rise in average per capita income, personal income distribution will be given greater attention. For the present, at least, income redistribution is not regarded as a top priority in China.

Nevertheless, in some areas of China poverty remains a problem, and its incidence tends to be higher in non-coastal regions. During the Eighth Five-Year Plan (1991–5) the Chinese government is to continue aid to poor areas. This requires the more prosperous coastal regions to provide funds and technical and managerial personnel to help develop resources in poor areas. Assistance will be for construction of farm buildings, for increasing grain yields, additions to regional infrastructure and the 'tapping' of natural resources. *China Daily* (31 May 1991, p. 3) reports that 'The aim will be to organise and encourage developed and poor areas to join forces to tap the natural resources in poor regions.' The aim therefore is to reduce the incidence of poverty in poor regions by increasing their level of production rather than by merely redistributing income.

In certain circumstances, it might be argued that freer migration from poor areas to richer ones would be a more effective way of relieving poverty and increasing national production. At least this option should be compared with that of 'pumping' outside capital into a region where incomes are low.

6.2 MEASURING POVERTY AND ITS INCIDENCE IN LESS DEVELOPED COUNTRIES

Determining who is and who is not in poverty can be a difficult task. This is often done by means of a *poverty line*. A poverty line specifies a level of income below which an individual or family unit is considered to be in poverty. It may be based on perceived nutritional and other needs and be a physiological minimum, in which case it is sometimes described as a line or level of income below which *absolute* poverty exists. But of course *perceptions* of poverty may be rather different, and may be influenced by comparative incomes in society, and by knowledge of the income of others and of other cultures.

As one would expect, absolute poverty is common in LDCs. Ahluwalia, Carter and Chenery (1979, p. 306) found that 'almost 40 per cent of the population of the developing countries live in absolute poverty defined in terms of income levels that are insufficient to provide adequate nutrition. . . . The incidence of poverty is 60 per cent or more in countries having the lowest level of real GNP.' By comparison, in Australia, even using a largely sociological or psychological standard for the poverty line, not more than 10 per cent of household units appear to be in poverty.

Most of those in poverty in less-developed countries are located in rural areas and are engaged in agriculture and associated pursuits (Todaro, 1981, p. 130). This is not surprising, because in LDCs those so located and so engaged constitute the bulk of the population. Indeed, from the percentages quoted by Todaro (1981, p. 131), the *incidence* of poverty in rural areas in LDCs (proportion of rural dwellers in poverty) seems higher but not all that much higher than in non-rural areas. Nevertheless, the number of rural dwellers in poverty is several times greater than the number of non-rural dwellers in poverty. For this reason, if no other, it is important not to neglect the rural sector in development plans. In China's case, per capita incomes in rural areas are on average much lower than in urban areas (about half the level in urban areas) and rural areas contain the largest number of people in poverty (Du Rensheng, 1989, p. 3).

6.3 ECONOMIC GROWTH, INCOME INEQUALITY AND POVERTY

On average, the distribution of personal income is more equal in developed countries than in less-developed countries, and the incidence of absolute poverty is smaller in more-developed countries. This suggests that, in the long term, economic growth provides a way for less-developed countries to increase equality of personal incomes, reduce the incidence of absolute poverty and raise per capita incomes on average. If this were so then economic growth would bring not only the benefits of higher incomes on average but more equality in their distribution.

In practice, however, the matter is not as straightforward as this. Kuznets (1963, 1973) has hypothesised that the relationship between the level of income per capita in countries and income inequality tends to be of an inverted U-shape, like that indicated by curve *ABC* in Figure 6.1. If this is true then as less-developed countries at first increase their per capita income due to economic growth, income inequality can be expected to increase. But if sufficient economic growth takes place and income per head rises enough then there is a tendency for greater equality of income to occur with continuing economic growth. Such a pattern can emerge, for instance, if the surplus (agricultural) labour theory of Lewis (1954) applies and industrialisation proceeds in a country. This is assuming that wages or income are higher in industry than in agriculture, as Lewis did.

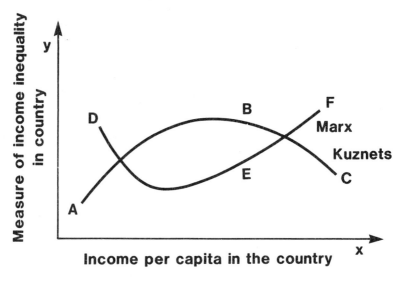

Figure 6.1   Some possible theoretical relationships between income inequality and levels of per capita income in countries

According to Kuznets (1963), economic growth in the poorest countries initially disadvantages the poor segment of the population, increasing income inequality. However, once a certain stage of development is reached, further economic growth is associated with increasing equality of income (Kuznets, 1963; Adelman and Morris, 1973; Chenery *et al.*, 1974).

Nevertheless, several different views about the relationship between inequality of income and economic growth have been expressed. Maitra (1988), drawing on the theories of Marx, suggest that at least for capitalist countries, a skewed U-shaped pattern like that indicated by the curve *DEF* in Figure 6.1 applies. This relationship is the opposite in essence to that hypothesised by Kuznets (1973).

Marx argued that during the initial period of economic growth the demand for labour rises in proportion to the growth of capital and results in the demand for labour exceeding its supply, even if population is growing. This results in excess demand for labour and rising wages. Consequently, rising wages cause capitalists to substitute capital for labour and the organic composition of capital (the ratio of capital to labour) begins to rise. In turn, this results in a fall in the demand for labour and unemployment for the working class. Thus, Marx believed, wages rise and income distribution improves initially with economic growth, but subsequently the opposite trend asserts itself under capitalism (Maitra, 1988).

Nevertheless, at least three other hypotheses exist that are different from those of Kuznets and Marx. These include the following: (1) The suggestion of a number of neo-Marxists that income inequality rises continually with economic growth. This would give rise to an upward-sloping curve in Figure 6.1. (2) The hypothesis of a number of neo-classical economists that income inequality declines continually as economic growth occurs. This implies a continually downward-sloping curve in Figure 6.1. (3) Vilfredo Pareto argues that the distribution of income tends to remain unchanged despite economic growth and changing institutions because the same élites in society tend to come to the top. Pareto's relationship would be depicted by a horizontal line in Figure 6.1.

Writers, mostly neo-classical economists, supporting the hypothesis that income distribution becomes less unequal, even initially, as economic growth occurs include Roberti (1974), Hayami and Kikuchi (1981), Prahladchar (1983) and Hayami and Ruttan (1985). For example, the experiences of South Korea, Taiwan, Hong Kong and Singapore are often cited in this regard. According to Ranis (1977, p. 54)

the Taiwan experience demonstrates that market allocations do not have to work on behalf of the rich, they can be made to work on behalf of the poor if two conditions are met: if assets, in both agriculture and non-agriculture are not very unequally distributed at the outset, and if relative prices are reasonably realistic indications of resource availability.

But, since the mid-1970s, income distribution has become more uneven in Hong Kong, Singapore and South Korea; this throws doubt on the above hypothesis, and has suggested to some scholars that a path like *DEF* in Figure 6.1 is being followed. Nevertheless, in practice, most neo-classical economists believe that economic growth is compatible with continually rising wage rates and improvements in the distribution of income (cf. Diwan and Kallianpur, 1985, p. 627; Samuelson, 1964).

In contrast, neo-Marxists predict a worsening distribution of income, and even falling wage rates, from the very inception of economic growth, as a result of a rise in the number of landless and of those without capital. According to this view, capitalistic economic development leads to a deterioration in the social position of the majority (Gimenez *et al.*, 1977; Griffin, 1979; Pearse, 1980), and it is claimed that the operation of the price mechanism reinforces the inequality of income that arises from inequality in the distribution of productive assets (Griffin and Khan, 1978, p. 299).

Empirical evidence about the relationship between income distribution and economic growth is inconclusive. Indeed, it suggests that there is *not* a very close relationship between economic growth, income per capita and the distribution of income, even though, in countries with higher per capita income levels, incomes seem broadly to be more evenly distributed than in countries with low per capita levels of income.

The extent of income inequality for LDCs with the same or similar levels of income per capita varies greatly, and shows greater variation than between more-developed countries (Todaro, 1981, p. 129). This indicates that factors other than average income levels help to a considerable extent to explain distributions of income. Further, the incidence of poverty varies considerably in less-developed countries with similar levels of per capita income. Thus the evidence supports Todaro's conclusion that

problems of poverty and highly unequal distributions of income are not just a result of natural economic growth processes. Rather they depend on the *character* of that economic growth and the political and institutional arrangements according to which rising national incomes are distributed among the broad segments of a population. (Todaro, 1981, pp. 130–1)

International empirical evidence indicates that inequality of income tends to be lower in relation to per capita income for socialist than non-socialist countries on average, to decrease with higher proportionate school enrolments, and to be low in countries dominated by small-scale or communal agriculture (Gillis *et al.*, 1983, Chapter 4). The quality of the population (or the workforce) in terms of education, health and similar factors appears (especially in developed countries) to be associated with greater equality of income.

China's leaders have emphasised the importance of improving the quality of China's workforce as a means to modernisation. This may also help to preserve greater equality in income. Zhao Ziyang (1987, p. 22) has said:

> . . . the revitalisation of the economy and indeed the progress of the whole society all depend on improving the quality of the workforce and training large numbers of competent personnel. Education is of fundamental importance to the fulfilment of our great long-range mission. We must therefore continue to stress the strategic role of education and do a better job of tapping intellectual resources.

After the ten years, 1966–76, in which the education system was run down in China, it became even more vital to give attention to education. More recently Jiang Zemin, the successor to Zhao Ziyang as General Secretary of the CPC, has also emphasised the importance for China of improving the quality of its workforce (*China Daily*, 24 May 1991, p. 1)

6.4 'TRICKLE-DOWN' OF ECONOMIC GROWTH, INCENTIVES, INEQUALITY AND ECONOMIC GROWTH

Views vary about whether it is important for LDCs to adopt policies to alleviate poverty and to reduce inequality of income in the early stages of their development. In the 1960s and for most of the 1970s, the popular view was that there is little point in worrying about inequality of income in the early stages of economic growth. It was believed that if economic growth could be achieved then its benefits would flow on or 'trickle down' to the poorest groups in society relatively quickly. While for some LDCs the poorest groups seem to have benefited relatively quickly from economic growth, in others the poor have not gained to any significant extent from overall economic growth (Todaro, 1981, p. 135).

The strategy of 'grow now and redistribute later' is today less popular. Popular alternatives are the *basic human needs* (BHN) approach and the *redistribution with growth* (RWG) approach. BHN policies are designed to satisfy the basic needs of the poor through government provision of commodities and services, subsidies and assistance. The BHN strategy requires the provision of

several basic commodities and services to the poor: staple foods, water and sanitation, health care, primary and informal education, and housing. The strategy includes two important elements. First, it requires finance to ensure that these basic needs can be provided at costs that the poor can afford. Second, the strategy includes service networks to distribute these services in forms appropriate for consumption by the poor, and especially in areas where the poor live. (Gillis *et al.*, 1983, p. 93)

Redistribution with growth (RWG) policies are designed to increase the productivity of low-income producers, improve their earning opportunities and see that they are supplied with the resources necessary to take advantage of these opportunities (Gillis *et al.*, 1983, p. 92). RWG policies provide economic opportunities for the poor to improve their earning power by their own effort.

Since 1949 China has tried to achieve a high rate of economic growth by maintaining a high savings and a high investment ratio, but during this period the focus of its income distribution policies seems to have altered. Prior to 1979, the main emphasis was on meeting basic human needs, mainly by individuals sharing in collectives, communes or similar groups. But now its emphasis seems to be on redistribution with growth, as in the case of economic aid for poor areas, and on a policy of 'grow now and redistribute income later'. This changed emphasis arises from the view (1) that basic needs are now fairly well satisfied in China and (2) that material incentives are needed to encourage economic effort and promote economic growth.

To what extent are material incentives and income inequalities necessary to promote economic growth? Lewis (1954) argued that inequality resulting from accumulation in the industrial sector is important for growth. This argument is however based on a particular theory and stresses profit as an important source of savings.

There seems to be no simple relationship between income inequality and economic growth. There is, for example, no evidence that economic growth increases with income inequality. Countries with great inequality of income often experience little economic growth. If there is a relationship between these variables, it seems likely that economic growth as a function of income inequality would at first rise with increases in this variable and then decline. Some income inequality may provide incentives or reflect the presence of economic incentives for effort, but great inequality may mean that a large proportion of the population is unable to meet their basic needs and the quality of the workforce is therefore low and unable to provide an adequate basis for economic growth. Furthermore, significant inequality of income can be a threat to political stability.

Nevertheless, if economic growth is to be achieved then effort and enterprise must be rewarded. Economic or material rewards in the shape of higher income have an important role to play in that regard. Recent Chinese leaders, such as Li Peng and Jiang Zemin, accept this view, which was clearly expressed by Zhao Ziyang (1987, pp. 39–40):

> The policies of distribution we formulate should encourage some enterprises and individuals to become prosperous before others through good management and honest work, thus widening the differences in personal income to a reasonable degree. But at the same time, these policies should prevent the polarisation of rich and poor, enable all people to move towards common prosperity and bring about social equity while improving efficiency.

6.5   JUSTICE AND EQUITY IN INCOME DISTRIBUTION AND EQUALITY OF OPPORTUNITY

Views about what constitutes a just distribution of income and about justice in the distribution of social opportunities inevitably reflect one's value system and views about the nature of the world. Even though it seems impossible to justify ultimate values scientifically, they are important because they are the basis of most social action. Furthermore, differences in values can make the difference between a civilised and progressive society and a barbaric one.

The issues involved in deciding on a just distribution of income and economic opportunity are complex (Tisdell, 1982, pp. 415–19, 452–5). Even when income is earned only from personal exertion and use of one's inherited abilities, the matter is complex. But let us concentrate just briefly on one issue, namely that involving economic reward according to work, a principle which is being increasingly emphasised in China. One principle of justice which we might agree on is 'the equal treatment of equals'.

Suppose that two individuals with *equal* inherited ability are given equal opportunities to develop their talents and to work, but one does not apply him or herself to the task. Is it just that their income payments be equal? It can be argued that this would not be just. To do so would actually in *psychological* terms give a higher income to the lazier person.

This can be illustrated by Figure 6.2. Let individual B be the lazier person and A the more industrious. Suppose that both have the same opportunity to trade off hours of leisure against income as shown by line *KM*. One individual chooses the combination of income and leisure hours per day corresponding to point *J* and the other person chooses the combination at *L*. Thus B, the lazier person, receives a lower income payment than person A. But, in the circumstances, this seems just since both have equal opportunities and abilities.

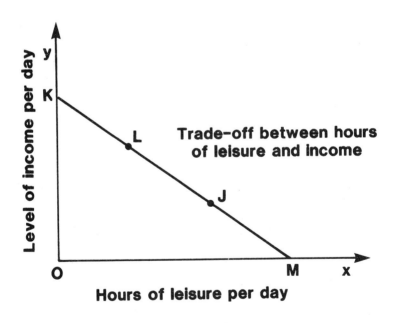

Figure 6.2   Given equal opportunities to earn income, differences in actual income do not necessarily indicate differences in 'real' income

The matter, however, from the point of view of justice is more complicated when individuals fail to develop their abilities over a *long period* of time, for example, through education. Suppose that two students have equal ability and equal access to education but one does not apply himself or herself, and therefore develops fewer skills and is less productive in later life than the more studious person. Should the studious person subsidise the income of the less studious? Strictly on the above principle, this should not be the case. On the other hand, we all make mistakes when younger or are more inclined to do so. Therefore there may be a case if the person who was less studious in his or her youth is in difficult economic circumstances to show compassion and redistribute some income. Many of us believe that principles of justice have also to be tempered by compassion and mercy.

This all inevitably raises deep philosophical issues. For example, to what extent are individual choices and personal development a function of the individual's environment? To what extent do individuals have free will? To the extent that it is believed that individuals are fully responsible for their decisions or choices in all circumstances, a harder line may be taken in requiring individuals to enjoy or suffer the consequences of their decisions.

However, natural abilities are not equally distributed among individuals in society, and this unequal distribution can be a source of income (and of social) inequality, even when individuals of equal ability develop and use these equally. This raises the question of the extent to which it is just to compensate individuals materially for lower differences in ability and the extent to which it is practical to do so.

According to the principle of justice put forward by Rawls (1971), incomes in society should be equal unless inequality is to the advantage of all. This is based on the type of agreement which individuals might be expected to reach if they were to confer before they were born, not knowing into what situation they would be born. It is said to be the type of agreement that would emerge behind a 'veil of ignorance', *given* that there is an equal chance of each being born into the circumstances of the others, for example with the natural abilities or handicaps of others.

Note that the Rawlsian principle of justice is not inconsistent with some income inequality. If it is the case, for example, that by giving extra economic and other advantages to the talented in society all would gain, as can be the case, then this inequality would be justifiable even given the Rawlsian principle. Furthermore, this principle is not inconsistent with the principle of 'equal treatment of equals', that is, equal treatment of those with the same ability as propounded above. In fact it suggests that inequality of income arising from differing attitudes to work and effort by equals is justified.

Income redistribution may be direct or indirect, coming about in the latter case because of changes in the resources made available to the poorer members of society. This raises the question of the extent to which resource compensation is a rational means of compensating for poverty in comparison with direct income transfers to the poorer members of society. The issues involved are complex and cannot all be canvassed here. But observe that if the poorer members use or are only able to utilise the resources transferred to them less productively than the better-off members of the community then aggregate production is reduced by this policy, and this implies a Kaldor–Hicks welfare loss. In other words, a potential Pareto improvement might be made by reverting to a less equal allocation of productive resources and compensating the losers by income transfers. However, the poor are not necessarily potentially less productive then the rich. There are 'deserving' and extremely talented individuals among the poor, and providing such individuals with adequate resources will actually and possibly significantly add to national production. The principle of equal treatment of equals of natural ability would also support a policy of providing equal access to resources for those of equal talent, whether they are from poor families or from rich ones. In this respect educational systems have an important role to play, and so does the state in ensuring that economic opportunities available to individuals are not based on social privilege.

While social privilege now plays a smaller role in China than in the past, together with contacts it still plays a significant role in determining the access of individuals' economic opportunities. *Guanxi* (informal social networks and contacts) are extremely important in China in influencing the economic prospects of the individual. However, such factors seem important in most less developed countries. They tend to become less-important as a competitive market system develops and economic growth occurs.

There is another aspect of income distribution which ought to be mentioned, that is, intergenerational equity in the distribution of income. In this respect Tietenberg (1988, p. 33), on the basis of Rawls's principle, suggests that 'at a minimum, future generations should be left no worse off than current generations'. Very often this is used as an argument for sustainable economic development and for conserving natural resources to ensure that the incomes of future generations can be maintained (Pearce *et al.*, 1989, p. 3). In this context, however, Rawls's principle of justice appears to involve a number of philosophical difficulties (Tisdell, 1990), possibly major one of these being that future population levels can be controlled and so resource conservation and population control need to be considered simultaneously. Nevertheless, profligate use of natural resources to achieve economic growth in China now can be at the expense of the ability of future generations to maintain their economic welfare. Some of these issues will be taken up in Chapter 12.

6.6 INCOME SECURITY AND EFFICIENT ALLOCATION OF RESOURCES

As economic growth proceeds in a country, not only do levels of income change, but the security of incomes obtained by individuals can alter. Although the incomes of individuals were often low in many traditional peasant and gathering economies, but not always so, as pointed out by Woodburn (1981) and Yellen (1990), individuals, were from an economic viewpoint, relatively secure in most cases because of the social sharing of commodities and the adoption of husbandry practices which encouraged natural resource conservation. Such economic security can disappear as a result of economic growth, the development of a market system, specialisation in work and the mobility of labour.

As economic systems develop, as social bonds disappear and job security is diminished, many states introduce social security or service schemes on a nationwide basis to compensate for this. If it is accepted that social security systems are more common in developed countries, then the income security of individuals appears typically to follow a U-shaped pattern with the economic development of societies. Thus the type of relationship indicated in Figure 6.3 may be common.

It should also be remembered that in some circumstances improved efficiency in the allocation of resources can help to equalise incomes and raise incomes overall. In some regions the productivity of agriculture may be low and difficult to raise, because of the poor natural environment in the area. The appropriate policy in order to alleviate poverty in the area may be to allow migration, if no other productive or sufficiently productive industry can be developed there. In the latter case, however, opportunity costs should be taken into account. Rather than establish an industry in a depressed region, it may be more economic (productive) to establish it elsewhere and allow or even assist individuals from the depressed region to migrate to the more productive region. The Chinese authorities still appear to take insufficient account of opportunity costs in making such decisions, as is evident, for example, from the continued government control over labour movement.

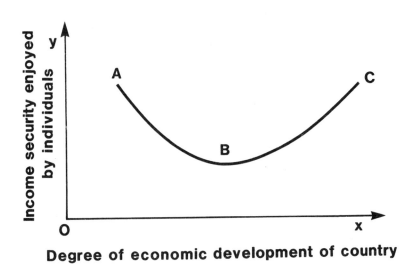

Figure 6.3   The level of income security enjoyed by individuals may be a U-shaped function of the degree of development of a country

6.7 CONCLUDING COMMENT

The topic of justice in the distribution of income and economic opportunities should be of fundamental importance in a socialist economic system given that Marx's main criticism of the capitalist system was that it led to the exploitation of labour and an unfair distribution of income. At the same time, Marx provided virtually no guide or particular policies for managing a socialist or communist state. The principle of 'to each according to need, from each according to ability' appears unworkable in practice because there is little or no incentive for those with greater ability to give of it fully and each may try to rely on the effort of others. Furthermore, equal sharing is not necessarily just nor is it likely to be very productive from an economic growth point of view. Thus new principles need to be considered and developed to guide socialism with Chinese characteristics. In doing so, it seems important to take account of the factors mentioned above.

REFERENCES

ADELMAN, I. and MORRIS, C.T. (1973) *Economic Growth and Social Equity in Developing Countries*, Stanford University Press, Palo Alto.
AHLUWALIA M.S., CARTER, N. and CHENERY, H. (1979) 'Growth and poverty in developing countries', *Journal of Development Economics*, 6 (3), pp. 299–341.
CHENERY, H., AHLUWALIA, M.S., BELL, C.L.G., DULOY, J.H. and JOLLY, R. (1974) *Redistribution With Growth*, Oxford University Press, Oxford.
DIWAN, R. and KALLIANPUR, R. (1985) 'Biological technology and land productivity: fertilisers and food production in India', *World Development*, 13 (5), 627–38.
DU RENSHENG (1989) 'Advancing amidst reform', pp. 3–10 in J.W. Longworth (ed.) *China's Rural Development Miracle*, University of Queensland Press, St Lucia, Brisbane.
GILLIS, M., PERKINS, D.H., ROEMER, M. and SNODGRASS, D.R. (1983) *Economics of Development*, Norton, New York.
GIMENEZ, M.E., GREENBERY, E., MARKUSEN, A., MAYER, T. and NEWTON, A. (1977) 'Income inequality and capitalist development: A Marxist perspective', in W. Loehr and J.P. Powelson (eds) *Economic Development and Income Distribution*, Westview, Boulder, Colo.
GRIFFIN, K.B. (1979) *The Political Economy of Agrarian Change: An Essay on the Green Revolution*, Macmillan, London.
GRIFFIN, K.B. and KHAN, A.R. (1978) 'Poverty in the Third World: ugly facts and fancy models', *World Development*, 6 (3), pp. 295–354.
HAYAMI, Y. and KIKUCHI, M. (1981) *Asian Village Economy at the Crossroads*, University of Tokyo Press, Tokyo.
HAYAMI, Y. and RUTTAN, V.W. (1985) *Agricultural Development: An International Perspective*, Johns Hopkins University Press, Baltimore, Md.
KUZNETS, S. (1963) 'Quantitative aspects of economic growth of nations, distribution of income by size', *Economic Development and Cultural Change*, 1 (2), pp. 1–80.
KUZNETS, S. (1973) 'Modern economic growth; findings and reflections', *American Economic Review*, 63, pp. 247–58.
LEWIS, W.A. (1954) 'Economic development with unlimited supplies of labour', *Manchester School*, 22, pp. 139–91.
MAITRA, P. (1988) 'Population growth, technological change and economic development – the Indian case, with a critique of Marxist interpretation',

pp. 9–34 in Tisdell, C. A. and Maitra, P. (eds) *Technological Change, Development and the Environment: Socio-Economic Perspectives*, Routledge, London.

PEARCE, D., MARKANDYA, A. and BARBIER, E. B. (1989) *Blueprint for a Green Economy*, Earthscan, London.

PEARSE, A. (1980) *Seeds of Plenty, Seeds of Want*, Clarendon, Oxford.

PRAHLADCHAR, M. (1983) 'Income distribution effects of the Green Revolution in India: a review of the empirical evidence', *World Development*, 11 (11), pp. 927–44.

RANIS, G. (1977) 'Growth and distribution: trade-off or complements?', In W. Loehr and J.P. Powelson (eds) *Economic Development, Poverty and Income Distribution*, Westview Press, Boulder, Colo.

RAWLS, J. R. (1971) *A Theory of Justice*, Harvard University Press, Cambridge, Mass.

ROBERTI, P. (1974) 'Income distribution: a time-series and a cross-section study', *Economic Journal*, 84, pp. 629–38.

SAMUELSON, P. A. (1964) *Economics: An Introductory Analysis*, 7th edn, McGraw-Hill, New York.

TIETENBERG, T. (1988) *Environmental and Natural Resource Economics*, 2nd edn, Scott Foresman, Glenview, Ill.

TISDELL, C. A. (1982) *Microeconomics of Markets*, Wiley, Brisbane.

TISDELL, C. A. (1990) *The Nature of Sustainability and Sustainable Development*, Discussion Paper in Economics No. 48, Department of Economics, University of Queensland, St Lucia, Brisbane.

TODARO, M. P. (1981) *Economic Development in the Third World*, 2nd edn, Longmans, New York.

WOODBURN, J. (1981) 'Egalitarian societies', *Man* (NS), 17, pp. 431–51.

YELLEN, J. E. (1990) 'The transformation of the Kalahari. !Kung', *Scientific American*, April, pp. 72–9.

ZHAO ZIYANG (1987) 'Advance along the road of socialism with Chinese characteristics', report delivered at the Thirteenth National Congress of the Communist Party of China 25 October 1987, pp. 3–80 in *Documents of the Thirteenth National Congress of the Communist Party of China (1987)* Foreign Languages Press, Beijing.

7 Agriculture and Agricultural Research Priorities

7.1 AGRICULTURE AND ECONOMIC DEVELOPMENT

Views about whether agricultural growth plays or can play a key role in the economic development of less-developed countries have varied considerably. Particularly, during the 1950s and into the 1960s, the dominant view in the Western World was as expressed by Hollis B. Chenery that 'industrialisation is the main hope of most poor countries trying to increase their levels of income' (Chenery, 1955). Models developed, for example, by A. W. Lewis (1954) propagated the view that returns to investment in agriculture were low or even negative, and that any surplus which might be generated in agriculture would soon be dissipated by population increases in rural communities. This led to the policy suggestion that capital formation should be directed towards industrialisation and urbanisation rather than towards agriculture. The net benefit of such a policy was seen to be the generation of a larger level of surplus or savings to promote capital accumulation and slower rates of population increase given that urban populations tend to increase, at a slower rate than rural populations. Writers such as W. W. Rostow (1956, 1960) speculated that such policies could eventually result in LDCs (less developed countries) embarking on sustained economic growth.

However, as suggested by Todaro (1981, p. 252) development economists today are less confident about placing such heavy emphasis on industrialisation. Todaro (1981, p. 252) says:

> the 1970s witnessed a remarkable transition in development thinking – one in which agricultural and rural development came to be seen by many as a *sine qua non* [an essential precondition] of national development. Without such agricultural and rural development, industrial growth would either be stultified or, if it succeeded,

would create such severe internal imbalances in the economy that the problems of widespread poverty, inequality and unemployment would become even more pronounced.

Presumably a significant factor in changing thinking was the apparent success of Green Revolution technologies in agriculture spearheaded by the development of new high-yielding rice varieties at the International Rice Research Institute (IRRI) in the Philippines. The development of new high yielding varieties (HYVs) of cereals and associated biological-chemical technology has continued at a rapid pace and has demonstrated that large increases in productivity and high returns can be generated from investment in some types of agriculture (Alauddin and Tisdell, 1991).

In a country such as China, where there is a large agricultural sector and much agricultural expertise, it is clear that the development of the agricultural and rural sector is important for overall economic development. Desirably, this should occur hand in hand with developments in other sectors, including appropriate industrialisation policies. This 'middle path' of development seems appropriate in China for several reasons including the following:

(1) The fact that a large proportion of China's population is engaged in agriculture and is located in rural areas. Estimates vary, but according to Du Rensheng (1989, p. 3) around 80 per cent of China's population lives in rural areas, and possibly more than 60 per cent have a direct involvement in agriculture. Mere logistics and the time required for structural change alone suggest that a large proportion of China's population will continue to be rural for some time. According to Du Rensheng (1989, p. 3), the per capita income of China's rural population is only about half that of its urban population and the incidence of poverty is higher in rural than in urban populations. Assistance for the rural population will require attention to the rural sector.

(2) In relation to capital available for investment, there will be many projects in rural areas including agriculture which will give higher returns than marginal projects involving industrialisation. Optimal allocation of scarce capital so as to maximise returns is likely to require a mixture of rural and urban (agricultural and industrial) investments, i.e. a mixed portfolio of investment.

(3) The returns obtained by enterprises and the income obtained by individuals in cities *may* overstate their social economic value. For

example, environmental costs imposed by enterprises in cities may not be properly accounted for in their own costs and the incomes of urban dwellers may be directly or indirectly subsidised out of general taxes; for example, they may be provided with subsidised housing or subsidised public transport as in China. In fact, the rural communities in China are more or less self-sufficient. They fund their own welfare programmes with few government subsidies, no housing subsidies, and so on. They have inherited the legacy of Mao's 'walking on two legs' policy. Such policies reflect 'urban bias' (Lipton, 1977).

(4) Economic development is likely to proceed faster and more securely when there is an appropriate balance between agricultural and industrial development because agriculture produces a surplus of wage goods (such as food) to support urban and industrial workers and its growth adds to the demand for or the market for industrial goods.

Apart from the above, given the geographical nature of China, agriculture is likely to remain an important industry in China even when China becomes more developed. Although the agricultural sector employs only a small proportion of their workforce, agriculture continues to be an important sector in most developed countries. This is true for example for the United States, the European Community, Canada and Australia. Thus it is appropriate that continuing attention be given to agricultural and rural development.

This chapter will concentrate on aspects of scientific and technological change in agriculture, emphasising the importance of agricultural extension of knowledge and difficulties involved in determining agricultural research priorities. Interindustry or macroscopic economic aspects of agriculture will be considered in the next chapter.

Jiang Zemin, General Secretary of the CPC, in an important speech delivered to the Soviet Academic Society emphasised the continuing importance of agriculture for China's development. He said:

To develop agriculture remains our top priority in the 1990s. To develop agriculture, we will continue to deepen the rural reform and popularise and advance science and technology in agriculture, increase agricultural input by the central and local authorities, and by the collective units and individual peasants. (*China Daily*, 20 May 1991, p. 4)

7.2   TECHNOLOGICAL/SCIENTIFIC CHANGE AND
PRODUCTIVITY INCREASE IN AGRICULTURE

Agricultural productivity and the ability of agriculture to meet the
wants of a population can be increased in several different ways. These
include

(1) improvements in the allocation of resources used in agriculture;
(2) increase in 'X-efficiency' (Leibenstein, 1966, 1978) on farms
    through keener management and greater application of farm
    personnel to their tasks;
(3) wider or better use of existing knowledge and information about
    improved agricultural techniques; and
(4) the development of improved techniques through research.

These means potentially promise greater agricultural output without
an increase in the amount of resources used in agriculture. They are
usually productivity enhancing measures.

Let us concentrate on the better use of knowledge and the extension
of knowledge as a means to raise agricultural productivity. Already
China is increasing the number of its agricultural extension officers.
After falling from 17 600 in 1979 to 14 000 in 1984, this number
increased gradually to 16 200 in 1989 (Chai, 1991, p. 27). China
intends to put greater emphasis on this aspect in the future. The
minister in charge of the State Science and Technology Commission,
Song Jian, said in mid-1991 that China intends to speed up the process
of transferring scientific findings to production.

During the Eighth Five-Year Plan period (1991–95), China will
apply around 20 000 scientific findings. In agriculture more fine
varieties of grain, cotton and oil-bearing plants will be introduced
along with other items of new technology for processing farm and
sideline products and for protection of the environment. (*China
Daily*, 8 June 1991, p. 3)

Existing agricultural knowledge is not always utilised to the full
extent that is economical. Education, communication and extension
services play an important role in the process of raising agricultural
productivity. Up to a point, it may also be worth while importing
knowledge and adapting it to the local environment. This may require
the country to engage in adaptive research and development (R & D).

Since the communication of existing knowledge, the adaptation of existing knowledge to the local environment, and research and development into new areas all require the use of scarce resources, an appropriate economic balance must be struck between these activities. This can be illustrated hypothetically by Figure 7.1.

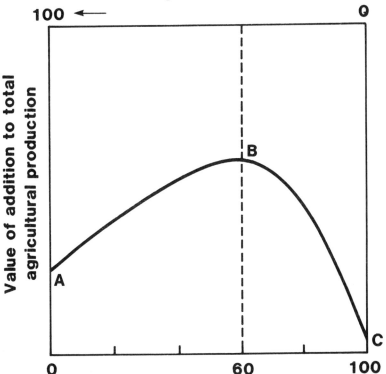

Figure 7.1   Optimal allocation of resources between R & D and the communication or extension of research results in agriculture

Assume that a given quantity of resources is available for R & D or for the communication and extension of agricultural knowledge. As the proportion of resources allocated to one activity rather than the other varies, we can expect the value of the addition to production to alter. We would expect this addition to the value of production to be low when all or most of the resources are used in R & D and communication and extension is neglected. Alternatively this may occur when R & D effort is low and most or all resources for knowledge creation and communication are used in communicating existing knowledge.

In the case shown in Figure 7.1, the curve *ABC* represents the (hypothetical) addition to the value of agricultural production of different allocations of resources for knowledge creation and communication between agricultural R & D and communication (and extension) of agricultural knowledge. In the case shown, the optimal allocation is 60 per cent of resources to R & D and 40 per cent of resources to communication or transfer of scientific results.

A 'correct' balance needs to be struck between the proportion of resources allocated to the communication of agricultural knowledge and that used to increase agricultural knowledge, that is in R & D.

7.3   PRIORITIES IN AGRICULTURAL RESEARCH

One matter which needs to be considered is whether national priorities should be established for agricultural research and what these ought to be. Research can proceed without such priorities being established. It then tends to be on an *ad hoc* basis and lacking direction, and can be inefficient. On the other hand, to direct all agricultural research centrally according to a comprehensive rationalistic plan may not be economic and runs the risk that planners can be out of touch with local needs and opportunities. It can stifle local initiative. A rational comprehensive plan is one in which objectives are completely and consistently defined. The aim is to ensure that all actions are in accordance with these objectives (cf. Tisdell, 1981).

While many regard the rationalistic comprehensive approach to planning as ideal, several factors need to be considered. It may involve considerable cost to formulate the plan, to collect information and to monitor performance. In that respect it should be remembered that individuals are not programmable machines and that all have limited capacities for comprehending, collecting and processing information. Thus unbounded or complete rationality based on perfect information is in most cases impossible or uneconomic. The best that can usually be hoped for is bounded or limited rationality (Simon, 1957 a, b). From an economic point of view (and often from a humanistic viewpoint), systems based upon the assumption of bounded rationality are ideal. In relation to agricultural research, for example, this may involve some decentralisation of decision-making on a regional basis and then by research units, with plans becoming more detailed as one proceeds downwards. Note that China seems to have developed good information channels through the Party propaganda networks. Even at the basic production units there are propaganda cadres.

In devising agricultural research systems, we have to grapple with limits to information flows within research organisations, the restricted ability of individuals to handle information flows and the diversity of human nature. For example, presentation and transmission of information within organisations involves costs, and there is always the chance of errors (accidental or deliberate) occurring in transmission of information. A perfect system does not seem to be attainable but this does not imply that nothing ought to be done. Rather, we are led to the point of view that we should try to devise the best imperfect or attainable system (cf. Tisdell, 1985, 1986).

One of the problems that may arise when national priorities are being determined is that those determining them can be out of contact with those they affect most directly. This is a particular danger in so-called top-down planning, that is, plans devised at the top and flowing downwards. Top planners or controllers may be out of contact with wants and opportunities, especially where they are only, academically trained and are employed in the bureaucracy in a city far from the farmers primarily affected by the research. It is therefore sometimes suggested that it is better for planning to be bottom-up. While this merthod will ensure an input from many of those affected and is likely to bring to light opportunities and needs which otherwise would not be considered, it is not without its difficulties. For example, priorities expressed by those at the bottom may conflict. Again, those at the bottom are likely to lack the general and comprehensive knowledge and perspective of top planners.

The problem is that individuals all have different sets of information. Those at the bottom, at the top and inbetween in an agricultural organisation, as well as farmers and others, have different sets of information relevant to the setting of agricultural priorities and planning. The problem is to make appropriate use of the different sets of information and abilities of individuals to obtain the best attainable result. As a rule, such a system will involve information flows and suggestions both from the topdown and from the bottomup, and at levels inbetween, with some sort of appropriate filtering taking place. Such a system of management or planning has been described as side-by-side. But clearly such a system can take many different forms, and much more research is needed to determine the type of side-by-side systems that may yield the best results.

7.4 COST–BENEFIT APPROACH TO EVALUATING AGRICULTURAL R & D

One approach sometimes used in market and mixed market economies for evaluating agricultural R & D is social cost–benefit analysis. This method aims to evaluate all the costs and benefits of projects in monetary terms. In turn, its objective is to select projects so as to maximise the total of net returns on resources or capital invested in projects. It is recognised that market returns may not coincide with social returns, owing, for example, to externalities or spillovers, and that some adjustment may need to be made to market-determined returns in order to evaluate social returns. Adjustments can be made using a variety of social welfare criteria, each of which involves value judgments of one kind or another. No evaluation system is value-free. However, a measure of objectivity can be obtained in cost–benefit analysis by specifying exactly the social welfare criterion being used.

The most commonly used basis for cost–benefit analysis in mixed market economies is the Kaldor–Hicks criterion. Since most projects involve gains for some individuals and losses for others, a means must be found to take this into account. The Kaldor–Hicks criterion calculates social benefit as being the difference between the maximum sum of money which gainers from a project are willing to pay for its implementation less the minimum amount of money that those losing from the project are willing to accept for it not being carried out. A social net benefit is said to exist if those gaining from the change *could* compensate the losers and be better off than before the change. This criterion does not require that actual compensation be paid to losers. It is based on the concept of a *potential* Paretian improvement rather than an actual improvement. A Paretian improvement is said to occur when some gain and no one loses from implementation of a project or a social change.

For example, in Australia the Industries Assistance Commission (1985) used social cost–benefit analysis to evaluate the economics of introducing biological control agents to Australia and releasing these to control species of weeds of the genus *Echium*. Such a project was found to benefit some farmers and create losses for others. The project was estimated to increase the profits of wheat producers and graziers, mostly in the eastern states of Australia, but to result in reduced income for apiarists, and for graziers in South Australia where the weeds were used as a drought fodder. However, the total increase in profits of farmers benefiting was predicted to far exceed the loss in profits of those losing.

The difference between the increase in profits, *G*, of those gaining, less the loss in income, *L*, of those losing, can be taken to measure benefits, *B*, of the project if the Kaldor–Hicks approach is used. Thus mathematically the benefits are

$$B = G - L.$$

Benefits, *B*, then need to be compared with costs, *C*, to determine whether benefits exceed cost and to estimate the return on costs on the investment. The Industries Assistance Commission (1985) found that benefits exceeded costs by a considerable margin and that the project was justified on the basis of cost–benefit analysis, and would yield a high return.

In some cases supply-and-demand analysis is used to estimate the social benefits from a research project or the introduction of a new technique in agriculture (Davis *et al.*, 1987; Davis and Ryan, 1989). If the research project or new technique will result in the reduction in the cost of production of a particular product, say rice, in a country, then it can be viewed as leading to a shift outward or downward in the supply curve of the product. In the *normal* case, benefits will consist of two parts: (1) an increase in the surplus (profits) obtained by producers and (2) an increase in the surplus obtained by consumers. The latter occurs if the market price of the product falls as a result of greater supply.

In the case shown in Figure 7.2, suppose that the cost of producing a product, say wheat, is reduced and the supply curve of wheat shifts from S_1S_1 to S_2S_2 as a result. Given that the demand curve for the product is DD, the market equilibrium alters from E_1 to E_2. Thus the equilibrium price of the product falls from P_1 to P_2 and the supply of the product expands from X_1 to X_2. The increase in consumers' surplus as a result is shown by the equivalent of the hatched area in Figure 7.2, and, assuming for simplicity that the supply curve moves in a parallel fashion, the increase in producers' surplus is shown by the equivalent of the dotted area. The total benefit equals these areas combined.

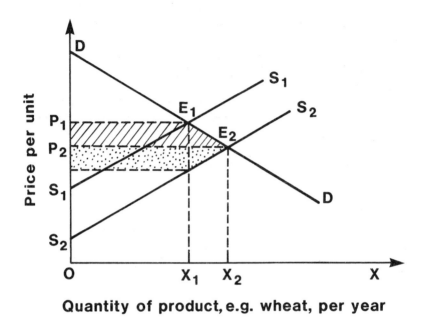

Quantity of product, e.g. wheat, per year

Figure 7.2   A case in which the economic benefits from reduction in supply of a product are shared by both consumers and producers

The exact distribution of benefits between producers and consumers depends on the relative slopes of the supply and demand curves. Indeed, technological progress does not always benefit *both* consumers and producers. While in terms of this analysis consumers can never lose, they do not increase their surplus if the demand for the product in question is perfectly elastic. In that case all the benefits are appropriated by producers of the product, as is illustrated in Figure 7.3.

In the case shown in Figure 7.3, market equilibrium shifts from E_1 to E_2 as a result of technological progress, but the equilibrium price of the product remains unaltered at P_1. There is no increase in consumers' surplus, but the surplus obtained by suppliers rises by the dotted area. If, by contrast, the demand for the product happened to be perfectly inelastic (and the demand curve for the product is therefore vertical) then all the benefits of technological change would be allocated to consumers (cf. Duncan and Tisdell, 1971; Edwards and Freebairn, 1982).

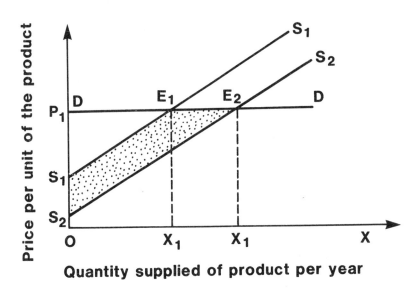

Figure 7.3   A case in which all the economic benefits from technological progress are appropriated by producers

A common procedure used in the West for estimating returns to agricultural R & D is to estimate the increased market surpluses generated by new technological innovations in agriculture arising from the R & D and compare these with the costs of the R & D. This enables social return on the R & D investment to be estimated.

Many agricultural research projects have yielded high rates of returns as estimated in this way (Marsden *et al.*, 1980; Arndt *et al.*, 1977). For example, as reviewed by Marsden *et al.* (1980) and Arndt *et al.* (1977), Griliches (1957) estimated the internal rate of return on R & D expenditure required for the development of hybrid corn in the USA to be 35–40 per cent. Audito and Bartletta (in Marsden *et al.* 1980) calculated the internal rate of return on R & D outlays leading to the development of high-yielding varieties of wheat in Mexico to be 90 per cent. Akino and Hayami (1975) estimated the internal rate of return on research leading to improved rice varieties in Japan to be 73–75 per cent. Using similar methods, Marsden *et al.* (1980) found high returns to research outlays by the CSIRO (a government research body in Australia) designed to find means to control insect pests in agriculture.

It might be objected that these are particular examples or cases and could therefore give a misleading picture of the overall returns to investment in agricultural R & D. But at least for the USA, available evidence suggests that returns from aggregate agricultural R & D are high. Peterson and Fitzharris (1977) found that in the period 1937–72 internal rates of return on aggregate United States agricultural R & D ranged from 35 to 51 per cent.

The above-mentioned returns have been estimated *after the event*. Is it possible to use similar cost–benefit analysis to estimate social rates of return to R & D projects *prior* to the projects being undertaken? To the extent that it is practical, it would provide a method of 'optimally' allocating R & D funds between alternative projects, or even alternative agricultural projects. In fact, Davis *et al.* (1987) and Davis and Ryan (1989) have suggested cost–benefit analysis based upon supply and demand curves be used to allocate R & D funds between agricultural commodities. However, application of this method may be subject to a number of limitations.

7.5 LIMITATIONS OF USING COST-BENEFIT ANALYSIS TO ALLOCATE AGRICULTURAL RESEARCH FUNDS

The level of benefits obtained from agricultural research depend not only on the economic value of results but on the productivity of the research in adding to knowledge; that is, the size of the technological advance or enhancement of knowledge likely in relation to the research outlay. In particular, scientific and technological productivity is extremely difficult to estimate in advance of research being under-taken. One is very much dependent on the views of scientists as to prospects for the scientific advance. If CBA is used as a top-down planning device then, the managers of the R & D budget may be out of contact with scientific possibilities and not in fact know of all possibilities. Worst of all, the initiative of scientific researchers may be stifled if the administrative system is very rigid and rule-ridden. If the motivation or the morale of researchers is low then this will adversely affect scientific productivity. Possibly morale is higher when researchers have some flexibility in their research and involvement in the process of resource allocation for R & D.

Cost-benefit analysis relies on all costs and benefits being reduced to a single dimension, namely a monetary dimension. This makes it one-dimensional. Consequently, important welfare aspects of decisions may be overlooked.

Three factors tend to be overlooked in cost–benefit evaluation (cf. Conway, 1985; Alauddin and Tisdell, 1991):

(1) the impact of projects on the variability of income;
(2) their consequences for the distribution of income and especially for poverty; and
(3) their implications for the sustainability of production, of communities and of society.

Apart from taking account of the anticipated or expected returns from projects, it can be important to take the above factors into account. For example, society may be prepared to forgo some expected returns to ensure greater stability in agricultural production, or to ensure that the poorest members of society are given special assistance through research programmes. One should also take into account the ecological and environmental *sustainability* of economic initiatives.

While cost–benefit analysis can in principle take these factors into account to some extent through its discounting procedures, environmental factors have tended in the past to be overlooked in orthodox economic project analysis. When using cost–benefit analysis one should be aware that all costs and benefits may not have been included in the evaluation and should not forget that non-economic factors, including the need to resolve human conflict, may have a bearing on the problem. Sometimes the optimal economic solution to a problem is not politically optimal, given that human conflict must be contained.

7.6 CONCLUSION

In a country such as China, agriculture and the rural sector can make an important contribution to economic development. Even though relative employment in this sector is likely to fall with economic development, the agricultural sector can be expected to remain a large sector in China for the foreseeable future, and an important source of production even when the country becomes more developed. Therefore it is appropriate that China should continue to improve productivity in this sector, especially through scientific and technological change. Zhao Ziyang (1987, p. 26) has stated that 'it is necessary to stress the question of agriculture, which is extremely important and has a direct bearing on overall economic development and reform. The steady growth of agriculture and the improvement of the structure of production in rural areas are the foundation for steady, long-term development of the entire economy.' He goes on to point out that the strengthening of agriculture is an important and urgent task in China. According to his successor as General Secretary, Jiang Zemin, development of agriculture remains a top priority in China (*China Daily*, 20 May 1991, p. 4). However, agriculture is still comparatively starved of investment funds, though not to the same unbalanced extent as in the past.

China should give careful consideration to its priorities in agricultural research and communication of agricultural information. But agricultural research in a large country involves many individuals in its conduct and management. This raises several difficulties, especially for top-down planning. A side-by-side method of management of agricultural R & D is probably optimal in the circumstances.

Cost-benefit analysis has been used to evaluate the returns from past agricultural research and development projects in market or mixed-market economies. The results indicate that returns are high and compare more than favourably with returns from industrial projects. While cost–benefit analysis may provide some guidance in the allocation of agricultural R & D funds, it does, as mentioned, have limitations as a management tool. Its use is subject to further limitations in an economy, such as China's, in which prices are distorted or controlled, because the actual price of products may not reflect relative values or opportunity costs adequately. As market mechanisms become more widely established, however, it does become more realistic to consider cost–benefit analysis as a possible planning or decision-making device in China.

REFERENCES

AKINO, M. and HAYAMI, Y. (1975) 'Efficiency and equity in public research: Rice breeding in Japan's Economic development', *American Journal of Agricultural Economics*, 57, 1–10.

ALAUDDIN, M. and TISDELL, C. (1991) *The 'Green Revolution' and Economic Development: The Process and its Impact on Bangladesh*, Macmillan, London

ARNDT, J. M., DALRYMPLE, D. G. and RUTTAN, V. W. (1977) *Resource Allocation and Productivity in National and International Agricultural Research*, University of Minnesota Press, Minn.

CHAI, J. (1991) 'Agricultural development in China, 1979–1989', mimeo., Department of Economics, University of Queensland, St Lucia, Brisbane.

CHENERY, H. B. (1955) 'The role of industrialisation in development programmes', *The American Economic Review*, 45 (2), pp. 40–57.

CONWAY, G.R. (1985) 'Agrosystem analysis', *Agricultural Administration*, 20, pp. 31–55.

DAVIS, J. S., ORAM, P. A. and RYAN, J. G. (1987) *Assessment of Agricultural Research Priorities: An International Perspective*, Australian Centre for International Agricultural Research, Canberra.

DAVIS, J. S. and RYAN, J. G. (1989) 'Evaluation of and priority setting for agricultural research: methodology and preliminary application for China', pp. 415–529 in J.W. Longworth (ed.), *China's Rural Development Miracle*, University of Queensland Press, St Lucia, Brisbane 4067.

DUNCAN, R. C. and TISDELL, C. A. (1971) 'Research and technical progress – the return to producers', *The Economic Record*, 47, pp. 124–29.

DU RENSHENG (1989) 'Advancing amidst reform', pp. 3–10 in J.W. Longworth (ed.), *China's Rural Development Miracle*, University of Queensland Press, St Lucia, Brisbane.

EDWARDS, G. and FREEBAIRN, J. W. (1982) 'The social benefits from an increase in productivity in part of an industry', *Review of Marketing and Agricultural Economics*, 50, pp. 193–204.

GRILICHES, Z. (1957) 'Hybrid corn: An exploration in the economics of agricultural research,' *Econometrica* 25(4), pp. 501–22.

INDUSTRIES ASSISTANCE COMMISSION (1985) *Report on the Biological Control of Echium Species (Including Paterson's Curse/Salvation Jane)* Australian Government Publishing Service, Canberra.

LEIBENSTEIN, H. (1966) 'Allocative efficiency vs X-efficiency', *The American Economic Review*, 61, pp. 392–415.

LEIBENSTEIN, H. (1978) *General X-Efficiency Theory and Economic Development*, Oxford University Press, London.

LEWIS, W.A. (1954) 'Economic development with unlimited supplies of labour', *Manchester School*, 22, pp. 139–191.

LIPTON, M. (1977) *Why The Poor Stay Poor: Urban Bias in World Development*, Harvard University Press, Cambridge, Mass.

MARSDEN, J.S., MARTIN, G. E., PARHAM, D. J., RISDILL SMITH, T. J. and JOHNSTON, B. G. (1980) *Returns on Australian Agricultural Research*, Industries Assistance Commission and CSIRO, Canberra.

116 *Economic Development in the Context of China*

PETERSON, W. L. and FITZHARRIS, J. C. (1977) 'The Organization and
Porductivity of Federal–State Research System in the United States', in
T. M. Arndt, D. G. Dalrymple and V. W. Ruttan (eds) *Research Allocation
and Productivity in National and International Agricultural Research*, University of Minnesota Press, Minneapolis, pp. 60–85.
ROSTOW, W. W. (1956) 'The take-off into self-sustained growth', *The
Economic Journal*, 66, pp. 25–48.
ROSTOW, W. W. (1960) *The Stages of Economic Growth*, Cambridge University Press, Cambridge.
SIMON, H. A. (1957a) *Administrative Man*, 2nd edn, Macmillan, New York.
SIMON, H. A. (1957b) *Models of Man*, Wiley, New York.
TISDELL, C. A. (1981) *Science and Technology Policy: Priorities of
Governments*, Chapman & Hall, London.
TISDELL, C. A. (1985) 'Project evaluation and social cost–benefit analysis in
LDCs: awkward issues for a useful approach', *Development Southern Africa*,
2 (1), pp. 16–25.
TISDELL, C. A. (1986) 'Cost–benefit analysis, the environment and informational constraints in LDCs', *Journal of Economic Development*, 11 (2),
pp. 63–81.
TODARO, M. P. (1981) *Economic Development in the Third World*, 2nd edn,
Longmans, New York.
ZHAO ZIYANG (1987) 'Advance along the road of socialism with Chinese
characteristics', report delivered at the Thirteenth National Congress of the
Communist Party of China, 25 October 1987, pp. 3–80, in *Documents of the
Thirteenth National Congress of the Communist Party of China (1987)*
Foreign Languages Press, Beijing.

8 Interindustry Development – Manufacturing, Services and Agriculture

8.1 INTRODUCTION – INTERCONNECTIONS BETWEEN INDUSTRIES IN DEVELOPMENT

The relative contributions of sectors of an economy (agriculture, industry including manufacturing, and service industries) to the employment of the workforce and to aggregate economic production vary as economic development proceeds. Whereas the relative economic contribution of agriculture tends to decline with economic development, that of the service sector tends to grow. As for industry, especially manufacturing industry, its relative contribution to total economic activity tends at first to rise with economic development and then to decline somewhat as tertiary industry continues to expand. Nevertheless, in more developed countries the size of manufacturing sector typically remains far in excess of that of agriculture. This has been the basic pattern of sectoral development of countries which have shown significant economic development in the last 300 years or so, and one might expect the economic development of China to follow a similar pattern.

Does the above pattern imply that industrialisation is the driving force or the primemover of economic growth and development? Such a view seems unwarranted. For example, the actual driving force for economic development in Britain may originally have been agriculture, which with its new technologies and farming methods increased agricultural production, thereby helping to provide investible funds for industry, wage goods to support industrial workers and a market for manufactures. But in time, through interindustry interdependence, industrialisation itself provided additional economic benefits for agriculture such as expanded markets, the improved processing and storage of agricultural goods and less-expensive and better-quality agricultural machines and tools. In fact the mechanisation of industry

117

seems to have led in the longer term to the 'industrialisation' of agriculture itself, for example the greater use of machines and chemicals in agricultural production. Thus Western economic growth seems to have involved a relatively balanced but changing interdependent process between industries and sectors, with new industries in this pattern rising and some old ones disappearing.

It is possible, indeed likely, that the development of manufacturing was not the prime moving force or leading sector in the original development process and that manufacturing *needed* for its sustainable development the development of agriculture, or the import of agricultural goods from abroad. From input–output analysis, it is clear that manufacturing expansion requires supplies from other sectors, so that the development of manufacturing as a rule requires the development of non-manufacturing sectors as well (Leontief, 1952; Tisdell, 1972, Chapter 12). This appears, however, not to have been the premise which guided economic development planning in the Soviet Union and in China in their earlier phases of development.

In its earliest phases of development planning after 1949, the Communist Party of China was greatly influenced by the Soviet model of development, as propounded by Stalin. This involved high levels of forced savings for capital formation, principally for the expansion and development of manufacturing, especially heavy industry. The expansion of heavy industry seems to have been viewed as the key to economic development, and this led to the neglect of agriculture (which was the prime source of forced savings) and the comparative neglect of light industry in development planning. Thus an unbalanced sectoral approach to economic development was adopted.

While this may have been useful for immediate defence purposes and manufacture of armaments, in the longer term it does not appear to have provided a sound basis for continuing economic development. This appears to have been more quickly realised and acted on by the Chinese leaders than by those of the Soviet Union. An important step forward in China in that regard was the introduction of the household responsibility system in agriculture beginning in 1978.

The co-ordination of the development of an economy is an extremely complicated task, and as economies become more advanced and diversified in production it becomes more complex still. While some imbalance in the growth of industries or sectors may provide a stimulus through backward or forward economic linkages for the development of other industries, interindustry (input–output) analysis indicates that large and permanent imbalances between industries result in the waste of resources and less growth than would be attainable by a more balanced approach. For example, if the manufacturing capacity of an industry is expanded but its supplies of raw materials are not, or are not expanded in step, then excess capacity or disguised excess-capacity may emerge in the manufacturing industry. The level of production of the manufacturing industry will be hampered by shortages of raw materials. This has commonly been the case in China and the Soviet Union in the past, partly as a result of inadequate planning but also as a result of a faulty conception of the interindustry requirements for economic development.

To the extent that a country engages in international trade, it will not need to follow as balanced a path in the domestic development of sectors as one not so doing (cf. Gillis *et al.*, 1983, Chapter 3). International trade provides greater scope for workable specialisation in production by a country and can reduce input constraints on the development of manufacturing which would become binding in the absence of international trade. Thus China's opening to the outside world since 1978 has provided it with greater leeway to sustain its economic development. At the same time, however, this opening up raises new issues, some of which were discussed in Chapters 4, 5 and 6. The greater use of markets in China is also assisting in the better co-ordination of its economic development, and this aspect will be discussed in the next chapter. The remainder of this chapter pays particular attention to China's policies in relation to agricultural and industrial development and the growth of its service industries.

8.2 ECONOMIC INCENTIVES AND THE LABOUR SURPLUS PROBLEM IN AGRICULTURE

8.2.1 Growth in Agricultural Output in China

As mentioned in the previous chapter, the continuing development of agriculture is of continuing importance for the economic development of China and the welfare of the majority of the Chinese people. It becomes even more important if one accepts the hypothesis of Perkins and Yusuf (1984, p. 37) that on the whole China will have to produce enough grain for its own needs rather than rely on imports.

During its 'open-door' stage of development and with its economic reforms, China's level of agricultural production expanded greatly.

The rate of growth was, however, much greater in the period 1978–84 (7.4 per cent) than in the period 1984–9 (3.1 per cent) (Chai, 1991, p. 20). The causes of this slowdown have been debated (Chai, 1991) but will not be discussed here to any great extent. However, note that even in the period 1984–9 the growth rate in agricultural production in China was more than 25 per cent greater than that in the period 1957–78 (2.3 per cent) and that with higher levels of production it tends to become increasingly difficult to maintain growth rates. The slower rate of growth in agricultural production in China in the period 1984–9 compared with 1978–84 is due largely to a substantial fall in cotton production. But such a decline is not necessarily undesirable, given that China's production of man-made fibres, such as nylon, is expanding and that cotton-growing land can be used to raise food crops.

Two important aspects of the Chinese agriculture require special consideration. These are (1) the household responsibility system and (2) the agricultural labour surplus problem. Let us consider these in turn.

8.2.2 Household Responsibility System

The household responsibility system in agriculture was introduced in 1978 and subsequently extended, so that by the end of 1982 almost 80 per cent of rural production brigades were using it. Under this system a household is assigned a plot of land and in return enters into a contract with the state through its production brigade or collective with a contracted agricultural output, retaining any excess output for itself. The excess may be sold to state or in most cases sold on the open market. For the contracted output the household is paid a price which is usually *lower* than the market price of the produce. The difference between the payment received by the farmer for supplying the official output quota and the total revenue which would have been attained had all the output been purchased at market price may be regarded as a rental payment. In some cases the household is allowed to meet its obligation to the state by a cash payment (Liu Guoguang *et al.*, 1987, pp. 162–3). This leaves the household completely free to determine its production and to dispose of it as it wishes.

The introduction of the household responsibility system has greatly reduced X-inefficiency (X-inefficiency refers to inefficiencies in resource-use within the enterprise and failure of management to adopt available appropriate techniques; that is, efficiency which is under the control of the enterprise), in Chinese agriculture as compared with the commune/collective production control system, and has also improved the allocative efficiency in agriculture. With the introduction of the system agricultural production in China grew at a very rapid rate. Liu Guoguang *et al.* (1987, p. 185) state:

> the contract responsibility system based on the household with remuneration linked to output has been introduced, which clearly defines the obligations, directly benefits the peasants, involves simple procedures and makes maximum use of the enthusiasm of the masses of the peasants by assuring them of their power to make decisions on matters relating to the management of production and by ridding the distribution system of the influence of equalitarianism.

Production is now managed by the household rather than the commune, so decision-making is decentralised and the maximisation of household gain or profit becomes the guiding principle of the household.

The effect of the household responsibility system, combined with a two-part price system (or double-track system) can be illustrated by Figure 8.1, taking a simple case. (There are other possibilities discussed by Chai (1991).) The figure shows the marginal cost curve and marginal revenue conditions faced by a household under the household responsibility system. In return for the land allocated to it, the household is assumed to be under contract to supply quantity x_1 of, say, grain to the brigade or commune annually, for which it is paid a price per unit of OA. It may sell the remainder of its output on the free market. If we assume that the free market price is OF per unit then the marginal revenue facing the household is the stepped function $ABDMR$. If the household's marginal cost of producing agricultural output is, say, as indicated by the curve MC_2, then in order to maximise its surplus or profit the household should produce an annual output of x_3. In the case shown, production is then such that marginal costs of production are equal to the market price, and, as discussed in the next chapter, this *may* result in allocative efficiency.

Note that increased X-efficiency, if input prices remain unchanged, shows up as a decline in the per unit costs of production. For example, under the system of direct control of production by the collective, marginal costs of production on the land allocated to the household might have been like that shown by the curve marked MC_1. This would mean, for example, that the marginal cost of producing output x_2 under the collective system would be GJ, whereas under the household responsibility system it is GH. Observe, further, that the household's 'rental payment' to the state in the case illustrated is equal to the area of rectangle $ABDF$.

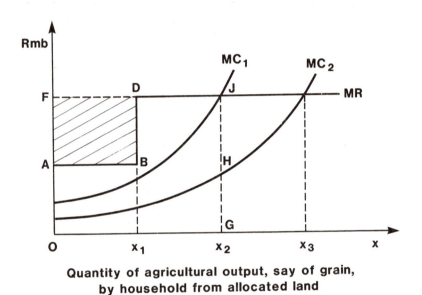

Quantity of agricultural output, say of grain,
by household from allocated land

Figure 8.1   A simple model of household economics under the household responsibility system

In the short term, the household responsibility system enabled greater agricultural output to be obtained using the same amount of resources as before. Along with associated reforms, farmers were now free to become more specialised in agricultural production according to their comparative advantage and/or to engage in non-agricultural production in their *local* area. This stimulated the growth of rural industry. The reforms resulted in greater freedom of economic choice by individuals. This freedom has yielded material economic benefits.

Nevertheless, a number of agricultural problems have become apparent since those institutional changes. Attempts were made to distribute land to households on an egalitarian basis, and to ensure that all households had an equal mix of land of varying qualities, as well as the same quantity. This policy resulted in small quantities of land being made available to households, in some cases with the plots owned by the household being scattered. The greater consolidation of holdings could increase economic efficiency and in some cases larger holdings could provide greater economies of scale. Measures therefore to permit officially the transfer and consolidation of holdings, which to some extent is already occurring informally, as pointed out by Cao Yang and Tisdell (1991), could lead to increases in agricultural output.

The introduction of the household responsibility system highlighted the agricultural labour surplus problem in China. China has adopted policies to absorb some of this surplus by employing farm workers in rural industries.

8.2.3 The Agricultural Labour Surplus Problem

Approximately one-third of China's total agricultural labour force is estimated to be surplus to that required to maintain its present level of agricultural production (Du Rensheng, 1989, p. 7; Chen Jiyuan, 1989, p. 212). Given that about 300 million labourers are employed in agriculture, this means that about 100 million are surplus. However, the precise basis of these estimates is not clear. If surplus labour is defined in the way suggested by A.W. Lewis (1954, 1965) then this would refer to the amount of agricultural labour which has a zero or negative marginal product. If on the other hand it refers to the concept of surplus labour as defined by Marglin (1976), it means the quantity of labour which needs to be removed from agriculture and employed elsewhere in the economy so as to equalise the marginal productivity of labour in agriculture with that elsewhere in the economy, e.g., in manufacturing industry. Whatever is the precise basis of these estimates, Chinese farmers do appear to be operating on the basis that 100 million labourers need to be absorbed elsewhere in the Chinese economy, and current plans are to absorb a large proportion of this surplus in rural industry.

Theoretically, there are at least three avenues for absorbing China's surplus agricultural labour force: (1) In agriculture, by the adoption of productivity-enhancing and labour-using techniques (techniques raising the marginal productivity of labour). (2) By the employment of this surplus in rural industries. This path has been preferred so far in China. (3) By the employment of this labour surplus in large cities. This is not a preferred method in China, but nevertheless a large number of rural labourers have been issued with permits to enable them to work *temporarily* in large cities. However, it is extremely difficult for rural dwellers to obtain an urban residency permit entitling them to permanent residence in cities, and those on temporary residence permits are denied a number of the economic privileges available to holders of a permanent urban residence card.

On the basis of experience in Japan, Taiwan and Korea, Ishikawa (1978) suggested that typically modernisation of agriculture in its first stages results in both rising labour requirements per hectare and rising productivity per hectare before giving way to a situation in which productivity per hectare continues to rise but agricultural labour requirements per hectare fall. Given this pattern, agriculture is labour-absorbing during the early stage of modernisation. This stage results in rising agricultural production and so makes available an increased wage fund or amount of wage goods to foster industrialisation, as well as providing a market for industrial goods. In stage one, modernisation of agriculture reduces the agricultural labour surplus while at the same time providing means for increasing industrialisation, which also helps to absorb the surplus agricultural labour force. By the time that the second stage of the Ishikawa curve is reached and the quantity of labour required in agriculture begins to fall, industrialisation may well be sufficiently under way to absorb easily the agricultural labour which needs to be transferred out of agriculture.

However, the typical Ishikawa pattern may not always apply. In some cases the first stage is absent or virtually absent. This means that modernisation of agriculture results from the beginning in falling labour requirements per hectare, even though rising productivity per hectare occurs. Thus a greater amount of wage goods are available for industrialisation, but the surplus agricultural labour force, rather than declining at first with agricultural modernisation, begins to rise immediately. This makes industrialisation a more urgent task and means that the industrialisation 'breathing space' suggested by the traditional Ishikawa curve is absent. In South Asia, available evidence suggests that the first stage of the Ishikawa curve may be absent (Tisdell and Alauddin, 1992; Jayasuriya and Shand, 1986). It may also be absent in China or almost so (Cao Yang and Tisdell, 1991). But whether or not this is so, China now has a significant agricultural labour surplus which can at best be only marginally absorbed by agricultural expansion. Industrialisation is an important means for absorbing China's surplus agricultural labour force. In this regard, the expansion of rural industry in China has played an important role.

8.3 RURAL INDUSTRIES

The expansion of rural industry has done much to absorb China's surplus agricultural labour force. At the end of 1990, rural industry was estimated to be employing 92 million of China's estimated 400 million *rural* labour force, that is about a quarter of it. Plans are in hand for rural industry to employ an additional 30 million rural labourers by the end of this century (*China Daily*, 30 March 1991). If the rural population remains constant, then it is predicted, this will still leave about 60 million surplus labourers in rural areas by the end of this century. But rural population is still increasing and at the end of this century there may be a much larger labour force to absorb. Thus China's surplus agricultural labour force could rise from the present estimated 100 million to 200 million by the end of this century (*China Daily*, 20 May 1991, p. 4), posing a continuing economic problem for the country. While this estimate may be too pessimistic, the importance of bringing population increase under control in the countryside is difficult to overemphasise.

The growth in the economic importance of rural enterprises (covering industrial, commercial and service industries) since 1978 has been very significant. In 1978, rural enterprises employed 28 million people. This rose to 30 million in 1980 and to 95 million by 1988. But the numbers employed were somewhat lower in 1989 and 1990, e.g. 92 million in 1990, owing to government policies and the economic recession. By the end of 1991, employment in rural enterprises is expected to be back to 95 million, and by the year 1995 rural enterprises are expected to employ a workforce of 117 million. The government is to continue 'to encourage the growth of rural enterprises to help promote rural economic growth, increase farmers' income, and absorb the surplus labour force' (*China Daily*, 3 June 1991, p. 1). Nevertheless, rural pressures for migration to large cities are likely to remain. Rural migration to large cities has been severely restricted in China since the early 1960s when the household registration system was introduced.

Rural industry is making a significant contribution to China's industrial output, in 1990 accounting for 30 per cent. The rate of growth in this production (1991) by township and village firms far exceeds that of state industrial enterprises in the cities. Among other things, rural enterprises account for 63 per cent of nylon production, 60 per cent of garment manufacture, 80 per cent of farm machinery and equipment production and 90 per cent of the output of bricks (*China Daily Business Weekly*, 16 June 1991, p. 1).

About half of the employment in China's rural enterprises is in township or village enterprises (collectives), the remainder being accounted for by private businesses. Possibly because of differences in their organisational structure, the absence of state financial support in the advent of economic difficulties, and the fact that they face a more competitive market situation, rural industrial enterprises appear to be outperforming state-owned industrial enterprises in economic terms. As noted in the *China Daily Business Weekly* (June 16 1991, p. 1), 'the strong growth of rural enterprises is particularly significant when most of the state-owned large- and medium-sized concerns are plagued with poor economic returns'. Such enterprises provide considerable competition for relatively protected state-owned ones.

Government policies during 1988 and 1989 were adverse to rural industry, partly in response to urban-based criticism which may well have been encouraged by state-owned city-based enterprises. Nevertheless, despite these factors, production and sales of rural industry still rose in 1989. A comment from the Ministry of Agriculture summarised the situation as follows:

> Competition between rural and state enterprises for raw materials and the market had intensified at that time. State firms usually lost out in this particular battle because the rural entrepreneurs were more flexible in management, production and sales. The success of the rural enterprises, hard-won as they were, discredited the allegation that they were bound for bankruptcy in the austerity programme. . . . (*China Daily Business Weekly*, 16 June 1991, p. 2).

This statement suggests that the relatively cushioned and protective status given to state-owned industries and their institutional structure is an impediment to improvements in their economic performance. This issue will be discussed in Chapter 10.

8.4 MANUFACTURING AND INDUSTRIALISATION IN BALANCED DEVELOPMENT

8.4.1 Industrialisation Strategies

Prior to thr Eleventh Central Committee Meeting of the CPC in 1978, China had, except for a very short period of time, followed a strategy of unbalanced development in order to force the pace of its economic development. On the whole, under Mao, the industrial sector was regarded as a key to development and within that sector heavy industries, *especially* the steel industry were regarded a leading industries. These industries were seen as the key to industrialisation, so that if they were made to grow they would force all manufacturing industries to grow at least eventually. In turn, industrial growth was seen as the key to the eventual growth and development of the whole economy. Policies, therefore, for fostering the growth of steel production, heavy industry and industrialisation were adopted, but in an unbalanced and partial economic manner (Liu Guoguang *et al.*, 1987, Chapters 3 and 4). This sometimes meant that the purpose of economic production (namely, to serve the economic interests of the people) was lost sight of, because the expansion of heavy industry became an end in itself and often proceeded without regard to its economic value and its interdependence with other industries. In practice, a naive view of economic development and the economy prevailed.

Because of the failure to take account of interdependencies of industries in production, and to plan adequately the expansion of complementary industries, China's pre-1978 industrialisation strategy proved to be short-sighted. Often, the growth and production of manufacturing industry was severely restricted by lack of supplies of inputs from other industries (for example, shortages of raw materials from agriculture, of minerals and of energy supplies) and further hampered by transport and communication bottlenecks. If some of the resources allocated to expanding the production of 'key' industries had been allocated to the development of complementary industries, production of the key industries may well have been greater, and more valuable from an economic point of view, and total production could have been higher. Maoist industrialisation held back the development of complementary industries because the importance of interindustry relationships for production was not adequately grasped by politicians and planners. At the same time, central planning prevented demands of one industry for supplies from other industries being directly translated into practice. This resulted in the appropriate mix in production not being achieved and allowed key industries to concentrate on quantity rather than quality in production and to ignore to a large extent the demands of other industries (Liu Guoguang *et al.*, 1987, Chapter 4). Consumer sovereignty was absent, and so the discipline which buyers can impose on suppliers was absent.

As China's economy expanded and further growth was wanted, co-ordination problems became more obvious and it became clear that these were holding back appropriate industrialisation itself. Central planning authorities had shown themselves unable to co-ordinate supplies of commodities in the economy satisfactorily so as to avoid bottlenecks in production. In addition, the goods produced were often not what their users (even industrial users) wanted and were below the quality which could be achieved with the resources available. This was to a large extent because state administrations had broken the nexus between producers and users, imposing themselves as state middlemen between users and producers, and such administrations tended to set production targets in terms of quantity without including quality constraints. As the diversity of China's economy increased, and as its leaders became increasingly in favour of a diversified modern economy serving the needs of the people, the limitations of the old system became more evident.

To some extent this explains the pressure for the introduction of markets and market reforms and for the greater decentralisation of decision-making to the enterprise level. While much of the motivation for these reforms may have been to improve management and economic efficiency at the enterprise level (Jackson, 1992), they also had favourable effects on allocative efficiency, and provided means of better interindustry co-ordination in supplies, and more balanced development.

In the 1980s Chinese economists stated China's new industrialisation policy as follows:

> For the purpose of realising our envisaged objectives, we now advocate the adoption of a strategy of relatively balanced development or a balanced development strategy for short. This policy requires that balance and co-ordination should be conscientiously maintained between the various sectors of the national economy and the various links of social reproduction. (Liu Guoguang *et al.*, 1987, p. 122)

So in the post-Mao period China's emphasis has been on more balanced development. Market reforms have been of considerable assistance in pursuing this goal and were to some extent introduced in response to it. As suggested earlier in this chapter, economic development is likely to be more secure and rapid when the development of agriculture proceeds hand in hand with the development of industry. The pattern of *relative* emphasis on the development of first agriculture, then light industry and after that heavy industry seems more conducive to economic development than the reverse pattern (cf. Oshima, 1987). But under Mao Zedong, China, partly under the influence of Stalin's principles of economic growth, adopted the sequence heavy-industry–light-industry – agriculture as the preferred strategy for industrialisation and economic development. This emphasis was not reversed until after the Eleventh Central Committee Meeting of the CPC.

It should however be noted that the sequence of heavy-industry – light-industry – agriculture was followed despite Mao's politically professed priority for agriculture. Reasons for this may have included the pattern of Soviet growth and (aid-bias) in the earlier years of the People's Republic, plus an immediate response to perceived and actual military threats, which for defence purposes dictated an emphasis on industry. With the establishment of more harmonious international relations the bias in industrial development for defence purposes is no longer a 'necessity'.

Note that a policy of relatively balanced development does not imply necessarily the even development of all industries. However, it requires, co-ordinated development, taking into account the relative demands of industries and their interdependencies, particularly their infrastructure requirements, which have been greatly neglected by China in the recent past.

Chinese authorities and economists appear now to be wary of adopting a selected or key industries approach to development. But the economic importance of 'focal or strategic points' in economic development (industries or economic activities selected out for special economic encouragement by the state) has not been rejected, nor has a selective approach in relation to development of export industries, such as Japan has been reputed to follow, been rejected. Liu Guoguang *et al.* (1987, p. 128) state the position as follows:

We [China] should concentrate our energy on important sectors and key projects so that great headway can be made. On the other hand, we must see to it that the relationship between the important and less important projects is correctly handled with regard to scope, speed and time of development so they all can develop in a coordinated manner and any undue emphasis on important points which may upset the balance can be prevented.

These writers go on to point out that the appropriate focal points from the economy may alter with time. For example, today a focus on the development and use of computing and information-technology may be more appropriate than an emphasis on the steel industry.

8.4.2 State Industrial Enterprises and Manufacturing

For a less-developed country, China is relatively industrialised. This is so for example compared with India. In 1988, industry accounted for 48 per cent of gross domestic production in China and 30 per cent of that in India, with the respective shares for manufacturing being 33 per cent and 19 per cent (World Bank, 1990, p. 182). It is interesting to note that the broad composition of manufacturing output in 1988 was not significantly different between these two economies. The percentages of value added in manufacturing accounted for by (1) food, beverages and tobacco, (2) textiles and clothing and (3) machinery and transport equipment were much the same in China as in India, but chemicals were relatively more important in the Indian case (World Bank, 1990, p. 188).

The relatively large size of China's industrial sector is a result of its strategy of forced capital accumulation and its direction of capital formation in favour of industry, mainly for the use of state enterprises because of ideological preferences for state ownership. Although its unbalanced industrialisation policy has been modified, bias in favour of industrial and urban development remains, and within industry there is economic prioritism for state-owned enterprises.

State-owned enterprises accounted for 56.1 per cent of gross industrial output by value in China in 1989. Collective-owned enterprises accounted for 35.7 per cent, and other forms of ownership including enterprises owned by individuals 7.2 per cent (Jackson, 1992, Table 3.1; *1990 Statistical Yearbook of China*, p. 29). Thus state-owned enterprises dominate production in this sector; they tend additionally to be much larger than other enterprises. They are also capital intensive: for example, state-owned industrial enterprises absorbed a much greater percentage of China's investments in fixed assets in 1989 than was their percentage net contribution to industrial output.

State-owned enterprises tend also to be less profitable than non-state owned industrial enterprises (*China Daily*, 27 June 1991, p. 4). More than a third of state enterprises were reported in 1991 to be managed at a loss (*China Daily*, 27 June 1991, p. 4). Like public enterprises in many countries, they are usually politically defended by the ministries responsible for them. Consequently, even when they make persistent losses, they normally continue to operate. China's bankruptcy laws have not been applied to them. They can usually gain access to additional funds to keep them operating, e.g. loans from banks (*China Daily*, 1 July 1991, p. 1). Thus they enjoy a privileged position compared with enterprises owned by collectives and individuals. However, their 'protected' status and the consequent absence of economic discipline is detrimental to the efficient operation of China's industry and its development. This is exacerbated by political interference in the operation of these enterprises by politicians untrained in business management. While decentralisation is greater than in the past, state industrial enterprises remain a weak link in the Chinese economic system. The type of advance which has been made by the introduction of the household responsibility system in agriculture has not yet been achieved in the industrial sector. This aspect will be discussed in more detail in Chapter 10.

8.5 SERVICE INDUSTRIES

Classical economists and Marx described labour not directly employed in the production of physical goods as unproductive labour. Thus labour involved in the supply of services was on the whole regarded as unproductive. This view has led to the retardation of the service sector in planned socialist economies. An additional reason for such retardation may have been the difficulty of measuring the output of service industries, which makes central planning and control of them more difficult.

In China's case, services accounted for 21 per cent of its GDP in 1988, compared with 38 per cent in the case of India. In comparison, 70 per cent of the GDP of Hong Kong in 1988 was attributed to the service sector (World Bank, 1991, p. 182).

Defining the service sector to include service trades such as commerce, catering, repair, and sectors involved in non-material production, such as urban public utilities and scientific, cultural, educational and health organisation, Liu Guoguang *et al.* (1987, pp. 319–20) said that China concentrated too much on the 'development of industry and agriculture – sectors of material production – to the neglect of the development of the [service] trades, including those related to commodity circulation. We failed to recognise the role that these trades can play in providing employment.' In 1952 the percentage of China's workforce employed in the service trades was 35.3 per cent, but it fell continuously until 1978 when it reached 21.6 per cent. By 1982 it had risen again slightly to 23.3 per cent, but this was still markedly below the level of 1952.

While Liu Guoguang *et al.* (1987) stress the scope for labour employment in the service sector, one should not overlook the fact that the service sector is productive. It can, for example, provide services to agriculture and industry which help to increase their material production, and improvements in distribution of commodities can release resources for use elsewhere. In addition, by helping to improve the quality of the workforce, the service sector can add to production. It is by no means an unproductive sector. Observe also that if some of the agricultural labour force has zero productivity in agriculture then surplus labourers might be more productively employed in service trades to provide some economic benefit. At least one's eyes should not be closed by Marxian dogma to this possibility.

China plans to expand the relative size of its service sector in the 1990s. In part this will be necessary to support plans for improving the quality of its workforce and increasing the scientific and technological bases. In addition, if China wishes to continue to expand its tourist industry, as it plans to do (see Chapter 11), and to be internationally competitive in this area then it also needs to expand and improve the efficiency of its service sector. Furthermore, more attention should be given to the service sector as an outlet (directly or indirectly) for absorption of the agricultural labour surplus in China.

8.6 CONCLUSION

The development of industry in China has been unbalanced, and while it is now more balanced than in the Maoist period, problems of imbalance and inappropriate industry-mix still persist. Before 1978, economic development was attempted in accordance with untested economic–political dogmas which imposed severe social and economic costs on China. But after 1978 a more pragmatic and realistic view prevailed as far as structural and industry development is concerned. One hopes that with China continuing to lower the barriers to the outside world this more open view will continue to prevail. But whether or not it can do so when the Communist Party continues to reject pluralism is uncertain. Jiang Zemin, General Secretary of the CPC, on the occasion of the 70th anniversary of the party's founding, stated that one of the requirements for developing culture with Chinese features is to use Marxism-Leninism and Mao Zedong Thought as a guide and that 'pluralism should never be accepted as a guiding ideology' (*China Daily*, 2 July 1991, p. 4). The extent to which adopting this approach could reduce diversity of thought and eventually economic progress in China is unclear. However, it is in conflict with the traditional Western view that diversity of thought and expression are valuable ingredients in economic progress and human expression.

REFERENCES

CAO YANG and TISDELL, C. A. (1991) *China's Surplus Agricultural Labour Force: Its Size, Transfer, Prospects for Absorption and Effects of the Double-track Economic System*, Discussion Paper in Economics No. 59, Department of Economics, University of Queensland, 4072, Australia.

CHAI, J. C. H. (1991) 'Agricultural development in China', mimeo., Department of Economics, University of Queensland, St Lucia, Brisbane.

CHEN JIYUAN (1989) 'China's transfer of the surplus agricultural labour force (TSALF)', pp. 210–20 in J. W. Longworth (ed.) *China's Rural Development Miracle with International Comparisons*, University of Queensland Press, St Lucia, Brisbane.

GILLIS, M., PERKINS, D. H., ROEMER, J. and SNODGRASS, D. R. (1983) *Economics of Development*, Norton, New York.

ISHIKAWA, S. (1978) *Labour Absorption in Asian Agriculture*, International Labour Office, Bangkok.

JACKSON, S. (1992) *China's Enterprise Management: Reforms in Economic Perspective*, De Gruyter, Berlin and New York, forthcoming.

JAYASURIYA, S. and SHAND, P. T. (1986) 'Technical change and labour absorption in Asian agriculture: some emerging trends', *World Development*, 14 (3), pp. 415–28.

LEONTIEF, W. (1952) *The Structure of the American Economy*, 2nd edn, Oxford University Press, Oxford.

LEWIS, A. W. (1954) 'Economic development with unlimited supplies of labour', *The Manchester School*, 22, pp. 139–91.

LEWIS, A. W. (1965) *The Theory of Economic Growth*, Allen & Unwin, London.

LIU GUOGUANG, LIANG WENSEN and others (1987) *China's Economy in 2000*, New World Press, Beijing.

MARGLIN, S. A. (1976) *Value and Price in the Labour-surplus Economy*, Clarendon, Oxford.

OSHIMA, H.T. (1987) *Economic Growth in Monsoon Asia: A Comparative Survey*, Tokyo University Press, Tokyo.

PERKINS, D. H. and YUSUF, S. (1984) *Rural Development in China*, Johns Hopkins University Press, Baltimore, Md.

TISDELL, C. A. (1972) *Microeconomics: The Theory of Economic Allocation*, Wiley, Sydney.

TISDELL, C. A. and ALAUDDIN, M. (1992) 'The Ishikawa curve and agricultural productivity in Bangladesh: some new findings', *Hitotsubashi Journal of Economics*, in press.

WORLD BANK (1990) *World Development Report 1990*, Oxford University Press, New York.

9 Prices, Markets and Resource Allocation in China

9.1 INTRODUCTION – FUNCTIONS OF PRICE AND MARKET SYSTEMS

A major feature of change in China's economic system since 1978 has been its market reforms and its increased reliance on market mechanisms as means for guiding economic decision-making. In this respect, China proceeded further than the Soviet Union and Eastern European countries in the 1980s. But China is still far from having a complete market economy. So far its reforms have proceeded furthest in relation to product markets. While there has been some relaxation of central control over resource or factor allocation, markets either are not present for resources or are much restricted in their operation. So the extent of China's market reforms are uneven as between product and factor markets. This, as discussed below, is not surprising given the Marxian background of the People's Republic.

In most economies, prices perform a rationing role as far as commodities are concerned. When they are restricted in their capacity to do this, rationing may be performed by means of ration coupons issued by the government or by queuing and other transaction costs imposed on exchange by inadequate allocation mechanisms. But the use of prices to allocate commodities does not mean that a market system is operating fully. Supplies of commodities may for example be determined by central command and delivered to state marketing authorities which then use market prices to clear the available centrally determined supplies. But the composition of supplies is likely to reflect the views of the central government about what should be produced, not the views of purchasers about what they want. In this case there is no direct mechanism linking the wants or desires of purchasers to the decision of suppliers.

But when the market mechanism operates there is a direct link between suppliers and buyers – prices acting as a signal to buyers and profitability as a signal to sellers. The market system acts as a means to co-ordinate the whole economy. Central command systems have proven less effective and more costly (in terms of transaction costs) for co-ordinating large and relatively complex economies than systems involving the operation of market mechanisms, with some state intervention.

The competitive market system is a relatively effective method for reducing economic scarcity for the following reasons: (1) It *tends* to promote the most economic allocation of resources between productive units, industries and locations and to result in the composition of production (mix of production) desired by buyers. (2) Apart from promoting allocative efficiency of resources between productive units, it provides incentives for their most productive use *within* productive units. In this respect, it tends to reduce managerial slack and reduce X-inefficiency (see p. 120). (3) It provides incentives and rewards for entrepreneurship and economic innovation. (4) It rewards effort where the results accord with market demand.

However, the benefits to be obtained by individuals from this system depend upon their ownership of resources. When this ownership is very uneven, distribution of incomes also tends to be very uneven. Where resources have been distributed by past privileges or by blind chance, or where some individuals are naturally handicapped, then the distribution of income which emerges can be unjust. To prevent an unjust or unfair distribution of income from emerging (or where it exists from continuing) is a major goal of communism. Therefore, under socialism or communism, it is important that use of the market system should also be made compatible with justice in the distribution of income. However, that as discussed in Chapter 5, requires that the concept of a just distribution of income be clarified. It was not clarified by Marx, but it is important that it be placed on a firm philosophical footing.

In relation to the above matter, the position of those economists who advocated competitive socialism such as Lange (1938) is worth noting. They advocate basically that the role of the government be restricted to (1) determining the rate of capital accumulation in society, (2) the provision of 'collective' goods such as education and health services, and (3) redistributing income so that the distribution is just. Subject to these provisions, they say, markets should be used to determine the supply of commodities and their distribution. However, in the latter respect Lange (1938) did see a role for state marketing authorities. He believed that they could, by following appropriate rules, actually ensure that market *equilibria* are reached more quickly or more closely than is the case in practice.

Competitive socialists are opposed on the whole to trying to redistribute income by interference in the operation of the market system by the use of subsidies, price controls, or restrictions on resource allocation. They accept the neo-classical economic point of view that this is an inefficient approach. Rather they would prefer to see income redistributed without interference with or distortion of the price mechanism. So the economic problem is dealt with in a dichotomous manner and the basic recommendation which emerges is to get the distribution of income 'right' and then let the price mechanism work. Of course, their recommendations are not quite that crude, because there are also market failures, such as environmental externalities or spillovers to take into account. These may require some government intervention in the markets for 'private' goods.

In practice, perfect dichotomy is not possible. Redistribution of income is likely to affect economic incentives and can reduce total output. This adds an extra dimension to the problem, but does not destroy the basic viewpoint. To the extent that income redistribution reduces total output, this should be taken into account in redistributing income. The achievable ideal distribution of income taking this effect into account will usually differ from the ideal should the level of production be independent of the distribution of income or measures to redistribute income. China's economic and political theorists cannot ignore such issues now that China's market reforms are well under way.

9.2 MARKET REFORMS IN CHINA

The reasoning behind the introduction of market reforms in China has not been all that clearly articulated, possibly because of the political nature of social change. But these reforms have continued now for more than a decade. Nevertheless, the prime initial motivation for the reforms may have been to reduce organisational slack and increase economic efficiency *within* productive units. The main advantages of the household responsibility system in agriculture introduced in 1978 have been claimed by Chinese economists (Liu Guoguang *et al.*, 1987, p. 165) to be the more efficient use of resources within agricultural productive units, improvements in economic decision-making within these, and greater motivation on the part of farmers. The system also resulted in economic remuneration or income being more in accordance with work done than was the case with the preceding 'common rice-bowl' system. The household responsibility system in agriculture became a prototype for the wider introduction of a two-tiered or double-track price system. But, as will be apparent from the next chapter, its introduction to industry has involved more difficulties than its introduction to agriculture.

Whatever the prime motivation for market reforms, further reasons for them were advanced as they proceeded. Suppliers were accused of supplying low-quality products prior to the reforms because buyers lacked any economic power over them. In particular, it was charged that heavy industry was serving only itself and was not attentive to the buyers of its products. In Tianjin in 1981 a special meeting of executives of State Industrial and Communications Enterprises covered by the Ministry of Industry and Communications, demanded that heavy industry stop 'serving itself' (Liu Guoguang *et al.*, 1987, p. 145). It was said to be necessary 'to adjust the structure of heavy industry, to keep the manufacturing industry from developing blindly by turning it from running after quantity to paying attention to quality' (Liu Guoguang *et al.*, 1987, p. 152). In this context, the two-tiered system was seen as a way to give buyers increased power over suppliers and to provide incentives to increase the quality of products produced.

As for allocative efficiency, greater freedom of choice about products to be produced was given to suppliers, but allocative efficiency in relation to resource employment and use between productive units was increased only marginally. After the introduction of the household responsibility system, rural households were given greater freedom of movement in their *local* area to conduct economic activities, greater choice of occupation *locally*, and more choice about what products to produce and how to produce them (Cao and Tisdell, 1991). This extra economic freedom provided greater scope for specialisation and for the adjustment of production to needs as expressed though the market. Similar arrangements were extended to cover city-based enterprises, but *free* nation-wide movement of factors of production was not introduced, and there were still production quotas to meet in many cases. Nevertheless, these reforms did increase the flexibility of China's economic system and improve economic efficiency. They made for more balanced development and provided the economic system with enhanced ability to adjust to changing economic circumstances.

In the past, the advantages of the market system in relation to entrepreneurship and innovation do not appear to have been stressed by Chinese economists. However, economists such as Schumpeter (1954) have argued that this characteristic is an even more important quality of the market system than its performance in promoting allocative efficiency. In the promotion of major new industries and technology, the Chinese economic system appears basically to be still under state guidance, even though managers now have greater choice at the enterprise level about their methods of production. Although Liu Guoguang *et al.* (1987, p. 152) indicate that in reforming the economic system it is important to introduce policies

beneficial to the development of new products, to the specialisation and co-ordination of industry, to encourage the improvement of technology through competition and finally to ensure the realisation of the strategy of modernising industry,

they do not provide *exact* guidelines as to how this can best be achieved. However, they do suggest (ibid., p. 474) that

as time passes, the scope of mandatory plans will gradually diminish and that of guidance will expand. It is anticipated that in the immediate future, the scope of market regulation will be enlarged.

Chinese philosophies about what economic activity should or should not be directly controlled seems not to have been fully developed as yet. To say that the Chinese system of economic management is unique and is 'a Chinese affair' (Liu Guoguang *et al.*, 1987, p. 475) throws little light on the issues. In practice, the allocation of factors of production seem to remain to a large extent under central control in China as between productive enterprises, and the production of key or basic commodities is most closely controlled. There may be several reasons for this, as follows: (1) A view that markets operate in an inferior way in 'key' parts of the economy. (2) A belief that markets unless restrained in these areas will result in an unjust distribution of income. (3) A political view that continuing control is necessary in these areas to maintain the leadership role and power of the CPC. Undoubtedly these controls help to reinforce the power of the CPC.

It might be observed that very little attention appears to have been given in the past to the control of environmental spillovers or externalities as a reason for government intervention in economic activity. Presumably this will be rectified as Chinese economic thought progresses.

With this background in mind, let us discuss the possible economic implications of the two-tiered price system, particularly in relation to product markets, shortcomings in factor or resource allocation in China, and the susceptibility of China's economy to price inflation.

9.3 DOUBLE-TRACK OR TWO-TIERED PRICE SYSTEMS AND ECONOMIC EFFICIENCY

The double-track or two-tiered price system is now widely used in China to guide the supply and exchange of products (Byrd, 1987; Diao, 1987; Mao and Hare, 1989). Under this system productive units are required to supply annually a mandatory quantity (quota) of their output to the state. For this quantity, producers are usually paid an official price per unit which is lower than the open market prices of the product or products involved. Producers can sell any production in excess of their mandatory production quota(s) on the free or open market. This means that for many products the market system operates at the margin of production.

Note that China's market system differs in some respects from the system of market socialism suggested by Lange (1938) and Taylor (1938). In their model, mandatory quotas of production to be supplied to the state by productive units do not apply. However, all supplies are purchased by the state at a price determined by state marketing authorities and resold by these authorities.

But the state marketing authorities are instructed to try to determine prices so that they are market equilibrium prices. Conceivably, market equilibrium prices might be found by the marketing authorities in some cases by a trial-and-error process. The sole function of the state marketing authority for any product is to speed up the attainment of market equilibrium or to approach this equilibrium more closely than might be the case with an unregulated market system.

Lange (1938) believed that state marketing authorities would be more effective than an unregulated market in searching for market equilibrium. But there is no proof that this is in fact the case. Because a state marketing authority is unlikely to predict market equilibrium perfectly, it will need to rely on mechanisms such as buffer stocks or equalisation funds to carry out its policies. In the case of equalisation funds, if the marketing authority habitually overestimates market demand then its payments to suppliers will on average exceed its receipts from buyers and the state marketing authority will operate at a deficit. This deficit may have to be met from general state revenues, so as a result the industry is subsidised and becomes an economic burden. The subsidy provided to suppliers distorts the economic system. This particular problem does not arise in the two-tiered price system, and China's two-tiered price system has other economic advantages over the Lange–Taylor system, as discussed below.

Byrd (1989) argues that China's two-tiered price system can be relatively efficient from a Paretian welfare point of view. Relative to the resources or factors of production allocated to production units, it can result in an optimal composition of production, that is, an optimal array of output of products. In other words, it results in an optimal balance or mixture in production, taking into account what buyers want and the available production possibilities.

If productive units, relative to the resources allocated to them, find that at prevailing market prices they are not constrained (by mandatory production quotas) in their choice of a profit-maximising product mix then a Paretian optimum occurs. It occurs provided that managers aim to maximise profit and it is achieved relative to the resources allocated to the productive units. In this case, in formal economic terms, all productive units equate their rates of product transformation to the same relative market prices, which in turn result in these being equated with the rates of indifferent substitution of products by consumers (Tisdell, 1972). This can be illustrated by Figure 9.1.

In Figure 9.1, the curve *ABC* represents, relative to the resource allocated to it, the production possibility curve of a productive unit which can produce two products. In the case shown, the production unit is required to supply *OK* of product one to the state and *OH* of product two to the state. Therefore, the unit's 'free' set of production possibilities is the hatched area. The slope of the line *LBM* represents the relative prices of the two products in the open market, and this line is the highest attainable iso-revenue curve for the productive unit if it can sell all of its production on the open market. The segment of this line bounded by *LRJ* represents the highest iso-revenues available to the productive unit by selling its free production on the open market. Thus point *B* is its profit-maximising combination of output. At point *B*, the slope of the production possibility frontier of the unit, its rate of product transformation, is equal to the slope of the iso-revenue line *LBM*, that is the relative prices of the products in the market.

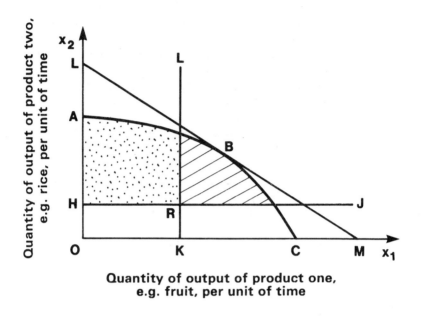

Figure 9.1   Case in which a two-tiered price system is consistent with efficiency relative to the resources distributed to productive units

If all the other productive units are similarly not constrained by official production quotas and if all maximise their profit then all will equate their rate of product transformation to the *same* relative market prices. Thus the rates of product transformation chosen by the productive units will be equalised. In turn consumers, in purchasing commodities in the market place, equate their rates of indifferent substitution of the products to the common market-determined price ratios. Thus the rates of indifferent substitution of products are equated to the rates of product transformation by productive units. Thus a necessary condition for a Paretian optimum is satisfied, relative to allocation of resources to productive units.

However, this condition will not be satisfied if the official quota of production to be supplied to the state constrains the production decisions of any of the units. This would occur, for example, in Figure 9.1 if the quota production line, *HRJ*, happened to be above point *B*. Other things being equal, the lower are the production quotas to be delivered by productive units to the state, the more likely is it that a Paretian optimal mix of production will be achieved.

Note that the above argument assumes profit maximisation by the productive units. For this to occur, managers (and those involved in production in the unit) must have an incentive to maximise their units' profits. This is likely to occur if their remuneration is an increasing function of this profit. Reforms in China, especially the introduction of the household responsibility system in agriculture, have attempted to establish such a link. The link, however, is more direct in the case of agricultural households than in state industrial enterprises, where, as discussed in the next chapters, the link is often weak. When there are little or no rewards to managers for production in excess of state quotas, production may occur at point *R* in Figure 9.1 rather than at a point like *B*, that is, at a point within the production possibility frontier rather than at a point on it. If production does occur on the production possibility frontier and is *fully* determined by the state then this mixture of production may not conform with what buyers or consumers want.

In China only some of the products which a productive unit or firm can produce may be subject to official production quotas. In agriculture, for instance, a unit's production of grain may be subject to an official quota, but its production and marketing of sideline products, such as fruit and vegetables, may be entirely free. In the case shown in Figure 9.1, this would mean that the constraint indicated by the line *LRK* would not apply, and the unit's production possibility (marketing possibility set also) after meeting the constraint on, say, rice deliveries to the state indicated by line *HRJ* would be equal to the dotted plus the cross-hatched areas. In this case, the Paretian optimal condition still holds. In fact, the fewer are the commodities subject to state regulation and the lower are the mandatory production quotas for products controlled by the state, the more likely is Paretian optimality to be achieved relative to the resources allocated to productive units.

9.4 COMPARISONS BETWEEN THE ECONOMIC EFFICIENCY OF THE MARKET SOCIALISM SYSTEMS OF LANGE, TAYLOR AND OTHERS, AND THAT OF CHINA'S TWO-TIERED PRICE SYSTEM

There are a number of differences and similarities between socialist market systems such as those proposed by Lange and Taylor and China's two-tiered price system. Both systems aim at balancing market supplies and demands. But the Lange and Taylor system requires the use of state marketing authorities. The two-tiered system only involves state authorities in exchange in relation to the portion of production subject to an official quota, and some products in China are not subject to any production quotas at all, so that the whole of supply and demand is subject to direct exchange between sellers and buyers in markets. Therefore, the Chinese system may be less costly in terms of market transaction costs than the Lange and Taylor scheme. Furthermore, it does not require the state to hold buffer stocks or to use equalisation funds to effect marketing, even though it makes prices more risky or uncertain for sellers than Lange's or Taylor's scheme. But if the price paid by the state to producers for official supplies under the two-tiered price system is higher than that charged to consumers, as has been the case in the recent past for grain in China, then a subsidy has to be paid from state revenue to meet the marketing deficit. In the past China has paid a considerable subsidy on grain to benefit *consumers*. But now official prices are being moved closer to market prices.

Note that this discussion assumes that under the two-tiered price system the state will *not* be forced to buy production in excess of the mandatory enterprise quota. In practice, the Chinese government has agreed in the past to purchase production in excess of an enterprise's mandatory production at a floor price if the enterprise requests it. It is assumed here that the floor price is always set so that it is well below the market price; otherwise, if the floor price regularly equals or exceeds the market price then the two-tiered system becomes very similar in practice to that of Lange and Taylor.

I have suggested elsewhere that the two-tiered price system may be more effective in modifying the behaviour of monopolists than the market system proposed by Taylor and Lange (Tisdell, 1992). The two-tiered system may entice monopolists to produce a greater output than would the system proposed by Lange and Taylor.

A disadvantage of the Lange and Taylor system is that it breaks the direct link between sellers and buyers in exchanging products. As a result, sellers do not receive valuable direct feedback on the quality of their products and the needs of buyers. The marketing authorities may also have to institute quality checks on the products supplied by sellers, and this can add to their costs.

The Chinese two-tiered system has the advantage that it is flexible and allows transition to a relatively free market economy. This can be achieved by reducing official production quotas over time and phasing them out entirely for selected products. Prior to phase-out, official prices for quota production can be gradually raised, so that they approach market prices before control ceases. China has adopted this approach and Byrd (1987) argues that it is therefore moving in the 'correct' direction as far as markets and economic efficiency are concerned.

But the two-tiered price system has some shortcomings. One disadvantage of the two-tiered system is the scope which it gives for corruption by officials. Corrupt officials may sell official supplies obtained at less than market prices at market prices or at prices exceeding the official prices and appropriate the gain. Supplies of resources or factors to productive units can also involve protracted bargaining, and bribes may also be paid to planners by productive units to obtain favourable treatment in the assignment of low-priced resources. These may be hoarded by the unit (cf. Ames, 1971) or resold at a profit or used to produce goods for the high-priced free market.

Where capital available to a productive unit is a function of its surplus then the two-tiered price system disadvantages units producing commodities for which official prices are low and official quotas are high (cf. Yang and Tisdell, 1991). This can distort capital formation in the economy. Industries such as energy industries in which official prices are low may be starved of funds for capital formation and be very reliant on central redirection of capital for their growth needs. Thus the two-tiered price system can lead to long-term distortion in the economy.

It should also be noted that the above theoretical discussion ignores the possible income effects on demand of the two-tiered price system, as does the discussion by Byrd (1989).

Despite Byrd's efficiency arguments, the Chinese economy is still a long way in practice from achieving allocative efficiency, because of restrictions on the operation of factor markets. Resources are not free to move in response to price signals, and consequently their rates of technical substitution are not equalised everywhere. Hence, the economy operates within its *attainable* production possibility frontier. This can be illustrated by Figure 9.2

In Figure 9.2, the curve ABC represents the production possibility frontier for a two-product economy, *given* the resources allocated to productive units. If official quotas do not constrain any of the units in their production decisions, and the two-tiered price system operates then point B is achieved. This results in a maximum of welfare or a Paretian optimum relative to the allocation of resources to units, given that iso-welfare curve $W_1 W_1$ applies. However, the allocation of

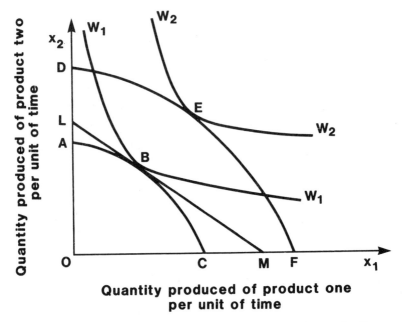

Figure 9.2   While a two-tiered system may achieve Paretian optimality
relative to resources allocated to productive units, the absence of
free markets for resources means that the best possible optimum
(*optimum optimorum*) is not achieved

resources may not be such as to maximise production in the economy
as a whole, because the marginal productivities of resources may differ
between units. If resources happened to be free to move to equalise
marginal productivities everywhere, instead of the economy being
constrained to production possibility frontier *ABC*, it could reach
frontier *DEF*. In that case, the economy might reach equilibrium at
point *E*, and this enables a higher level of economic welfare to be
attained. At present, factor market limitations and imperfections
greatly restrict the allocative efficiency of China's economic system.
Let us consider this matter further.

9.5 FACTOR MARKET CONSTRAINTS AND LIMITATIONS IN CHINA AND ECONOMIC EFFICIENCY.

While China has made great strides in improving its allocation of
factors of production and in providing material incentives to producers

for the more productive use of resources, restrictions on and short-comings in the operation of factor markets remain a serious obstacle to greater economic production and growth in China. Greater advance has been made in reforming product markets than factor markets (cf. Diao, 1987).

Ideologically this is to be expected from a Chinese perspective. The creation of fully fledged factor markets may lead to the reinstitution of private ownership of the means of production and the acceptance of market-determined values for labour and other means of production. This would run counter to communism and traditional Marxist-Leninist views. Nevertheless, increased inequality of income related to productivity and market-influenced prices is now widely accepted in China as being necessary to provide economic incentives and promote economic growth. Even *de-facto* ownership means of production is emerging, e.g. land allocated to families (cf. Cao and Tisdell, 1991).

Economic reforms have helped to reduce X-inefficiency in Chinese productive units. The contract management responsibility system and two-tiered market system itself have helped in this respect by enabling producers to retain profits from sale of output for which profit exceeds profit-targets. In state enterprises, bonuses to employees based on profit have been introduced and these provide incentives for improvements in the internal productive efficiency of enterprises (Chai, 1991; Jackson, 1991a 1992; Jackson and Littler, 1991). State enterprise managers also have more leeway than formerly to hire and dismiss employees.

Nevertheless, factor mobility is still limited. Rural dwellers cannot live permanently in cities without a permit. While temporary residence may be allowed, a temporary urban resident is denied several economic privileges available to permanent urban residents. However, rural residents now have freedom of choice within their rural region as to occupation and place of residence. They can for example work in village industries if they wish.

Inadequate mechanisms exist for allocating financial resources and capital from an efficiency point of view. Markets are not used to allocate capital and financial resources so as to equate the marginal efficiency of capital to the rate of interest everywhere. Allocation of capital is greatly influenced by political factors.

Non-market influences on the allocation of factors of production in China result in the rate of technical substitution of factors of production not being equalised. Resources are not allocated in a manner which would equate the value of their marginal products.

Consequently, considerable interregional income inequality exists and the Chinese economy operates below its potential production possibility frontier. In other words, the Byrd (1989) production frontier is within the potential one, as discussed in the previous section. Bankruptcy laws are not enforced in the case of all state-owned enterprises, including provincial and local government enterprises. These enterprises are often kept financially viable by soft loans. This is a source of inefficiency, especially of industrial enterprises. All this is exacerbated by the fact that no provision exists for financial (market) takeover of inefficiently managed firms by others because of the absence of markets in such assets. In capitalist economies, financial markets provide a spur to managers of companies to be efficient and maximise profit because otherwise they risk takeover by financial raiders (see next chapter; Marris, 1964). How far China will go in creating financial markets and allowing private trading in these remains to be seen.

9.6 PRICE INFLATION AND CHINA'S ECONOMIC REFORMS

Another feature of the Chinese economy in its transformation stage is its susceptibility to price inflation. While Liu Guoguang *et al.* (1987, p. 468) suggest that a shortcoming of thorough-going or complete market socialism is that macroeconomic control e.g. of inflation is difficult, this seems to be a greater problem for the Chinese economy in its present stage of reforms. The main reason for this may be the absence of disciplined financial markets or of effective direct forms of financial discipline.

Since 1978 China's sources of inflation have been several. Wage push has contributed. Decentralisation of decision-making has made it more difficult for state industrial managers to resist claims by workers for wage increases and bonuses. The availability of soft finance and the failure to implement bankruptcy laws fully means that managers suffer little penalty by allowing cost 'hikes'. Managers also remain subject to a considerable amount of interference by politicians (with varying interests and degrees of power), and it can be unwise for managers not to take account of their wishes.

Political interference adds to economic inefficiency by encouraging political rather than economic choices by managers. It may at the local level make managers more willing to concede to wage demands or follow non-profit-maximising policies. The fact, too, that there is no risk of financial-market-determined economic takeover and of enforced bankruptcy or closure may also give rise to laxity in management (see next chapter).

Apart from wage-push, demand-pull factors have also made for inflation and are difficult to control in China's current development stage. In the period 1982–7, for example, aggregate demand exceeded aggregate supply at constant prices by amounts ranging from around 11 per cent to over 25 per cent. This is not surprising, given China's strong urge to modernise and therefore to invest in new capital and equipment, and this comes on top of demands for greater consumption.

Greater decentralisation of economic decision-making in the public sector, e.g. to provincial and local government level, has resulted in much-reduced direct central control over the level of aggregate investment in China, and this control has not as yet been replaced by effective indirect macroeconomic and market mechanisms of control. It is very difficult for the central government, for instance, to reduce the amount of lending by banks at the local level, because local managers are appointed on the advice of local politicians and to some degree depend on them for their job security. In general, local politicians can be expected to urge local bank managers to follow an easy monetary policy so as to promote growth in the local economy and to be accommodating in periods of economic difficulty (Yang and Tisdell, 1991). This can result in local managers acting to some extent independently of the wishes of the central financial authority, e.g. failing to reduce credit quickly when called on to do so.

In the absence of adequate financial markets, it is difficult for China to follow effective inflation-avoiding macroeconomic policies, and this adds to political and economic instability. The operation of free economic forces in the current situation is liable after a period of time to generate considerable inflation with a risk of the macroeconomic system getting out of control. In the past such inflationary crises seem to have led to political upheaval, with changes in the ruling group followed for a period by increased central discipline but with a gradual return to a more liberal situation (cf. Yang and Tisdell, 1991). For how long cycles of this nature will be a feature is hard to say, but further economic reform seems to be needed to avoid them. Because such reforms involve further changes in the control of property or its ownership, it is understandable that making such reforms involves significant ideological issues for the CPC and that it is likely to baulk or delay in making them.

9.7   CONCLUSION

The two-tiered price system in China has provided an evolutionary means of reform towards a complete market system, and on the whole has been a source of increased economic efficiency. However, the two-tiered price system has been uneven in its introduction and has been instituted principally for product markets. While significant reforms have given individuals some freedom of economic choice in factor markets, less progress has occurred in market-making in this area than in product markets. This constitutes a major remaining source of economic inefficiency in the Chinese economic system. Furthermore, with greater decentralisation in decision-making, the absence of adequate financial and capital markets has added to China's difficulty in ensuring effective macroeconomic control, particularly of inflation.

Despite its market reforms, China's economic system continues to be plagued by inadequacies in the management of state industrial enterprises. China is far from attaining economic efficiency in its operations. This lack of economic efficiency is a problem, because such enterprises dominate the industrial sector and Chinese authorities still place considerable store on this sector as a vehicle for economic growth. Possible reasons for the poor economic performance of state industrial enterprises are discussed in the next chapter.

REFERENCES

BYRD, W. A. (1987) 'The impact of the two-tier plan/market system in Chinese industry', *Journal of Comparative Economics*, 11, pp. 295–308.
BYRD, W. A. (1989) 'Plan and market in the Chinese economy: a simple general equilibrium model', *Journal of Comparative Economics*, 13, pp. 329–32.
CAO YANG and TISDELL, C. A. (1991) *China's Surplus Agricultural Labour Force: its Size, Transfer, Prospects for Absorption and Effects of the Duble-track Economic System, Discussion Paper in Economics No. 59*, Department of Economics, University of Queensland, St Lucia, Brisbane.
CHAI, J. C. (1991) 'Incentive and profit sharing in Chinese industry 1978–1989', *Hong Kong Economic Papers*, 21, (pp. 47–57).
DIAO XINSHEN (1987) 'The role of the two-tier price system', pp. 35–46 in B. Reynolds (ed.), *Reform in China*, M. E. Sharpe, Armonk, New York.
JACKSON, S. (1991) *Market-plan controversy in China, Discussion Paper in Economics No. 63*, Department of Economics, University of Queensland, St Lucia, Brisbane.

JACKSON, S. (1992, forthcoming) *Chinese Enterprise Management: Reforms in Economic Perspective*, De Gruyter, Berlin and New York.
JACKSON, S. and LITTLER, C. R. (1991) 'Wage trends and policies in China: dynamics and contradictions', *Industrial Relations Journal*, 22, pp. 5–19.
LANGE, O. (1938) 'On the economic theory of socialism', pp. 55–142 in B. Lippincot (ed.) *On the Economic Theory of Socialism*, University of Minnesota Press, Minneapolis.
LIU GUOGUANG, LIANG WENSEN and others (1987) *China's Economy in 2000*, New World Press, Beijing.
MAO YU-SHI and HARE, P. (1989) 'Chinese experience in the introduction of a market mechanism into a planned economy: the role of pricing', *Journal of Economic Surveys*, 3, pp. 137–58.
MARRIS, R. (1964) *The Economic Theory of 'Managerial' Capitalism*, Macmillan, London.
SCHUMPETER, J. (1954) *Capitalism, Socialism and Democracy*, 4th edn, Allen & Unwin, London.
TAYLOR, F. M. (1938) 'The guidance of production in a socialist state', pp. 41–54 in B. Lippincot (ed.) *On the Economic Theory of Socialism*, University of Minnesota Press, Minneapolis.
TISDELL, C. A. (1972) *Microeconomics: The Theory of Economic Allocation*, Wiley, Sydney.
TISDELL, C. A. (1992) 'Microeconomic efficiency and macroeconomic policy effectiveness in China's transformation phase', *International Journal of Social Economics* (in press).
YANG RUILONG and TISDELL, C. A. (1991) *Inflation in the Transformation Phase of the Chinese Economic System: its Occurrence, Causes and Effects*, Discussion Paper in Economics No. 61, Department of Economics, University of Queensland, St Lucia, Brisbane.

10 Management of Enterprises, Separation from Ownership, and More on Markets

10.1 INTRODUCTION

Debate in China about the country's market and related economic reforms is continuing. Relevant questions include the extent to which markets increase economic efficiency, whether the market system results in a just or socially acceptable distribution of income, and the extent to which the market-related reforms add to inflation. A number of these matters were discussed in the previous chapter. All are important questions. But in some ways, a more fundamental question is whether separating the management of business enterprises from their ownership will improve their economic efficiency and the performance of the Chinese economy.

Zhao Ziyang (1987) emphasised in his report, delivered to the Thirteenth National Congress of the Communist Party of China on behalf of the Party's Twelfth Central Committee, that it is essential for China to proceed with institutional reforms, such as the effective separation of management from 'ownership', if the operation of the Chinese economy is to be improved. The problem of improving the management of China's state enterprises remains a pressing one, and Premier Li Peng has promised that during the Eighth Five-Year Plan (1991–5) further progress will be made in resolving this problem (*Beijing Review*, 15–21 April 1991). The basic problem, which has not changed fundamentally since Zhao Ziyang's report, is that although the whole people in theory or collections of people own most of China's resources, the ownership is administered by representatives who cannot be made completely accountable to the people, if for no other reason than the costs and difficulties of the people in obtaining information.

Most of these representatives are appointed through political processes and others through administrative processes, and many have few business or management skills. They may therefore direct the use of resources to uneconomic activities, use resources to serve special interests, or even exploit them to satisfy their own self-interest. Scope for consumption expenditure, the use of certain political processes which can add to inefficiency, organizational slack and paternalism does exist. Thus the slogan that 'the people own the resources, but there is a black spot in the commune office' gains force. But to what extent can the separation of management and ownership of business enterprises overcome these problems? How can the nexus between ownership-trustees and management be broken and economic efficiency achieved? This is the main question to be addressed in this chapter.

In addition to considering the nature of material incentives to the staff of Chinese state-owned industrial enterprises, and the effective separation of ownership from management, this chapter addresses briefly points additional to those discussed in previous chapters about market failure and efficiency in relation to market socialism, and also some aspects of justice and the distribution of income.

10.2 INCENTIVES AND THE MANAGEMENT OF CHINA'S STATE-OWNED INDUSTRIAL ENTERPRISES

As mentioned in Chapter 8, state industrial enterprises dominate China's industrial sector and their poor economic performance is a continuing problem. Almost 40 per cent of these enterprises were reported to be running at a loss in 1991 (*China Daily*, 28 June 1991, p. 1). There are several reasons for such losses. *Partly* they are in some cases a result of very low state-set official prices, especially in the case of those enterprises producing raw materials and energy commodities such as oil, coal and gas. All enterprises in the latter category had incurred losses for several years (*China Daily*, 28 June 1991, p. 1). But low prices do not apply in all cases, and are not the only reasons for poor economic performance by state industrial enterprises. Difficulties also arise because of several other factors.

The ministries responsible (at least indirectly) for state enterprises tend to be protective of them. These enterprises have not been subjected to the bankruptcy laws, and in times of need they can usually rely on soft loans to tide them over their economic difficulties. Furthermore, while material incentives have been introduced to encourage managers to maximise profits and increase economic efficiency, these measures have proven to be imperfect.

Beginning experimentally in 1979, China started a programme of increasing the autonomy of state industrial enterprises. The reforms involved the following features: (1) Instead of requiring all profits to be handed over to the state, as previously, provision was made for some retention of profit by enterprises for the purposes of reinvestment, the payment of bonuses to individual staff, and the funding of collective welfare benefits for staff. (2) The scope for enterprise managers to make their own production and marketing decisions was extended. Enterprises, after meeting the targets set by the state plan, can within the limits of their available resources decide what to produce and how to market it. (3) The reforms also aimed to increase management's flexibility in relation to labour employment and wage payments. While this has been the theoretical aim, Li Xuejun (1991, p. 13) points out that 'in practice the "flexibility" in labour and wage management has been largely a matter of paying higher bonuses to workers and cadres' (cf. also Jackson and Littler, 1991).

The introduction of responsibility systems spread rapidly in 1981–2 and continued with modifications until 1987 (Jackson, 1984, forthcoming 1992, Chapter 5). In 1987, payments to the state by state industrial enterprises were revised, so that they consisted of tax payaments plus a payment from after-tax profit. Whereas the earlier system was called the enterprise responsibility system, the 'new' one was designated the contract responsibility system (CRS).

The contract responsibility system was applied generally throughout China in 1987, although it had been used experimentally from 1981 onwards. Under the CRS the staff of state enterprises (directors) contract to complete certain production tasks for the state, and, apart from tax payments, agree to pay the state a specified portion of their after-tax profits. All profits after tax in excess of this specified portion may be retained by the enterprise to use as expansion funds, to pay bonuses to staff or to provide collective welfare benefits. If an enterprise fails to meet agreed targets then the shortfall must be made up from the enterprise's own funds (Li Xuejun, 1991, p. 18). The central role of the CRS has been confirmed by Premier Li Peng in the Eighth Five-Year Plan (1991–5) (*Beijing Review*, 15–21 April 1991).

There are several variations on the method used under the CRS to determine payments to the state (Jackson, 1992, Chapter 5). In some cases, for example, an absolute amount of after-tax profit of the enterprise is required to be delivered to the state, and in other cases the profit to be delivered to the state is increased annually at a constant percentage rate. But in any case the contracted rates are initially subject to political bargaining and are intended to apply for a contract period of several years. At the end of the contract period, after-tax profits payable to the state are reviewed and may be increased.

In practice, this system involves several problems. Profit rates payable to the state do not appear to be determined systematically, e.g. at rates equal to the average or normal rate of return on capital.

Directors may be reluctant to make high profits, even if they can, for fear that the level of their profit payable to the state will be increased at the time new contracts are entered into. Furthermore, once the enterprise starts operating at a deficit, it may continue to do so, because it would otherwise have the task of repaying accumulated losses plus unrealised profit contracted to the state. It may also remain in deficit because it hopes by bargaining to have its contracted profit level reduced at the beginning of the next profit period or to be given other concessions such as the increased delivery of raw materials, a reduction in official production quotas or a rise in official prices paid for its mandatory level of production.

While in theory managers or directors are supposed to be autonomous, they are not in practice. Sometimes it is unclear whether the party secretary in the enterprise or the managers are directing the business. In any case, political consultation processes are involved. Also, some managers are now elected by the workers. To some extent, this results in their appointment by a political process rather than on the basis of professional competence. In effect the workers become the electorate of the managers, who and may feel a political obligation to provide favours to them, so eroding discipline.

Government departments also retain control over industrial enterprises through production planning, appointments to management staff and the control of raw material supplies.

Note that the profits of state industrial enterprises are extremely dependent upon the level of official prices paid for their mandatory (plan) production. Variations in these factors can have a much greater influence on changes in the level of the profit of enterprises than can any improvements in their efficiency. Those 'targets' may be altered by political bargaining, as can be other factors of consequence for profit such as supplies of raw materials to an enterprise. A considerable amount of time may therefore be spent by management in 'politicking' rather than in improving industrial productivity.

While incentives have been given to managers and staff of state industrial firms to maximise profit, as already observed, such maximisation is unlikely to occur for the institutional reasons outlined. Furthermore, in those cases where enterprises do earn above contract profits or maximise these, their excess profit is likely to be used for consumption expenditure (increased wage and salary bonuses to managers and workers and collective welfare benefits within the enterprise), rather than for investment in and the expansion of the enterprise (cf. Jackson and Littler, 1991). Because of the availability of soft loans, directors are likely to try to rely on these for investment rather than invest their *discretionary* funds in the enterprise at their possible personal expense (e.g. bonuses forgone). *Elected* managers may be especially under political pressure from workers to follow such a path. Policies to yield quick profit at the expense of long-term profit may be adopted. In some cases, for example, machinery is operated beyond designed capacity and worn out quickly to obtain rapid profit, and other inefficient practices are also followed.

In order to obtain efficiency within enterprises, not only rewards are required for economic results but also penalties need to be applied for failure to achieve economic results. In capitalist market societies, the penalties are (1) bankruptcy or (2) *competitive* takeover by other companies or (3) personal losses to individuals owning the assets in the enterprises. These measures operate in a non-political and *impersonal* way. But such mechanisms are virtually absent in China's system for state industrial enterprises. Both carrots and sticks are needed, and it is the latter that are especially lacking in China, except maybe 'political sticks', which are usually ineffective in increasing economic efficiency. Until China can bring about institutional changes involving the three elements mentioned above, there is little hope of it having efficient industrial enterprises. In particular, note that *both* the application of bankruptcy laws and the scope for competitive takeover seem essential to encourage economic efficiency.

Currently (1991), some of China's state officials are suggesting that the way to revitalise state industrial enterprises is to invest more in them, renew their capital and ensure that they adopt modern technology. This may help, but it does not address the real issue, because account is not taken of the opportunity cost of providing extra economic advantages to state enterprises. Already the capital–output ratios of such enterprises are very high, and the question must be faced of whether the highest return on capital will be earned by giving extra resources to these enterprises rather than to say, collective enterprises or those operated by households or individuals. While politics and dogma may combine to favour state-owned firms, the costs of such an 'indulgence' must be carefully weighed up.

The problems involved in China's current industrial system can be seen more clearly by drawing upon Western theories and experience in relation to the separation of ownership and control of enterprises. Let us consider this aspect.

10.3 SEPARATION OF OWNERSHIP AND MANAGEMENT – DOES IT INCREASE ECONOMIC EFFICIENCY?

In the Western World opinion has been divided about whether the separation of management and ownership of business enterprises increases economic efficiency. Indeed, the earliest views on this subject as, for example, put forward by Berle and Means (1932) suggested that where owners lose control over managers, as in large public companies, there is scope for managers to engage in organisationally slack and even fraudulent practices without being disciplined by owners, e.g. by dismissal. It was assumed that where owners had more control over managers they would dismiss managers who failed to maximise the profitability of the company and would replace them by others. However, in most cases owners might be expected not to meddle in the day-to-day affairs of the business but to leave its operations to professional managers, thereby maximising business returns.

With the growth of the joint stock companies, the ownership of business enterprises becomes diffused among large numbers of shareholders, who, lose effective control over management. Consequently, managers may be given scope to pursue discretionary behaviour of a non-profit-maximising kind, thereby adding to economic inefficiency (cf. Williamson, 1964). Therefore several theories of the firm have developed which are based on the assumption that companies are operated, subject to some constraints, in accordance with the aims of managers (Baumol, 1959; Williamson, 1964; Marris, 1964; cf. Ames, 1971). These theories suggest that under managerial capitalism (a situation in which a large amount of capital is controlled by professional managers divorced from company shareholders) there may be widespread failure of business management to maximise profit.

On the other hand, the scope available to managers for deviating from profit maximisation under managerial capitalism can easily be exaggerated. Several factors limit the scope for such deviation or the actual deviation, even when management and ownership of business enterprises are separated. These are:

(1) *The existence of competitive commodity markets.* Under perfect competition, above-normal profits are eliminated and consequently managers may have little scope to deviate from profit maximisation without making a loss. If losses occur and continue for a company, the company will become bankrupt and will be liquidated.

(2) *Business growth-orientation by managers.* Many managers have a strong motivation to promote the growth of their enterprise. The profitability of the enterprise may play an important role in this. Retained profits can be an important source of funds for investment (Penrose, 1959), and shareholders have to be ensured a satisfactory return on their funds in order to subscribe additional funds for growth of the enterprise (Baumol, 1959). But in imperfect product markets scope for deviation may still exist.

(3) *The threat of financial takeover of companies which fail to maximise their profit.* Companies which fail to maximise their profit run the risk of being 'raided' and being taken over by other companies. The acquiring company can offer shareholders in the company to be acquired a payment slightly in excess of the market value of the shares in the company and, on takeover by more effectively using the resources of the company, increase returns. For example, suppose that the market value of a share in a company tends to reflect the discounted future earnings on the share. For instance, when a discount rate of 12 per cent is the current appropriate rate then the market value of the share may be 1 yuan. A raider, by reorganising the company, may be able to raise the stream of returns and dividends so that the discounted value of the share becomes 1.20 yuan. If shareholders in the company to be acquired are willing to accept 1.08 yuan per share, i.e. 8 per cent more than the market value of a share, then the raiding company stands to make a capital gain of over 10 per cent if, with reorganization and more profitable use of resources, the market value of a share rises to 1.20 yuan. Whenever a company fails to maximise its return on capital, there is always a risk of it being taken over and hence of its existing managers losing their positions or power. This acts as a constraint on managerial behaviour (see for example,

Marris, 1964). Thus managers are disciplined through the capital market as investors seek to maximise their returns on capital.

Even if there is imperfect competition in the product market, e.g. the existence of monopoly, a perfectly operating capital market would force managers to maximise profit in order to forestall the takeover of their company. But, of course, perfect capital markets and frictionless economic adjustment do not exist in reality. For example, transaction costs and uncertainties are involved in attempting to acquire other companies, and it is always a matter of judgement as to how much returns can be raised in an existing company by reorganising its activities. So, in reality, managers may have some discretion to trade off profit for other goals. But the more perfectly competitive are capital markets, the smaller will be the amount of this discretion.

(4) *Linking of managers' incomes and/or prestige to the profitability of a company.* In as much as the levels of managers' salaries are positively linked to the profitability of their company, either directly through bonuses or indirectly through market competition for managers, this can provide an incentive for profit maximisation. Those managers demonstrating greater ability to earn profit may be in greater demand and therefore, via market competition for managers, may earn a higher salary. Furthermore, if profit is an important indicator of social status among the peer group to which managers belong, this will *encourage* maximisation of profit. For example, the American business magazine *Fortune* lists the top companies according to profit and value of sales.

(5) *The certainty of bankruptcy for non-government owned enterprises which make continued losses.* This provides an incentive for business enterprises to make a profit, even if it does not in itself ensure profit maximisation.

Under managerial (or corporate) capitalism, even when owners lose control over management of a company, managers may still have an incentive to maximise profit or approximately to do this. As indicated above, both rewards and punishment mechanisms play a role.

While the ownership of companies is frequently so dispersed in Western countries that no shareholder is able to exert considerable control over managers, this is not always so. Institutional investors are important shareholders in many companies. These include insurance companies, especially life insurance companies, superannuation funds, investment companies and in some cases banks and other financial bodies. In some cases, institutional investors are powerful enough to be able to exert control on management. But they are unlikely to do so other than to promote profit maximisation. This is because institutional investors must compete in the market for investment funds and their companies in turn may be subject to takeover if they fail to maximise the returns on their funds. Furthermore, management may be resistant to any manipulation which might reduce profit if the market for managers tends to determine their salary in the long term and this is linked to their record in making profit. A further element that may restrain an individual investor in a company from manipulating its management for personal gain is the possible geographic distance between the investor and the seat of operation of the company.

This is not to suggest that shareholders are provided with perfect protection by market forces under managerial capitalism. Unscrupulous individuals sometimes float and manage companies to 'milk' unsuspecting shareholders, sometimes using offshore companies in tax havens to facilitate the process under the secrecy provisions existing in such places. Certainly a state watchdog, e.g. a Corporate Affairs Commission, is needed to curb such fraudulent practices.

10.4 POSSIBLE IMPLICATIONS FOR CHINA'S INSTITUTIONAL REFORMS

What implications can be drawn from the above for China's reforms in relation to the separation of management from business enterprises? What institutional changes are required to ensure that managers are guided by returns on resources rather than by non-economic factors such as political or personal intervention by local government leaders or other government leaders?

Separation of ownership from management of companies must be effective, and those managing should be disciplined by *impersonal* forces to maximise returns on resources, subject of course to the government providing guidance to markets where necessary. (The question of government guidance of markets will be discussed later.) These reforms are important in China's case since, because of widespread state ownership of enterprises, so much of its resources is held or administered on trust for the people by their agents or nominal agents. In the allocation of these resources, those responsible have no particular interest in maximising returns on their use *per se*, unlike the old fashioned sole owner in the Western World. They are more likely to be motivated by political considerations and by the possibilities for personal gain, since they owe their status and power primarily to political and/or bureaucratic support, that is forces which are not impersonal. How can a system of effective separation be instituted under a socialist form of the ownership of resources? How can all parties be disciplined by impersonal forces to maximise returns? This is an important problem.

First, it seems necessary that ownership trustees and management of business enterprises be separated in more than name. Where a single investing body has a 100-per cent equity or a dominant equity in an enterprise, it is unlikely really to be separated from management, even if the business enterprise is an independent legal entity. The investing body has an interest in obtaining special favours or treatment for the business enterprise if this can be done through the political process. For example, the investing body, such as a local municipal authority, may be able to obtain low-interest loans or grants from the central government for the enterprise, or it may favour the enterprise in the allocation of land, say, in competition with an enterprise owned outside the municipality wishing to operate within it. Consequently, resources are poorly allocated. The more diffused, however, is the ownership of the enterprise, the less likely is it that a single investing body will find it worth while to go to the trouble of trying to obtain or give political favours and the less likely are managers to seek such assistance.

Effective separation of ownership and management involves more than a legal statement. If management is dependent on one body, e.g. a local government body for additional funds and economic support then it can ill afford to ignore the advice of the leaders of the investing body, even if it is a separate legal entity. The survival of the business or its ease of survival is at stake, and rational managers will respond to their environment and use it to their best personal advantage. Thus management continues to be subject to political meddling and guidance by individuals who mostly have no special training or expertise in business management and who also have no direct responsibility for the management decisions made. Moreover, since the investors are not using their own money for investment purposes, but that of the community or the people held on trust, the unscrupulous may by various means and schemes make personal gains for themselves or their families by abusing the trust placed in them. Diffusion of ownership should help to reduce the scope for this.

However, this is not enough. Competitive capital markets are required for the supply of capital both to investing bodies and to productive units. In addition, a more competitive market for managers and the promotion of profit as a status and success symbol should help, even though the legacy of Confucian antipathy to profit and previous Communist Party criticism of it has to be overcome. It is also very important, for disciplinary purposes that company takeovers should be facilitated and bankruptcy rules enforced. In relation to these preconditions, China still has a very long way to go before they are met. In China serious failure by productive units to maximise their returns on their capital does not result in their takeover. Even in the case of negative returns, economic units may be propped up indefinitely with soft loans and grants. This adds to economic inefficiency as well as to *inflation*.

Can the preconditions for the increased economic efficiency of business enterprises be achieved under the socialist ownership of resources? What laws or rules are necessary to make this possible? Some limitations on the degree of equity or ownership of productive units by *individual* investment bodies would seem necessary. Also, professional investment companies (possibly state-owned) need to be promoted, and again it may be desirable that ownership of these should be diffused and, of course, made subject to market competition for their capital. All of these commercial units should be subject to commercial takeover. The amount of funds allocated directly through political processes should be reduced as quickly as is practical, and central government support should be ensured by creating an appropriate business *environment* for these commercial units. Within this system, some private ownership of shares may be allowed if this is desired. But even under socialist ownership, much more progress can be made in China in improving economic efficiency and increasing economic growth, especially in industry and commerce.

Of course, these are not the only reforms which may help to improve the efficiency of business in China and help to prevent the waste and misappropriation of the people's resources. Other changes which can assist include the following:

(1) More widespread use of effective accounting systems and greater accountability by those in charge of resources.
(2) Improved and more widespread training of managers.

(3) Greater scope for the promotion of managers by ability rather than seniority.
(4) Greater mobility of managers and scope for the marketing of managerial talent.
(5) Improvements in the legal system as it affects business, e.g. the improved codification and enforcement of business laws. Greater attention needs to be given to the penalties for misleading advertising and for the sale of defective or deficient goods, e.g. those goods injurious to health. Consumer protection law in China seems to be very weak. This is not to say that the same degree of consumer protection may be justified in a less-developed country such as China, but the sale of products patently dangerous to buyers or completely ineffective in their claimed benefit should be curbed.

10.5 MARKETS – WHAT GUIDANCE DO THEY NEED?

The idea that markets may be used successfully to guide a socialist economic system is by no means new. Both Taylor (1938) and Lange (1938) advocated a competitive market system as a means of guiding a socialist economy, as did Lerner (1946). They had in mind atomistic competition or perfect competition as the ideal model for resource allocation, with the role of the state being limited to a few defined tasks. Lange (1938) envisaged that there would be a central planning board with relatively limited tasks. Briefly these would be:

(1) to determine the aggregate level of investment or capital formation in the economy;
(2) to determine the supply of social or public goods such as defence and education;
(3) to determine and adjust the prices of all marketable commodities so as to attain market equilibrium by a trial-and-error process as quickly as possible.

In the system envisaged (see Tisdell, 1972, Chapter 22), all resources other than labour are collectively owned, labour is freely mobile, consumers have freedom of choice so that consumer sovereignty prevails, productive units are collectively owned and are managed by socialist enterprise managers who are instructed to or encouraged to maximise profit by bonuses, and for each industry a board of socialist industrial managers is appointed to control the number of firms in the industry, to ensure that the marginal firm just earns a normal profit. The price system is not used to redistribute income, but this is done independently by the government in an attempt to avoid the allocative inefficiency which can result from tampering with market equilibrium prices.

The Lange model involves a comparatively straightforward adaptation of the Paretian welfare economics model (the New Welfare Economics model) (Tisdell, 1972, Chapter 13) to a socialist system. Under various conditions, it can be shown theoretically that perfect competition leads to the maximum satisfaction of human wants relative to available resources *and* a given distribution of income. Therefore, it is concluded that in order to maximise social welfare the state should adjust income distribution so that it is 'ideal', and let perfectly competitive markets operate. Thereby, it is argued, static allocative efficiency in the use of resources is obtained.

But the model does not take account of the more dynamic aspects of the economy, such as the possible conflict up to a point between perfect competition and technological change (Schumpeter, 1942; Tisdell, 1972, Chapter 21; 1982, Chapter 10). Furthermore, it is not apparent that it is ideal for the central planning board to determine the price of all marketable commodities, for example, because the board may be slower in adjusting prices to equilibrium than unregulated market forces would be, and its administration will involve a cost. The socialist market system envisaged for China appears in the end to be one in which only the prices of a few commodities are regulated. It was accepted at the Thirteenth National Congress of the Communist Party of China that 'We [China] should gradually establish a system under which the state sets the prices of a few vital commodities and services while leaving the rest to be regulated by the market.' (Zhao Ziyang, 1987, p. 36) It was also recognised that

> The socialist market system should include not only a commodity market for consumer goods and for means of production but also markets for other essential factors of production such as funds, labour, technology, information and real estate. If there is only a commodity market it is impossible to give play to market forces. (Zhao Ziyang, 1987, p. 36)

However, at present, the Chinese economic system still has a long way to go in establishing markets for the means of production. Nevertheless, Zhao Ziyang recognised the essential problem.

Observe that the model of Lange does not take adequate account of the growth of new institutions such as multiproduct firms, large public companies and economies of scale and scope in some industries. In itself, it does not provide an adequate formula for creating a modern market-type socialist economy. There is a need to search for a better way which makes use of market forces up to a point. In this respect, it may be useful to recall the traditional arguments canvassed in the Western world both in favour of and against the use of perfectly competitive markets as a means for guiding economic activity. The basic arguments in favour have been as follows:

(1) It leads to allocative economic efficiency, that is an ideal allocation of resource.
(2) It eliminates organizational slack or X-inefficiency.
(3) It promotes economic growth through both incentives and penalties. For example, those who seize new economic opportunities and adopt new technology will be rewarded, whereas those who fail to do so will be forced out of business.
(4) It leads to increased division of labour and specialisation in production and other economic benefits by extending the scope for the exchange of commodities.
(5) It economises on the amount of information needed for economic decision-making and guidance. Each decision-maker decides, using a limited amount of information, what to do, and the cost of a bureaucratic state planning and controlling body is avoided.
(6) There is individual sovereignty or liberty in economic choice. The individual (in normal circumstances) is seen as the best judge of his or her own self-interest, but there are some exceptions to this rule (Mill, 1963).

The main arguments against letting markets have free rein appear to be the following:

(1) Failure of markets to maximise social welfare in the sense of Vilfredo Pareto, even in equilibrium, or to achieve equilibrium quickly. Such failures in the attainment of economic efficiency can occur even under perfect competition. Factors which can cause this to occur are

(a) externalities or spillovers from economic activities;

(b) indivisibilities in resource utilisation and large economies of scale in economic activity;

(c) the existence of pure public goods;

(d) uncertainty about economic variables and the importance of learning by doing.

(2) There is no guarantee that perfectly competitive markets will be effective stimulants for economic growth and, particularly, technological change. This is because of the market failures involved in scientific and technological change (Tisdell, 1981, Chapter 1) and the type of factors discussed by Schumpeter (1942). Schumpeter believed that oligopolies and monopolies could be more important vehicles for innovation and technological progress in business than could small competitive firms, given that the former are subject to long-run competition from substitutes for their products.

(3) Sometimes it is also argued that particular goods should be treated as merit goods and that their production and consumption should be encouraged by state support. For example, activities which preserve and transmit culture and which may be important in achieving national or group cohesion provide a possible case.

(4) Various arguments may also be advanced for restricting freedom of choice in consumption. This might be justified in the case where the knowledge of consumers is very limited, as with minors or the insane, or where the consumption can result in behaviour or side-effects which damage others, e.g. the use of drugs.

(5) Some argue that an unjust or unfair distribution of income is likely to result under a market system and that this at least requires state intervention to adjust the distribution of income.

What is and what is not a fair distribution of income is an extremely difficult question to answer, and a number of differing views exist. I shall not attempt to discuss this subject in detail here, but it is relevant to the debate about markets and was discussed to some extent in Chapter 6. However, it might be noted that the orthodox position of the New Welfare Economists is that markets as such should not be used to redistribute income. According to them, if income is to be redistributed, this should be done directly by the state through income transfers, since total welfare will be greater than if market prices are distorted through subsidies or other means.

Nevertheless, some economists believe that the competitive market system is relatively just, because individuals are paid the value of their marginal product (as determined by the market system), and those who work harder or make successful business innovations obtain greater rewards.

On the other hand, Rawls (1971) argues that the incomes of all should be equal unless inequality can be shown in particular instances to be to the benefit of all. He bases his view on the concept of a social contract or agreement which we might all reach (in theory) before we are born because then we do not know into what situation we might be born or whether we will be born handicapped. But could we have been equally as well have been born into any other situation? Could we have been born in another country or of a different race, for example? Could we have been born to be a living thing other than a human being? If so, should Rawls's principle be extended to all living things? Hindu philosophers and those believing in reincarnation and rebirth according to conduct in a previous life might find difficulty in accepting Rawls' concept of justice.

While a number of Marxists believe in equality of income, the slogan 'from each according to ability, to each according to need' gives little guide to policy unless need is defined. Furthermore, what is to be done about those who do not contribute according to their ability? Should they be allowed to consume according to their 'need'? Current Chinese thinking suggests that they should be penalized and this seems to be just (See Chapter 6). The Chinese slogan in the post-Mao period is 'to each according to his work' (*An lao fen pei*).

A number of the utilitarians, especially the Fabian socialists, argued that income should be made equal in order to maximise the total level of utility in society. Their argument was based on the proposition that all obtain approximately equal utility from the same level of income and that utility increases at a diminishing rate. However, they ignored the fact that individuals with the same ability and opportunity may have a different preference for leisure. One individual may be prepared to forego income for more leisure. It would therefore be unjust to redistribute income to this person from another person with the same income-earning opportunities who decides to work longer and obtain a higher income (Tisdell, 1989a). To do so would actually give the individual desiring more leisure a higher 'real' income than the other, equally placed in terms of income earning opportunities (see Chapter 6).

Edgeworth (1881, Tisdell, 1972, Chapter 13) disagreed with the Fabian socialists about whether individuals receive the same amount of utility from the same level of income. He was of the view that aristocrats and educated people obtained more utility than the others from the same level of income and that men obtained more utility than women. Hence, he argued that utility maximisation for society requires inequality in the distribution of income – more income to aristocrats and the educated than to others, more income to men than to women.

Another important issue is the extent to which equality of opportunity should be created. To what extent should all be given equal access to resources, e.g. educational opportunities, at the start of their life so that all start off with some equality in the race of life? To what extent should those handicapped by natural misfortune be given more resources? All of these are important issues and all may require state intervention in the market system to provide a fairer distribution of economic opportunities (see Tisdell, 1982, Section 14.7).

State intervention in the market system to create a fairer distribution of income and greater equality of economic opportunity seems to be called for in practice. At least there should be an aim to create equal opportunity for those with equal ability and potential to contribute to the economy – opportunities should not be a function of privilege. While some improvement in the distribution of income, especially through income supplements for those who have very low incomes due to misfortune, e.g. being born physically handicapped, seems justified under the market system, there seems to be no good reason why the incomes of all should be made equal. Furthermore, in a market system the state may need to intervene to correct for market failures and so improve economic efficiency. However, in considering such intervention the possibility of political and bureaucratic failure in achieving economic efficiency must be considered and the agency costs of the intervention must be taken into account (cf. Tisdell, 1982, Chapter 16).

Often one has to compare imperfect policy alternatives. In China today, for instance, industrial pollution is causing a loss in social welfare, but the political and administrative system has proven incapable of dealing with the problem. Often the state will not control its own enterprises correctly because of political connections between those involved. This is especially regrettable in a socialist state.

10.6 CONCLUDING COMMENT

In their theory and approach to market socialism, Taylor and Lange failed to take account of modern institutional developments such as

₂ rise of multiproduct firms, of large corporations in which management and ownership are frequently divorced, of the possible superiority of non-atomistic firms in the quest for technical progress and economic growth; that is, of Schumpeterian-type dynamics. Their theories are rooted in the concepts of perfect competition developed at the turn of this century and seem at least to require adaptation to modern economic structures. China, in developing its approach to market socialism, may well need to forge a new path. In that regard, it may need to build a system which provides both incentives and penalties to enterprises (managers) to maximise returns, and in that context to follow through the new Chinese motto 'markets guide enterprises, the state guides markets'. The state needs to guide markets appropriately by correcting for market failures, by effectively separating the ownership and management of business enterprises (bearing in mind the principles discussed earlier), and to interfere to the extent that is needed to ensure a fair distribution of economic opportunities and incomes. Neither central direction of the economy nor a *laissez-faire* market system provides the best attainable solution to our economic problems. A mixed economic system is likely to give the best economic results. However, a wide range of mixed economic systems is possible, and, in practice, one has to accept that it is probably impossible to create an absolutely ideal economic system. But this is no excuse for being satisfied with an economic system that is inferior to what is attainable. At present there is scope for improving the operation of the Chinese economic system. To realise this will require additional economic reforms.

REFERENCES

AMES, E. (1971) 'The economic theory of output-maximising enterprise', pp. 270–86 in G.C. Archibald (ed.) *Theory of the Firm*, Penguin, Harmondsworth. Reprinted from E. Ames, *Soviet Economic Processes*, Richard D. Irwin, Homewood, Ill. 1965, pp. 50–65.
BAUMOL, W.J. (1959) *Business Behaviour, Value and Growth*, Macmillan, New York.
BERLE, A.A. and MEANS, G.C. (1932) *The Modern Corporation and Private Property*, Macmillan, New York.
EDGEWORTH, F.Y. (1881) *Mathematical Psychics*, Kegan Paul, London.
JACKSON, S. (1984) 'Profit sharing, state revenue and enterprise performance in the PRC', *The Australian Journal of Chinese Affairs*, no. 12, pp. 97–112.
JACKSON, S. (1992, forthcoming) *Chinese Enterprise Management: Reforms in Economic Perspective*, De Gruyter, Berlin and New York.

170   *Economic Development in the Context of China*

JACKSON, S. and LITTLER, C. R. (1991) 'Wage trends and policies in Chir dynamics and contradictions', *Industrial Relations Journal*, 22, pp. 5–19.

LANGE, 0. (1938) 'On the economic theory of socialism', pp. 55–142 in B. Lippincot (ed.) *On the Economic Theory of Socialism*, University of Minnesota Press, Minneapolis. Reprinted from *Review of Economic Studies*, 1936–7.

LERNER, A. P. (1946) *The Economics of Control*, Macmillan, New York.

LI XUEJUN (1991) Enterprise management in the People's Republic of China: Development and issues', mimeo., Faculty of Business, Queensland University of Technology, Brisbane.

MARRIS, R. (1964) *The Economic Theory of 'Managerial' Capitalism*, Macmillan, London.

MILL, J. S. (1963) 'On Liberty', in *Six Great Humanistic Essays of John Stuart Mill*, Washington Square Press, New York.

PENROSE, E. (1959) *The Theory of the Growth of the Firm*, Blackwell, Oxford.

RAWLS, J. R. (1971) *A Theory of Justice*, Harvard University Press, Cambridge, Mass.

SCHUMPETER, J. A. (1942) *Capitalism, Socialism and Democracy*, 2nd edn, Harper, New York.

TAYLOR, F. M. (1938) 'The guidance of production in a socialist state', pp. 41–54 in B. Lippincot (ed.), *On the Economic Theory of Socialism*, The University of Minnesota Press, Minneapolis, 1938. Reprinted from *Review of Economic Studies*, 1936–7.

TISDELL, C. A. (1972) *Microeconomics: The Theory of Economic Allocation*, Wiley, Sydney.

TISDELL, C. A. (1981) *Science and Technology Policy: Priorities of Governments*, Chapman & Hall, London.

TISDELL, C. A. (1982) *Microeconomics of Markets*, Wiley, Brisbane.

WILLIAMSON, O. E. (1964) *The Economics of Discretionary Behaviour: Managerial Objectives in a Theory of the Firm*, Prentice-Hall, Englewood Cliffs, NJ.

ZHAO ZIYANG (1987) 'Advance along the road of socialism with Chinese characteristics', Report delivered at the Thirteenth National Congress of the Communist Party of China 25 October 1987, pp. 3–80 in *Documents of the Thirteenth National Congress of the Communist Party of China (1987)* Foreign Languages Press, Beijing.

11 Foreign Tourism: Benefits to China and Contribution to Development

11.1 GROWTH OF FOREIGN TOURISM IN CHINA

Since 1978, with China's adoption of new policies involving opening up to the outside world and the promotion of modernisation, the number of international visitors to China has increased dramatically e.g. by more than fourteen-fold in the period from 1978 to the end of 1988; investment in China's tourist industry has risen rapidly, and tourism has increased relatively as an earner of foreign exchange for China (Tisdell and Wen, 1991a, b; Zhang, 1989). This relative increase is noteworthy because China has greatly increased its volume of international trade and transactions since 1978. Another feature of the growth in China's tourism sector is the large role played in it by foreign direct investment, especially in hotels (Tisdell and Wen, 1991b).

The growth of this industry is indicative of China's new economic direction and its more pragmatic approach to economic policy than in the past. Its growth is all the more remarkable for the following reasons: (1) It is a service industry and therefore according to traditional Marxist thinking unproductive. (2) To a large extent it directly serves foreigners, although there has also been considerable expansion in domestic tourism in China since 1978. (3) Much of the direct investment in the industry is foreign, that is by foreign 'capitalists'. (4) It involves direct rather than indirect interaction with the outside world, and therefore has a considerable potential to be culturally disruptive. For these reasons it is necessary to consider why the growth of this industry has been encouraged by China.

Since 1978 the Chinese government has looked upon foreign tourism as a means to accumulate funds for the modernisation programmes, to enhance the friendship of the Chinese people with the rest of the world and to increase income and employment levels. After 1978 China's tourism policy focused on the economic benefits of foreign tourism, whereas in the past its main emphasis was on the political benefits (cf. Uysal *et al.* 1986, p. 113). Nevertheless, political and cultural benefits are not entirely ignored at present, e.g. 'suitable' literature about China is available free at many hotels and airports for tourists.

The Thirteenth National Congress of the Communist Party of China (1987) adopted the view that the growth of foreign tourism is important to economic development because tourism is a significant means for earning foreign exchange. In that regard Zhao Ziyang stated:

> Our capacity to earn foreign exchange through export determines, to a great extent, the degree to which we can open to the outside world and affects the scale and pace of domestic economic development. For this reason, bearing in mind the demands of the world market and our own strong points, we should make vigorous efforts to develop export-oriented industries and products that are competitive and can bring quick and high economic returns. (Zhao Ziyang, 1987, p. 28)

This report (on behalf of the Central Committee of the CPC) goes on to mention specifically that more should be done to expand the export-oriented tourist industry and so increase the amount of foreign exchange available to China.

Following China's relaxation in 1978 of its restrictions on foreign tourists, China's receipts from international tourism expanded greatly. They increased at current prices from $US 262.9 million in 1978 to $US 1845.27 million in 1987, that is by more than seven times in a decade. The number of international tourist arrivals in the same period rose from 1.8 million to 26.9 million, with the total number of foreigners arriving going up from 0.23 million to 1.7 million, the remaining expansion in arrivals being accounted for by arrivals of overseas Chinese and compatriots. The latter (from Hong Kong, Macao and Taiwan) are not regarded by China as foreigners. By 1988, China earned $US 2220 million per year from foreign tourists, and there were 1.84 million *foreign* visitors to China.

After the protests of mid-1989 and the Tiananmen tragedy of 4 June, foreign tourism to China fell sharply, but in 1990 it began to recover again and by 1991 was on an upward path once more. China's gross earnings of foreign exchange from foreign tourism returned to the 1988 level of $US2.22 million in 1990 (*China Daily*, 8 June 1991, p. 4). The number of 'compatriots' visiting China, especially from Taiwan, rose sharply in 1990. However, the growth of China's tourism industry has not been without problems, some of them indicative of general problems involved in the management and development of China's economy and worth while considering. It can be argued that investment in China's tourism industry has made it a dynamic and leading industry in China and that this has given rise to unbalanced growth (cf. Chapter 8; McKee and Tisdell, 1990; Gillis *et al.*, 1983 Chapter 3; Hirschman, 1958; McKee, 1987; Perroux, 1950).

11.2 SOME PROBLEMS ENCOUNTERED IN THE DEVELOPMENT OF CHINA'S TOURISM INDUSTRY

A major feature of the development of China's tourism sector since 1978 has been its relatively unbalanced nature. The main emphasis in the period 1978–89 was on the building of hotels. Their capacity for housing foreign visitors was expanded in many cases beyond the availability of transport for such tourists. Bottlenecks in transport often resulted in long transport delays for foreign tourists and/or in hotels having excess capacity even in peak seasons. The expansion of tourism has placed considerable pressures on air and rail transport, roads, harbours, electricity supply and communications. Complementary production and services have not been expanded in step with the expansion in tourist accommodation (Tisdell and Wen, 1991b).

For example, *Economics of Tourism* (Beijing, 1988) reported that Guilin, in the scenic karst area of South China, received 450 000 international tourists in 1987. Together with domestic tourists, this resulted in a total of 15 tourist visitors per resident of Guilin in 1987. As a result, public utilities and services were put under severe pressure. Electricity supplies were sufficient to only meet 60 per cent of demand, the airport was operating 60 per cent beyond its designed capacity, main roads were congested and there was a major water shortage. Furthermore, only 16 per cent of sewage could be disposed of in an acceptable manner and the city was therefore threatened by severe pollution.

Comparatively speaking, the provision, upkeep, restoration and preservation of tourist attractions (as distinct from tourist accommodation) has been neglected. For example, in Suzhou 260 spots are rated as having tourist value, but only 20 have been renovated and opened. In peak seasons the number of tourists attempting to visit these attractions is up to ten times as great as their estimated appropriate capacity (Tisdell and Wen, 1991b).

Within the hotel sector of the industry, there has been excessive building of high-class hotels (Zhao Jian, 1989; Tisdell and Wen, 1991a, b). More than 60 per cent of hotels in the main tourist cities of China are estimated to be in the high-class category, but most tourists do not wish to stay in this class of hotel. According to a survey undertaken by CITS (China International Travel Service), only 10 per cent of international tourists wish to stay in such hotels. Thus the composition of hotels in China by type does not reflect demand conditions. Why?

One problem was the belief among China's administrators that all foreign tourists are fond of luxury and rich. Modern high-class hotels were seen as a way of profiting from this. This bias was further accentuated by seeking out foreign investors involved in high-class hotel chains such as Sheraton, Hilton and Holiday Inns. Furthermore, Chinese authorities investing in hotels often failed to undertake adequate economic appraisal of their hotel investments. Hotels were built in some cases, for example, in out-of-the-way places in the hope that they would attract tourists and as a result their occupancy rate has turned out to be low.

On the other hand, it should be remembered that to have foreign tourism as a major industry in China has been a new enterprise for China. The early phase of industry development can be regarded as a learning phase, and in it period errors are bound to occur. However, it is important that there comes a time when major past mistakes are no longer repeated.

Apart from providing direct economic benefits to China, the foreign tourist industry may have another advantage. It drives home the importance of being internationally competitive. If China is to expand its foreign tourism sector, it must be competitive in its provision of tourist services (Tisdell and Wen, 1991a; Tisdell, 1990). The evidence of whether or not it is successful in that regard becomes clear through changes in the flow of foreign tourists within China itself. Up to a point, the industry may act as a barometer of national competitiveness, albeit possibly a poor one. Furthermore, by the contacts made with foreign tourists, individuals in China gain additional information about economic conditions outside China. This may provide Chinese with an additional basis for the continual comparison and monitoring of China's economic performance.

Even among China's leadership there is not likely to be unanimity about the objectives which China should follow in encouraging international tourism and tourism more generally. In practice, multiple objectives are being pursued, but sometimes one objective is stressed more than another by politicians, e.g. foreign exchange earnings. The matter is complex. It is, therefore, worth while listing some of the more important objectives and discussing the difficulties which may be involved in satisfying them.

11.3 POSSIBLE OBJECTIVES FOR CHINA IN ENCOURAGING FOREIGN TOURISM

11.3.1 List of Possible Objectives

In encouraging foreign tourism, a country may have several objectives, and not all of these may be economic ones. Furthermore, not everyone may agree entirely about which objectives are desirable or most desirable.

The following, each of which will be discussed in turn, may be important 'target' variables or considerations in relation to foreign tourism:

(1) The amount of foreign exchange earned.
(2) Net national profit or surplus obtained from foreign tourists.
(3) Domestic employment generated by foreign tourists.
(4) Cultural and sociological impact of foreign tourists on the host country.
(5) Conservational impact on the host country of foreign tourists.
(6) Promotion of international understanding and co-operation through international contact.
(7) Income distribution.

11.3.2 Foreign Exchange Earnings

In relation to foreign exchange earnings from tourism, one should differentiate between *gross* and *net* foreign exchange earnings. Net foreign exchange earnings take into account leakages from the domestic economy for imports of commodities necessary to enable gross export receipts to be earned. Particularly in small economies, these leakages can be quite high. They may also be especially high in a developing country such as China in the case of the luxury segment of the foreign tourist market. In general, however, they will be much higher for foreign than domestic tourism.

From the point of view of maximising the available amount of its foreign exchange funds for discretionary use, a host country needs to maximise its net foreign exchange earnings in relation to the net value of its resources used to attract foreign exchange. For an industry in which the import leakage is relatively high, this means that fewer resources should be allocated to its promotion than if only gross foreign exchange receipts are considered. This is not to say that an export industry with high import leakages should not be encouraged, but merely that the leakages should be taken into account. This can be illustrated by Figure 11.1.

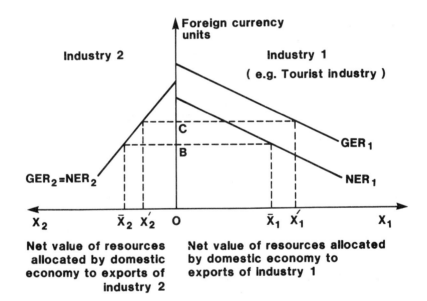

Figure 11.1 Illustration of the differences in net and gross foreign exchange earnings between industries and the implications for foreign reserves

In Figure 11.1 the curve (line) indicated by GER_1 represents the marginal *gross* foreign exchange receipts earned by industry 1 (e.g. the tourist industry) and the curve indicated by NER_1 represents the marginal *net* foreign exchange receipts earned by this industry. The difference between these two curves represents marginal leakages of foreign exchange from gross exchange receipts earned by industry 1. The leakages may be for import of goods used by the industry. In the case of industry 2, no leakages of foreign exchange receipts are assumed to occur, so its marginal gross foreign exchange receipts equal marginal net foreign exchange receipts as indicated by the line marked $GER_2 = NER_2$ in Figure 11.1.

In the case shown, maximisation of *gross* foreign exchange earnings requires X'_1 of resources to be allocated to industry 1, say the tourist industry, and X'_2 to be allocated to industry 2, given that $X = X'_1 + X'_2$ of resources is available for allocation between the two export industries. This allocation equates the marginal gross foreign exchange earnings of both industries. However, if *net* foreign exchange receipts are to be maximised then $\bar{X}_1$ of the available resources used in the domestic economy to promote exports should be allocated to industry 1, and $\bar{X}_2$ to industry 2. This combination equates the marginal *net* foreign exchange earnings by each industry. Thus, compared with the situation where the maximisation of gross foreign exchange earnings is the objective, industry 1, say the tourist industry, would be allocated fewer resources for export purposes than industry 2 when maximisation of net foreign exchange earnings is the objective. Nevertheless, the tourist industry would still be allocated more resources for export purposes than should industry 2.

Although China's statistics and statements by China's authorities tend to emphasise gross rather than net foreign exchange earnings by industries, including the tourist industry, the importance of net rather than gross foreign exchange earnings should be clear. Only the amount of net foreign exchange earnings adds to foreign exchange reserves or is available for discretionary imports by a nation, e.g. imports which may be decided on by its government. On the other hand, the fact that an industry has a large leakage on imports does not mean that it is a poor earner of foreign exchange. The opposite may be the case, and its imports may be essential for its success in attracting net foreign exchange. In fact, the case illustrated in Figure 11.1 illustrates the very point that an industry with a high import leakage or foreign exchange loss *can* be an excellent net foreign exchange earner. In that case, industry 1 has the largest export leakage but is the best earner of net foreign exchange. On the other hand, one can construct cases where this is not so.

As mentioned above, some import leakage may be necessary if an industry is to attract foreign business and attract foreign exchange. This seems necessary up to a point in the foreign tourist industry. From the point of view of maximising net foreign exchange earnings there is probably an *optimal import leakage* (falling somewhere between zero and unity), and measures which restrict imports for such an industry *may* actually reduce the net foreign exchange earnings of the industry.

In relation to international tourists, the marginal import leakage is likely to differ for different categories of tourists. It may be greater for high-income than low-budget tourists, less for Chinese compatriots than for Americans and Europeans, and so on. But net foreign exchange earnings would *not necessarily* be maximised by concentrating the development of the tourist industry on those tourists for which the foreign exchange leakage is low. In order to make a rational decision in this respect, empirical evidence is needed about the level of *net* foreign exchange earnings from different categories of tourists. However, one may also wish to question whether the level of foreign exchange earnings by an industry should be the sole consideration or even an important consideration in industry development.

11.3.3 Net National 'Profit or Surplus'

Not all governments, nor all economists, are convinced that maximising foreign exchange earnings is the most desirable economic policy. Few would wish to concentrate on this objective to the exclusion of others. An alternative objective might be to try to maximise the net national benefits obtained from foreign tourism as measured by the extra profits (surpluses) obtained by domestic producers plus the changes in surpluses obtained by domestic consumers. National benefits will as a rule be less than world economic benefits. Let us indicate this formally by relating the elements involved to China.

World economic benefits of foreign tourism to China = Extra profits or extra producers' surplus obtained by China's suppliers of tourist services + profits or surpluses obtained by foreign producers involved in tourism to China + consumers' surplus obtained by foreign visitors to China + change (positive or negative) in surpluses obtained by Chinese tourists or consumers.

China's benefits from foreign tourism = Extra profits or producers' surplus obtained by China's suppliers of tourist services + change (positive or negative) in surpluses obtained by Chinese tourists or consumers. If as a result of foreign tourism to China the price of tourism services rises in China, this reduces the surplus obtained by domestic tourists but raises the profits or surpluses obtained by suppliers of tourism services in China. The net effect, if China's tourism attractions are not damaged as a result of the increase in tourist numbers, is for China's benefits as measured by the above formula to increase.

11.3.4 Employment

Increased employment is sometimes seen by governments as an advantage of growth in the tourism industry. It has been estimated that in 1988 400 000 people were directly employed in China's tourism industry and that more than 1.57 million people were directly or indirectly dependent on it for their employment (The China State Administration for Travel and Tourism, *Yearbook of China Tourism Statistics*, 1989). However, expansion of the tourist industry does not *always* result in a substantial rise in domestic employment. This appears to be particularly so in many less-developed countries, where tourist facilities are provided for foreigners through foreign direct investment. In order to cater for foreign tourists, some relatively skilled labour is required. For example, hotel staff with knowledge of foreign languages and foreign tastes need to be employed. Often imported labour is used to fill key hotel positions requiring these skills. This has occurred in China to some extent. Sometimes the management of particular hotels in China is contracted out to overseas companies, e.g. management of the New China Hotel in Guangzhou has been contracted to a Hong Kong firm. Such arrangements may be necessary *initially* to ensure appropriate standards and service for foreign tourists.

11.3.5 Cultural and Sociological Impact

Some countries are concerned about the possible deleterious cultural and sociological impact of foreign tourists on their society. In the Maldives, for example, this has resulted in a policy of separating foreign tourists from the bulk of the population. Tourist resorts are as a rule located on islands which are not inhabited by Maldivians (Sathiendrakumar and Tisdell, 1985). However, foreign tourists do not always have an adverse impact on the culture and society of host countries. Sometimes local culture revives under tourist demand for local cultural objects and entertainment. Furthermore, as a study from Singapore indicates (Khan *et al.*, 1988), foreign tourists are not always a source of immorality and corruption.

11.3.6 Conservational and Environmental Impact

The impact of tourism on the conservation of natural resources and unique man-made resources is a factor to be taken into account in policy formulation. For example, some countries, such as China, prohibit the export of antique items of particular historical or cultural value. In some cases, governments *discourage* foreigners or even domestic tourists from visiting particular areas so as to minimise their impact on the natural environment. For example, New Zealand has a policy of not putting roads into some parts of the Fiordland National Park, located in the south of New Zealand. Visitors can only visit these parts by backpacking. This policy is designed to help preserve the wilderness of the region.

11.3.7 Promotion of International Understanding and Co-operation

Direct contact between peoples from different countries, such as can come with international tourism, can foster international understanding. Governments may be prepared to forego some economic benefits to promote such understanding. Just what form of tourism or what type of tourist does most to promote international understanding is a matter which may be worth investigating.

11.3.8 Income Distribution Consequences

A large influx of foreign tourists can have significant consequences for the distribution of income. Gains from tourism may be unevenly distributed in the economy, and domestic consumers and domestic tourists may suffer an economic loss in competition with foreign tourists. In the latter respect, competition for commodities in demand by foreign tourists can force up their prices or can result in their availability to domestic consumers being rationed. For example, with increased tourism to Australia, inner city areas of Sydney have been 'redeveloped' to provide accommodation for tourists. Some of these areas provided low-cost accommodation for Australians, who are now forced to live in other areas or under conditions they do not like. Thus they have suffered a reduction in their real income. Nevertheless, income distribution is unlikely to be the sole consideration in policy. Furthermore, situations can occur in which foreign tourism does not worsen the distribution of income or worsen it significantly.

11.3.9 Tourism Objectives or Target Variables in Summary

Several target variables that may be of interest or concern to governments in their foreign tourism policy have been identified. These are listed in Table 11.1 so as to provide an overview. However, a further two factors have been added, namely, the uncertainty and variability of the economic benefits from tourism.

Table 11.1   List of target variables of possible importance to governments in formulating tourism policy

---

1. Foreign exchange earnings (*gross* or *net*).
2. Net national economic benefits as measured by changes in economic surpluses.
3. Employment generation.
4. Cultural and sociological impact.
5. Conservational or environmental impact (including sustainability).
6. Promotion of international understanding and co-operation.
7. Income distribution consequences.
8. Uncertainty of economic benefits.
9. Variability of economic benefits.

Foreign tourism can be uncertain, and can be subject to both seasonal and cyclical fluctuations. This may be taken into account in government policy. For example, a country may try to diversify its sources of foreign tourists so as to reduce its vulnerability to changes in demand from a particular source. Some of these aspects are discussed by Tisdell and Wen (1991a) in relation to China.

Thus governments often have multiple target-variables to take into account in encouraging foreign tourism, and different governments may place different weights on these variables in their policy formulation. Furthermore, socioeconomic assessment of foreign tourism is complicated by uncertainty about the relationship between foreign tourism and the various target variables, as well as by the heterogeneous nature of foreign tourism itself.

11.4   SOME ASPECTS OF THE TAXING AND PRICING OF
THE SUPPLY OF TOURIST SERVICES

The taxing and pricing of tourist services, especially those provided for
or used by foreigners, is sometimes a matter of interest to governments. This is so for several reasons.

Foreign tourism, and increased tourism generally, usually involves
the provision of extra public infrastructure, which is to a large extent
financed by public funds. If foreigners are significant users of this
infrastructure, then, on the user-pays principle, it is important to ensure
that foreigners (directly or indirectly) make an adequate contribution to
public revenue. A second reason for interest in this subject is that a
national government may wish to ensure that the nation appropriates
as much as possible of its Ricardian-type rents from its unique, natural
and cultural tourist attractions (Tisdell, 1991). Such rents arise from
absolute scarcity of such assets. A third reason for interest in taxation
and pricing policy in relation to tourism is to ensure that the pricing of
access to tourist attractions is such as to ensure adequate environmental
protection or the conservation of tourist attractions (Tisdell, 1991), e.g.
to ensure that the number of visitors to tourist sites does not exceed the
'carrying capacity' of the sites.

The environmental and conservation aspects of tourism, even
though they are important, will not be discussed formally here (but
see Tisdell, 1991, Chapter 10). However, worthwhile use can be made
of a simple model in analysing the possibilities for the extraction of
rent from foreign tourists by a host country (for further discussion of
models see for example Tisdell, 1983, 1984). This model can also be
used to illustrate possible conflict between the goal of maximising
foreign exchange earnings and other goals. This is relevant in China's
case, because increased foreign exchange earnings remain an important
goal of China's National Tourism Administration (*China Daily*, 8 June
1991, p. 4).

If the demand curve for visits to the host country is less than
perfectly elastic then its government may either impose a tax on the
provision of tourist services to foreigners or promote a national cartel
in their supply, so as to increase national gain. Such a tax might, for
example, take the form of an entry or exit tax on visitors to the country
or might be levied on hotel services and similar services. The essence of
the matter can be seen from Figure 11.2.

Let the curve marked *DD* in Figure 11.2 represent the demand of
foreign tourists for tourist services in the host country, and, for

simplicity, assume that they alone demand such services. The demand for tourist services is not perfectly elastic in this case, because the demand curve is downward-sloping. The marginal revenue curve from sales of tourist services to foreigners (marked MR) therefore lies below their demand curve for these services. Given that the curve marked AS represents the industry supply curve of tourist services catering for foreigners in the host country, an amount X_2 of tourist services would be provided for foreign visitors under competitive conditions, and the host country would appropriate an amount of producers' surplus equal to the area of triangle ACE.

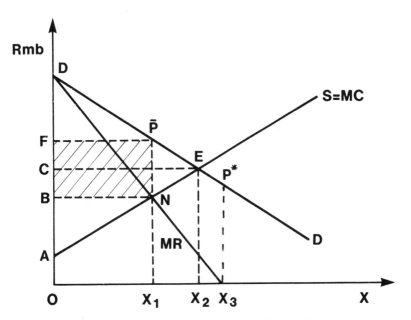

Figure 11.2 Appropriation of 'rent' from foreign tourists by pricing or tax policies

In these circumstances, by imposing a tax of BF on each unit of tourist services sold to foreigners (and thereby raising their effective price from OB to OF per unit), the government of the host country will maximise the net economic surplus appropriated by the country. This taxation level ensures that X_1 tourist services for foreigners are supplied and that the marginal cost of their supply is equalised with marginal revenue obtained from their provision. The government of the host country receives revenue of *BF* times X_1 (an amount equal to the hatched rectangle) from its tax and the surplus appropriated by the domestic industry is equal to the area of the triangle *ABN*.

If a cartel happened to be promoted in the domestic industry, this could also result in maximum gains from foreign tourists being appropriated by the host country if the cartel members belong to the host country and adopt a joint profit-maximising strategy. But, in this case, the above normal profit goes to the cartel members rather than to the government of the host country.

Note that policies of the above type require the host country to be able to discriminate between domestic and foreign tourists. If there are few domestic tourists then, for all intents and purposes, all demand in the domestic tourism sector may be regarded as foreign. Otherwise, it must be possible to distinguish between the two sources of demand in pricing or taxing policy if rent appropriation from foreigners is the main aim of policy. In relation to supply of some services this is indeed possible. For example, as in China, accommodation may only be supplied after identification using an identity card or a passport. Note that in China's case domestic tourism is significant and is growing.

Other means of increasing the amount of money appropriated from foreign tourists include *price discrimination* according to the apparent income of the tourists. But, in all such cases, it must not be easy to trade rights to tourist services, otherwise some individuals will be able to make a profit by arbitrage in the market.

The matter of whether a host country should try to appropriate the maximum possible amount of money from foreign tourists is debatable. To do so will reduce the degree of satisfaction obtained by the visitors. Consequently, they will be less likely to recommend the host country to friends and contacts. Adverse comments of previous visitors reduce future foreign tourism to the host country. *In the long term*, this may reduce total national profit or returns from foreign tourism. Furthermore, extraction of maximum financial benefit may conflict with the goal of increasing international understanding and sympathy for the host country, and the transaction costs involved in extracting extra income from foreign tourists have to be taken into account. For the latter reason, carrying price discrimination to extremes may be counter-productive.

11.5 CONFLICTING OBJECTIVES IN FOREIGN TOURISM POLICIES – THE CONFLICT BETWEEN NATIONAL GAIN AND THE MAXIMISATION OF FOREIGN EXCHANGE EARNINGS

The above simple model, involving rent appropriation from foreign tourists, can be used to illustrate conflict between objectives in foreign tourism policy. For instance, it can be used to illustrate possible conflict between the maximisation of foreign exchange earnings from overseas tourists and the maximisation of national surplus from such tourists. In particular, China's authorities need to be aware of this problem, because of the continuing emphasis they put on foreign exchange earnings.

In the simplified case illustrated in Figure 11.2, maximisation of net national gain (surplus) from foreign tourism requires national tourist services to be priced at a level which equates marginal revenue obtained with the marginal cost of supplying the services. Given that the marginal cost of supplying such services is positive, this equalisation results in marginal revenue being positive. But if the total revenue obtained from foreigners (equals total *gross* foreign exchange earnings) is to be maximised then marginal revenue must be zero. This requires the price of tourist services to be lower than the price level which maximises rents (surpluses) appropriated from foreign tourists.

The *nature* of the conflict and trade-off possibilities can be illustrated by Figures 11.3 and 11.4. In Figure 11.3 the curve *GHJ* indicates 'profit' obtained from foreigners at different prices for tourist services, and the curve *KLM* indicates total amount of (gross) foreign currency obtained from foreigners. These relationships can also be seen by referring back to Figure 11.2. Up to a price for tourist services of P^* per unit, both total profit (surplus) obtained by the host country and its gross foreign currency receipts rise, but for a price between P^* and $\bar{P}$ these objectives are in conflict. In this situation, profit rises, but the amount of gross foreign exchange receipts falls. At prices higher than $\bar{P}$, both target variables decline.

In Figure 11.4 the options available in terms of profit or surplus appropriated by the host nation and foreign exchange receipts obtained can be represented by a trade-off frontier such as *STUVW*. Outside the segment *TUV* of this frontier, both the national profit or surplus obtained from foreigners, and the foreign exchange receipts, can be increased by varying the policy instrument, the price of tourist services, but within this range one objective must be traded off against

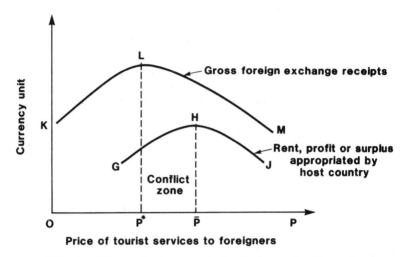

Figure 11.3   Possible conflict between the level of gross foreign exchange
earnings from foreign tourists and the rent or surplus
appropriated from foreign tourists by the host country

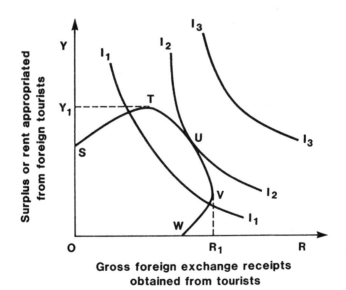

Figure 11.4   Policy choices involving a trade-off between the amount of rent
or surplus appropriated from foreign tourists and the gross
foreign exchange receipts obtained from these tourists

the other. *TUV* is the efficiency frontier, given that both appropriated profits and gross foreign receipts are desired. A preference function showing willingness to tradeoff national profit against gross foreign exchange receipts is required to determine optimal policy. If, for example, the indifference curves marked I_1I_1, I_2I_2 and I_3I_3 represent social welfare indifference curves, or the indifference curves adopted by the relevant policy-makers, then the combination corresponding to point *U* is optimal, and the price level for tourist services corresponding to that point is also optimal.

11.6 CONCLUDING COMMENT

Trade-off possibilities of the above type do not seem to have been considered seriously or stressed in China. Politically, there is a need in China to justify the tourism industry and its expansion, and the main argument used by China's National Tourism Administration has been the ability of the tourism industry to earn foreign exchange. But the industry has also assisted to some extent in the absorption of China's surplus labour force, and, as suggested in a previous chapter, expansion in employment in service industries may be one means by which China can directly or indirectly reduce the size of its surplus labour force in agriculture.

Just how inelastic is the demand for foreign tourism to China is difficult to say. There are natural and cultural attractions in China that either do not occur elsewhere, or, if they do, may be regarded as unsatisfactory substitutes for China's special assets. But it would be easy to exaggerate the significance of this. Not all travellers seek such attractions and for some the pull of other ancient civilisations, e.g. India or Thailand, is as strong or stronger (Tisdell, 1990).

The world tourism market is competitive. It is still difficult for China to compete in that market, especially in the provision of those tourism services which are dependent on recent investment and quality human services (Choy *et al.*, 1986). In the provision of tourist attractions Hecksher–Ohlin type, as distinct from Ricardian rent-type, mainland China does not compare well with Hong Kong, e.g. in providing shopping facilities and entertainment. Nevertheless, in relation to the quality of tourism personnel, China is making considerable effort to improve training and education (Zhang, 1987), while retailing and entertainment seem to be areas requiring more attention.

There are good prospects still for expanding the size of China's foreign tourism industry. In 1988 Japan was the most important source of *foreign* visitors to China, followed by the United States and the United Kingdom. In 1988 Japan accounted for one-third of foreign visitors to China, and the United States was the source of one-sixth of such visitors. So, between them, these two countries accounted for half of China's foreign visitors. European countries accounted for almost one-sixth of such visitors. More than half of China's visitors were from the East Asia–Australasia region. This area is likely to increase in importance as a source of foreign tourists to China because of Japan's recent emphasis on encouraging foreign tourism by Japanese to reduce its trade deficit, and the rising incomes of individuals in the nearby industrialising countries of the region. East Asia (excluding the People's Republic of China) has been identified as a rapidly growing source of international tourists (Garnaut, 1989). Foreign tourism tends to be an income-elastic good. China can also expect an increase in the number of compatriots visiting from Taiwan, and the number of ethnic Chinese visiting from other East Asian countries. Still, Chinese success in foreign tourism will depend upon the competitiveness of its tourist industry – particularly if it wishes to attract 'big spenders' from Japan and the United States.

It is impossible here to determine how much China has benefited from foreign tourism since 1978, and the extent to which such tourism has contributed to its development. However, its foreign tourism industry has undoubtedly played a large role in its opening up to the outside world and has been an important source of gross foreign exchange earnings for China. The contribution of foreign tourism to China's *net* foreign exchange earnings is unclear, but even if foreign exchange leakages in the industry were on average as high as one-third then the industry would still have been a very important foreign-exchange earner for China. In addition, the symbolic and diplomatic significance of foreign tourism in China should not be underestimated.

REFERENCES

CHOY, D. J. L., LI, DONG GUAN and ZHANG WEN (1986) 'Tourism in P. R. China: market trends and changing policies', *Tourism Management*, 7 (3), pp. 197–201.

CHINA STATE ADMINSTRATION FOR TRAVEL AND TOURISM (SATT) (1989) *The Yearbook of China Tourism Statistics*, SATT, Beijing.

GARNAUT, R. (1989) *Australia and the Northeast Asian Ascendancy*, Australian Government Publishing Service, Canberra.

GILLIS, M., PERKINS, D. W., ROEMER, M. and SNODGRASS, D. R. (1983) *Economics of Development*, Norton, New York.

HIRSCHMAN, A. O. (1958) *The Strategy of Economic Development*, Yale University Press, New Haven.

KHAN, H., CHOU, F. S. and WONG, K. W. (1988) 'The economic and social impact of tourism on Singapore', pp. 131–156 in C. A.

TISDELL, C. J. Aislabie and P. J. Stanton (eds), *Economics of Tourism: Case Study and Analysis, Institute of Industrial Economics*, University of Newcastle, NSW 2308.

McKEE, D. (1987) 'On services and growth poles in advanced economies', *The Service Industries Journal*, 7, pp. 165–75.

McKEE, D. and TISDELL, C. A. (1990) *Developmental Issues in Small Island Economies*, Praeger, New York.

PERROUX, F. (1950) 'Economic space: theory and applications', *Quarterly Journal of Economics*, Vol. 64, pp. 89–914.

SATHIENDRAKUMAR, R. and TISDELL, C. A. (1985) 'Tourism and development in the Maldives', Massey Journal of Asian and Pacific Business, 1 (1), pp. 27–34.

TISDELL, C. A. (1983) 'Public finance and appropriation of gains from international tourists: some theory with ASEAN and Australian illustrations', *Singapore Economic Review*, 28, pp. 3–20.

TISDELL, C. A. (1984) *Tourism, the Environment, International Trade and Public Economics*, ASEAN-Australia Economic Papers, No. 6. ASEAN-Australia Joint Research Project, Kuala Lumpur and Canberra.

TISDELL, C. A. (1990) 'Foreign tourism in China, in Australia, and between Australia and China: some observations and comparisons', *China Report*, 26 (3), pp. 261–71.

TISDELL, C. A. (1991) *Economics of Environmental Conservation*, Elsevier, Amsterdam.

TISDELL, C. A. and WEN, J. (1991a) 'Foreign tourism as an element in P. R. China's economic development strategy', *Tourism Management*, 12, pp. 56–68.

TISDELL, C. A. and WEN, J. (1991b) 'Investment in China's tourism industry: its scale, nature and policy issues', *China Economic Review*.

UYSAL, M., WEI, L. and REID, L. M. (1986) 'Development of international tourism in P. R. China', *Tourism Management*, 7 (2), pp. 113–19.

ZHANG GUANGRUI (1987) 'Tourism education in P. R. of China', *Tourism Management*, 8 (3), pp. 262–6.

ZHANG GUANGRUI (1989) 'Ten years of Chinese tourism: profile and assessment', *Tourism Management*, 10 (1), pp. 51–62.

ZHAO JIAN (1989) 'Overprovision in Chinese hotels', *Tourism Management*, 10 (1), pp. 63–6.

ZHAO ZIYANG (1987) 'Advance along the road of socialism with Chinese characteristics', Report delivered at the Thirteenth National Congress of the Communist Party of China on 25 October 1987, pp. 3–80 in *Documents of the Thirteenth National Congress of the Communist Party of China (1987)* Foreign Languages Press, Beijing.

12 Population Policy, Environmental Protection and International Issues Raised by China's Development

12.1 INTRODUCTION

China has the largest population of any country in the world, but it does not, as already observed, have the highest average density of population in the world. India, for example, has a higher average density of population. So also do Japan and many European countries, e.g. the Netherlands, Belgium and the United Kingdom. But, among other things, the industrialisation of the latter countries enables them to support high population densities. Nevertheless, China's leaders in the post-Mao period, unlike previously, have been concerned to slow down population growth in China because population growth is seen as a hindrance to economic development.

However, Chinese leaders have not, at least until recently, displayed the same degree of concern for environmental protection as they have for curbing population growth. But significant environmental problems have arisen in China as a result of population growth and growth in economic production. It has become obvious within China that more attention needs to be given to such issues if the country's economic development programmes are not to be stultified. Even within a socialist system there are strong incentives for enterprises to engage in polluting and environmentally damaging activities to their own economic advantage, despite the fact that these are to the detriment of society. This problem needs to be addressed by China more forcefully than in the past.

Concern has also been expressed in the West about the possible global environmental consequences of China's industrialisation and economic growth, especially the potential emissions of carbon dioxide and other greenhouse gases from its industries, which could add significantly to the threat of global warming. But there are additional possible environmental changes in China of global and international consequence. Furthermore, interest continues in the likely future international influence and power of China, which can be expected to grow with its economic development. Let us consider each of the above aspects in turn.

12.2 CHINA'S POPULATION AND POPULATION POLICY

12.2.1 Some Background Theory

Most economists consider human population levels to be an important influence on income levels and economic welfare. While opinions differ about the exact relationship, there is general agreement that human population levels *can* exceed levels which maximise per capita income or human welfare on average. (However for pro-population-growth points of view see, for example, Boserup, 1965; Clark, 1969, 1970; Simon, 1981.) This allows for the possibility that when population levels are low, increasing these levels may at first increase per capita income, while at high levels of population it may decrease it; this is the Marshallian case of increasing returns in production with population increase, followed by decreasing returns (cf. Tisdell, 1990). In the Marshallian case, the graph of the relationship between the average income per head of population and the size of the population is an inverted U-shape, the top of which corresponds to the level of population which maximises per capita income (Gillis *et al.*, 1983, Chapter 7). This can be illustrated by Figure 12.1.

In Figure 12.1, the curve OAC represents per capita income, or per capita output of a country as a function of the level of the country's population, and curve $ODAE$ represents marginal product, all things other than population being held constant. In the case shown, the level of population which maximises income per head is P_1. Larger population levels result in reduced income per head. If the population should exceed a level of P_2 then, in the case shown, it is too high to maximise total production or GDP. Total output reaches a maximum when marginal product equals zero.

A-priori evidence for China suggests that the level of its current population exceeds that for maximising its output. As discussed in previous chapters, China has a large surplus agricultural labour force. Possibly 300 million agricultural labourers are in surplus and have a zero or negative marginal product, and it is not clear, either, that they all would produce a positive marginal product in other sectors, given other resource restrictions. Thus China's present population may roughly correspond to a level like P_3 in Figure 12.1. This suggests that a reduction in China's total population would increase both per capita income in China and the level of its national production.

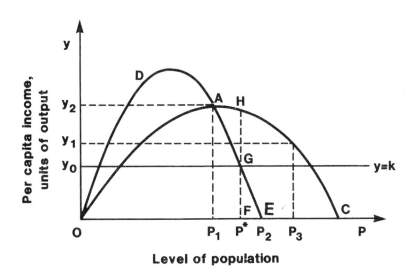

Figure 12.1   Optimal population levels assuming Marshallian relationships

However, it is possible that there may be more interest in the rate of capital accumulation rather than the level of per capita income. A *possible* national goal might be to maximise the rate of capital accumulation (aggregate amount of savings) subject to a minimum level of per capita consumption being provided for the population. Suppose that this minimum level of per capita consumption is $y_0 = k$. Then, where $f(P)$ is the national production function and S represents savings, $S = f(P) - kP$. This is at a maximum when the level of population is such that the required minimum level of per capita consumption equals the marginal productivity of the extra population. In Figure 12.1, this corresponds to a population level of P^*. Note that this level will as a rule be higher than the level of population which maximises income per capita, but less than that which maximises aggregate production. As already suggested, China's population seems to be greater than that needed to maximise its production. Therefore, *a fortiori*, it is higher than the level of population which maximises China's level of savings and its rate of capital accumulation. Overpopulation, apart from reducing per capita income and consumption levels, slows down the rate of capital accumulation. When population levels and consumption levels are controlled by the state, so too are savings levels. The state then has trade-off possibilities between population levels, consumption and savings levels. China, at least in the past, placed the greatest weight on high levels of savings and rates of capital accumulation as an objective. But its present level of population is too high to maximise its level of savings.

The above is a static theory. But that does not make it irrelevant, given the prevailing circumstances. At present, China does appear to be overpopulated from an economic point of view, although it is conceivable that in the future, with new technology and other economic developments, this would no longer be so. For the present and for some time to come it will be its overpopulation problem that China will need to address.

12.2.2 China's Response to its Overpopulation Problem

Basically, China's response to its overpopulation problem has been fourfold: (1) to promote capital accumulation and technological change, (2) to enforce birth control policies, (3) to foster industrialisation and (4), to a lesser extent, to promote urbanisation. But the People's Republic of China has not always recognised its level of population as being an economic problem. In Maoist China, 'Malthusian' theories were rejected. Both Marx and Engels had attacked Malthus's overpopulation thesis and took the point of view that scientific and technological progress would be sufficient to offset any deleterious effects from population increase (cf. Section 3.3). Marx believed that the basic cause of poverty was a maldistribution of income arising from capitalism and inequality in ownership of property rather than overpopulation, and he saw the overpopulation thesis as a 'redherring' and an attempt to blame poverty on the fecundity of the poor, mainly the workers. But in Maoist China, although income was relatively equally distributed, poverty remained a major problem, and was exacerbated by high fertility rates and high birth rates. High levels of military expenditure possibly added to this problem.

In the waning years of Mao's influence, as early as 1970, policy moves towards reducing the birth rate began, and in 1979 the policy of encouraging one-child families was adopted. Since this time, policies for controlling population increase have continued to be given a high priority by China's leaders.

Currently (1991), China's level of population is approximately 1.1–1.2 billion. In 1955 it was about 551 million and possibly was around the 1 billion mark at the end of 1980. Compared with the Maoist period, the rate of population increase is now much lower. For instance, the crude birth rate per thousand of population fell from 38 in 1965 to 21 in 1988 and the crude death rate from 21 to 7, and the total fertility rate from 6.4 to 2.4. If current policies continue and can be strengthened in rural areas, China will attain a net reproduction rate of unity by the year 2000, according to World Bank (1990, p. 230). Population levels in China are predicted to be around 1.6 billion in 2025 and to stabilise eventually at around 1.835 billion given current trends. Thus, even with current policies, substantial increases in China's population can still be expected. Reversing the growth of a population takes a considerable period of time because of the time lags involved.

There can be little doubt that China's policies have been effective in reducing fertility rates, and to a considerable extent this may be attributed to the administrative means used to regulate child-bearing (Lavely, 1989, p. 67). But, of course, increased urbanisation and better education have also played a role.

In 1970 China began a policy encouraging late marriage, greater spacing between children and fewer children per female (*wan, xi, shao*). Registrars often refused to issue marriage permits to persons below the government's recommended minimum age for marriage, permitted births were allocated in accordance with quotas by factories and for rural communities, and women were discouraged by birth planning officers from having more than two children. Then, following the perception of the true magnitude of China's population problem, in 1979 the one-child-per-couple policy was adopted with a view to achieving zero population growth by the year 2000, at which time it was hoped to hold China's population stationary at around 1.2 billion. But, especially because this policy has been difficult to enforce in rural areas, it is now clear that China's population will exceed 1.2 billion by

2000. However, the government is redoubling its effort to achieve its goal of zero population growth as soon as possible, and rural areas have been targeted for particular effort.

Lavely (1989, p. 68) points out that the implementation of the policy draws on the powerful administrative resources available to the Chinese state. Particularly in cities, where most employees work in state enterprises, government officials use numerous administrative means to reward those who conform to the policy and to penalise those who do not (cf. Liu Guoguang, 1987, p. 305). Economic advantages to couples who sign a one-child pledge include longer maternity leave, wage supplements and school privileges for their single child. Penalties for non-compliance may include reduced access to housing and slower promotion. But in the countryside this policy has been difficult to enforce, especially with the end of collectivisation in agriculture. Rural families still wish to have sons and are prepared to accept some state economic penalties to achieve this goal. Furthermore, with the introduction of the household responsibility system in agriculture, the state has reduced its direct control over farmers and their economic welfare. It is therefore more difficult to place economic pressure on farming couples if they have more than one child.

It is also possible that the economic costs to families of raising children in the countryside are lower than in the cities. Children can, for instance, assist in farm work from a relatively early age, whereas in the city there is little scope for them to contribute to family income through employment in economic activity. Furthermore, pensions are payable in the city to those with urban residence cards, but no pensions are payable in the rural areas. The incentive of farmers to have at least one son to work their assigned household- responsibility agricultural land for them in their old age and so support them is strong. On the principles put forward by Gary Becker (1960) that the size of families is heavily influenced by the *private* economic considerations of parents (that is, by the benefits and costs to parents of additional children), one would expect a stronger desire for larger families in the countryside than in the city, and indeed China's experience seems to be consistent with Becker's theories. This matter, however, requires further investigation.

One of the reasons why urbanisation may help to reduce the birth rate is that it reduces the net economic benefit to parents of larger families. In China's case, urbanisation also increases the effectiveness of administrative controls. This suggests that further progress can be made in rural areas by reducing the benefits to farmers of additional children and by improving income security, especially for the rural elderly who do not have male children.

12.3 SOME ENVIRONMENTAL CONSEQUENCES OF POPULATION INCREASE

Environmentalists see population increases and rises in per capita income (output) as factors accelerating environmental deterioration, if major technological innovations favourable to the environment are absent.

Increased aggregate production (production per head times level of population) in modern economies usually accelerates the rate of depletion of non-renewable resources, increases emissions of pollutants (both industrial and human wastes) and increases pressures on renewable resources. As the geographical area subject to economic production is extended and production is intensified in existing areas, larger tracts of natural area are radically transformed by economic activity. In the latter respect, for example, natural forests are increasingly felled for agriculture, industry and urban settlement and wildlife suffers. At the same time as modernisation occurs, technology may be increasingly adopted of a type giving rise to greater adverse externalities or which even adds significantly to global pollution. For example, much technology developed in the West is carbon-using and so adds to greenhouse gases. It has been claimed that China's economic growth and industrialisation using carbon fuels and this technology will make China a *major* contributor to this form of global pollution in the future (Oppenheimer and Boyle, 1990; Myers *et al.*, 1990; see also Tisdell 1991a). On the other hand, as pointed out by Mao Yu-shi (1991), pollution created now in China per unit of product with present technology is generally higher than in the USA.

Demographic changes, other than population increase, are also occurring in China which have environmental implications. For example, increased urbanisation in China has resulted in disposal of human wastes, including sewage, becoming a major problem. It also brings with it a new set of environmental health problems, both physical and psychological. Epidemics and human-communicated diseases can spread more rapidly, for example, in cities. Since urban communities tend to be less closely knit psychologically than rural communities, psychological disturbance may be more common in city environments. Furthermore, the problem of dealing with industrial wastes is a serious one in urban areas, though where an industry exists in the countryside unfavourable externalities from it can still be a problem. Indeed, one of the criticisms repeatedly made about rural industrial enterprises (which are usually not state-owned) is that they ignore pollution regulations and cause serious pollution. Such accusations tend to be encouraged by state-owned urban industrial enterprises which have found it increasingly difficult to compete with rural enterprises, but the accusations are not baseless (Mao Yu-shi, 1991).

12.4 POLLUTION CONTROL

Economists point out that the environmental or pollution externalities or spillovers in market systems may result in the private costs of activities diverging from social costs of these activities, that is, in the private net benefits of activities differing from social net benefits. Consequently, by following their own individual self-interest, economic units may fail to maximise social economic welfare. Economists usually recommend action to ensure that private marginal net benefits from activities are brought into line in the market system with social marginal net benefits. If an unfavourable externality is involved, one way in which this can be achieved is by placing a suitable tax on the offending activity, but other control methods are also possible (Tisdell, 1991b).

Because in theory a communal point of view is taken, one might expect in a socialist system environmental externalities to be taken better care of, but this does not necessarily occur in practice. Even in a socialist system, individual economic units can adopt a selfish point of view.

Serious pollution problems do occur in China, and the country has not yet fully systematised its pollution and environmental control policies. While in a less-developed country one might expect less weight or value to be put on environmental quality than in a higher-income country, if for no other reason than the fact that the demand for better environmental quality seems to be income-elastic, institutional factors in China make for poorer environmental quality than appears to be socially optimal. In introducing China's Ten-Year Programme for National Economic and Social Development (1991–2000), Premier Li Peng pointed to the need for China to give greater attention to environmental protection.

While penalties can be imposed in China on enterprises which cause external environmental damage, pollution control laws are not always enforced, particularly in the case of state enterprises. For example, it was reported in the *China Daily* in 1989 that an industrial enterprise near Wuhan (in Sashi City) had discharged poisonous chemical wastes into the waterway near its factory. Subsequently, when the water was used for irrigation, crops were damaged, livestock died and the fertility of the soil irrigated with the polluted water was reduced. Although the factory was ordered to pay damages, it did not do so, claiming that its financial situation did not permit it to pay. Furthermore, it continued to dispose of the chemically polluted effluent into the waterway. In practice, pollution laws are not impersonally and rigorously enforced. Politics often intrudes, especially when state-owned or collectively owned enterprises are the source of the pollution (Mao Yu-shi, 1991).

Under the contract responsibility system, directors of state-owned enterprises have an incentive to take maximum economic advantage of the environment, if its use is treated as a free good or almost so. Under the contract responsibility system discussed in Chapter 10, directors or employees of a state industrial firm have discretionary use of any after-tax profit of the enterprise that is in excess of the agreed target level of profit to be paid to the state. If the profit of profitable enterprises can be increased by making greater use of the environment then the directors have an incentive to do that for their own personal gain and that of their employees. The situation is not materially different from that under capitalism.

Where an enterprise is making a loss or a negligible profit, and is exploiting the environment to do so, its financial situation would be much worse if it paid for the full social cost of its economic activity, that is the cost actually borne by the enterprise *plus* the cost to others of its damage to the environment. If it had to do this, then in normal circumstances it would soon become bankrupt unless it could control, say, its pollution emissions at little cost. But it is appropriate that the enterprise should pay its social cost, and, if it then still cannot make a profit that it should be closed down, assuming that the prices of the commodities product reflect their economic values (which, in China, they do not always do; see Mao Yu-shi, 1991). However, as noted in Chapter 10, in cases where state-owned industrial enterprises have made continuing losses, China has not applied its bankruptcy laws to close them down and they have been subject to 'soft budget con-straints'. For this reason, enterprises often keep operating and cause a net social loss, particularly when the environmental damage they do is are taken into account. However, the true social interest dictates that such enterprises should be closed down or else should be required to alter their operations so that a net social benefit results. This is not to say that full social costs can be easily estimated and there are not controversies about appropriate methods of measurement of these. Nevertheless, this does not justify ignoring obvious social costs such as obvious damage from pollution.

Nevertheless, there are cases in China where the polluter-pays principle has been successfully applied. Take the case of a non-ferrous smelter in Daye County, Hubei Province. This smelter was a source of cadmium pollution in the nearby villages. Cadmium is emitted from a factory in water-wastes and in the air, water-borne cadmium was a serious source of contamination in the surrounding villages. The enterprise was required to pay the cost of the medical treatment of persons in the locality who had their health adversely affected by cadmium intake. The cost to the enterprise of paying for these medical services was found to exceed the cost of installing and operating a waste-water treatment plant to reduce emissions of cadmium to negligible levels. The factory therefore installed the plant. The social benefits from installing the waste treatment plant exceeded its costs by a wide margin (Hong *et al.*, 1990). Although the smelting works did not bear all the social costs of its cadmium pollution, it was required to pay sufficient of these costs for it to make a decision which resulted in a social gain.

Under its Environmental Protection Law, China has in principle a wide range of economic measures to protect its environment. According to Mao Yu-shi (1991, p. 12), China employs 'more economic leverages to protect the environment than the Americans do. China has promulgated a full spectrum of pollution charges including air, water, solid waste, radio-activity and noise charges'. The money collected from pollution charges is said to amount to 15 per cent of the total investment in environmental improvement projects. But such charges appear to be 'haphazardly' enforced, and it is not clear that the allocative aspects are consistently examined.

In practice, the main policy for environmental pollution, apart from propaganda, has been the state fund for environmental protection, which has resulted in large state-owned factories obtaining funds for investment in environmental protection, e.g. the purchase of pollution-reducing equipment. In effect, this is a subsidisation approach and favours state-owned enterprises. Indeed, these funds may be only *partially* used by the enterprises for pollution control. Also, attention must be given to enterprise *operations* apart from investment by enterprises in capital equipment or durable assets, if the environmental effects of economic activity are to be fully addressed. In any case, the subsidisation approach adopted allows for considerable political bargaining, which may cause distortions and provides some scope for dishonest practices. In practice there is clearly considerable room for improvement in China's environmental protection measures (Nickum and Dixon, 1989; Mao Yu-shi, 1991). As mentioned, this aspect has also been recognised by Premier Li Peng.

As the market system is extended in China, it is possible that the polluter-pays principle may also become more widely imposed and enforced. Whether or not China will adopt pollution-tax systems generally (it has some pollution charges now) or tradable pollution permits to control pollution, which have been suggested by some economists in the West to be efficient control systems, remains to be seen. However, it is reported that China is seriously examining marketable pollution rights as a possible means of controlling industrial pollution in Shanghai and Shenyang (Mao Yu-shi, 1991, p. 14).

12.5 INTERNATIONAL ENVIRONMENTAL ISSUES RAISED BY CHINA'S ECONOMIC DEVELOPMENT

Environmental developments in China are of international interest from a number of points of view. First, the continuing economic development of China will have a major global environmental impact. It is expected that with this development China will increase substantially its burning of fossil fuels, so contributing further to global greenhouse gases. Any international undertaking to limit carbon emissions would need to include China. But what control measures, if any, China would agree to internationally is unclear. The problem of the levels of global emission of greenhouse gases, if it is a problem, is still far from being solved. China, for example, might not be expected to agree to a uniform worldwide tax on carbon fuel use (cf. Mao Yu-shi, 1991). Secondly, China is the source of major river systems flowing into South and South-East Asia. Policies which it pursues in the headwaters of these rivers can have environmental consequences in neighbouring countries. For example, deforestation in the headwaters of these rivers could increase the severity of flooding in nearby or neighbouring countries such as Bangladesh and Thailand and increase the variability of river flows. Thirdly, China has many unique species of wildlife and natural landscapes of global interest (Liu Jianjun, 1990;

Liang, 1991). Loss of these, as well as a number of its historical treasures, would be the world's loss.

Despite the fact that China has increased the number of its nature reserves and national parks, China's natural resources are under continuing threat as a result of its economic growth. Recently, Mao Yu-shi (1991, p. 9) has suggested that 'the major problem of the environment in China is not industrial pollution but the abuse of natural resources'. How to resolve all its resource conflicts is a serious problem for China. Furthermore, migration to the more remote provinces in the West of China and Tibet has led to greater intensification of natural resource use in these areas and may compound future environmental problems. In addition, Chinese agriculture has become more intensive. Artificial fertiliser use has increased greatly, the adoption of high-yielding varieties of crops has increased the incidence of multiple cropping, pesticide use has risen and water supplies such as underground aquifers are being put under increasing strain to supply irrigation water. In several parts of the country, owing to the over-pumping of water for urban use and irrigation, water tables are dropping.

China has come to rely increasingly on modern petro-chemical agriculture as a means of expanding its food production. The extent to which production from modern agricultural systems is sustainable is uncertain but there clearly can be difficulties in the long term for sustaining production using these systems (Conway, 1985, 1987; Alauddin and Tisdell, 1991; Tisdell, 1991b). In remote areas where poverty exists, local residents, as mentioned in an earlier chapter, are being encouraged to use their natural resources more intensively to increase their income. Once again, attention must be given to the environmental consequences of this and the extent to which it is ecologically sustainable.

12.6 CONCLUDING OBSERVATIONS

A further aspect of interest is to what extent China's international power and influence will expand with its economic development (Harding, 1989, Chapter 9). Within the East Asian–Australasian region, Japan is currently the major economic power. With the end of the Cold War and reduced Soviet and United States military presence in the region, Japan can be expected to take a more active role in regional affairs and is likely to retain its predominant position in the short and medium term. But in the longer term, if China can maintain political stability and achieve its economic growth goals, it is likely to overtake Japan in its regional influence, and may even counterbalance Japan in the medium-term.

While gross domestic product (GDP) is a relatively poor indicator of relative economic power, it provides some indication of the relative sizes of economies. With Japan's GDP treated as unity, the relative sizes of selected economies in East Asia–Western Pacific are indicated in Table 12.1. As can be seen, in terms of size of GDP China's economy is the second largest in the region, even though its level of GDP still remains well below that of Japan.

Table 12.1   Relative sizes of GDP for selected countries or groupings in East Asia-Western Pacific 1987 in comparison to Japan

Country or group	Relative size of GDP
Japan	1
China	0.4
ASEAN	0.17
Australia + New Zealand	0.15
Australia	0.13
S. Korea	0.08
Taiwan	0.05
Hong Kong	0.03

Source: Partially estimated from Garnaut (1989) Table 1.1.

Chinese Premier Li Peng has set an annual average growth rate of GNP for China of about 6 per cent per annum for the whole of the period 1991–2000. This will result in China's GDP approximately doubling in this period. Thus, by early in the second millennium, China's GDP will be comparable to that of Japan currently, if China can achieve its growth target. Possibly by the middle of the next century, if not earlier, China's GDP will have overtaken that of Japan, although per capita incomes in China will still be much lower than in Japan. Because the Japanese economy is now entering a mature phase, it is unlikely to maintain its past economic growth rates, whereas the Chinese economy is still in a developing phase. China is rich in energy and mineral resources and these will be an asset for its economic development. However, even though China did achieve rates of GDP in excess of 6 per cent in the period 1978–88, we cannot be sure that it will achieve Li Peng's target for the 1990s.

China's economic development path is a difficult one, and involves approximately one-fifth of humanity. Support for the country's present government seems to be dependent on its promises to improve economic welfare, and we have had an opportunity to look at many diverse problems involved in trying to achieve this goal. It will be a major achievement for China if it is able to reach its goal of joining the middle-income countries in the next century, manages to attain zero-population growth by around the year 2000 and combines all of this with policies for sustainable and ecologically sound economic development. Despite growing materialism in China, the traditional attachment of Chinese to nature, as expressed in poetry and prose, remains. This, combined with the traditional Chinese belief in the importance of ecological balance, may result in environmental preservation and the conservation of nature becoming more important goals in the future (cf. Liang, 1991).

In theory, a socialist country should have good prospects for being able to achieve sustainable economic development (cf. Liu, Liang and others 1987, p. 303). But whether China will achieve sustainable development in practice is still unclear. Nevertheless, in its 'march along the road of socialism with Chinese characteristics', China has recognised that the type of economic development policies pursued by Mao Zedong are unsustainable and inadequate in the modern world. Thus it has already taken an important step towards more sustainable development, even though it has much further to go.

REFERENCES

ALAUDDIN, M. A. and TISDELL, C. A. (1991) *The Green Revolution and Economic Development*, Macmillan, London.
BECKER, G. S. (1960) 'An economic analysis of fertility', In National Bureau of Economic Research, *Demographic and Economic Change in Developed Countries*, Princeton University Press, Princeton.
BOSERUP, E. (1965) *The Condition of Agricultural Growth*, Aldine, Chicago.
CLARK, C. (1969) 'The population expansion myth', *Bulletin of the Institute of Development Studies*, Sussex, May.
CLARK, C. (1970) 'The economics of population growth and control: a comment', *Review of Social Economy*, 28, pp. 449–66.
CONWAY, G. (1985) 'Agroecosystems analysis', *Agricultural Administration*, 20, pp. 31–5.

CONWAY, G. (1987) 'The properties of agroecosystems', *Agricultural Systems*, 24, pp. 95–117.

GARNAUT, R. (1989) *Australia and the Northeast Asian Ascendancy*, Australian Government Publishing Service, Canberra.

GILLIS, M., PERKINS, D. H., ROEMER, J. and SNODGRASS, D. R. (1983) *Economics of Development*, Norton, New York.

HARDING, H. (1989) *China's Second Revolution: Reform After Mao*, Allen & Unwin, Sydney.

HONG ZHIYONG, BAO KEGUANG and TISDELL, C. (1991) 'Cadmium exposure in Daye County, China: environmental assessment and management, health and economic effects', *Environmental Management and Health* 2 (2) pp. 20–25.

LAVELY, W. (1989) 'Demographic and social change in China', pp. 63–73 in C. E. Morrison and R. F. Dernberger (eds.) *Asia-Pacific Report 1989 – Focus: China in the Reform Era*, East-West Center, Honolulu, Hawaii.

LIANG CHONGGI (1991) 'Nature reserves in China', *Tigerpaper*, 18 (1), pp. 2–5.

LIU GUOGUANG; LIANG WENSEN and others (1987) *China's Economy in 2000*, New World Press, Beijing.

LIU JIANJUN (1990) 'Saving wildlife: a nation mobilized', *Beijing Review*, 33 (16), 16–22 April, pp. 18–23.

MAO YU-SHI (1991) 'Environmental problems in China and the USA and its international collaboration', Paper presented at an international conference, 'The United States and the Asia-Pacific Region in 20th Century', Institute of American Studies, Chinese Academy of Social Sciences, Beijing, 23–25 May.

MYERS, N., EHRLICH, P. R. and EHRLICH, A. H. (1990) 'The population problem: as explosive as ever?', Paper delivered at the Fourth International Conference on Environmental Future, 'Surviving with the Biosphere', Budapest, Hungary, April.

NICKUM, J. and DIXON, J. (1989) 'Environmental problems and economic modernization', pp. 83–91 in C. E. Morrison and R. F. Dernberger (eds) *Asia-Pacific Report 1989 – Focus: China in the Reform Era*, East–West Center, Honolulu, Hawaii.

OPPENHEIMER, M. and BOYLE, R. H. (1990) *Dead Heat: The Race Against the Greenhouse Effect*, Basic Books, New York.

SIMON, J. (1981) *The Ultimate Resource*, Princeton University Press, Princeton.

TISDELL, C. A. (1990) *Natural Resources, Economic Growth and Development*, Praeger, New York.

TISDELL, C. A. (1991a) 'The environment and economic welfare', pp. 6–16 in D. L. McKee (ed.), *Energy, Environment and Public Policy*, Praeger, New York.

TISDELL, C. A. (1991b) *Economics of Environmental Conservation*, Elsevier, Amsterdam.

Index